SYSTEMS ANALYSIS AND DEVELOPMENT

SYSTEMS ANALYSIS AND DEVELOPMENT

Methods, Strategies and Tools to Successfully Develop Efficient Technology-based Business Solutions

First Edition

Eric M. Bunts

Binghamton University

Bassim Hamadeh, CEO and Publisher
Gem Rabanera, Senior Project Editor
Casey Hands, Senior Production Editor
Susana Christie, Senior Developmental Editor
Monica O'Keefe, Editorial Assistant
Jessica Delia, Graphic Design Associate
JoHannah McDonald, Licensing Coordinator
Natalie Piccotti, Director of Marketing
Kassie Graves, Senior Vice President, Editorial
Alia Bales, Director, Project Editorial and Production

Printed in the United States of America.

ACTIVE LEARNING

This book has interactive activities available to complement your reading.

Your instructor may have customized the selection of activities available for your unique course. Please check with your professor to verify whether your class will access this content through the Cognella Active Learning portal (http://active.cognella.com) or through your home learning management system.

Contents

Acknowledgments

To my wife, Stacy Bunts, thank you for all your support!
To my daughter, Molly Bunts, you pushed me to do my best!
To my father, Mike Bunts, a true systems analyst and a testament to the profession!

Introduction

Description

Systems Analysis and Development: Methods, Strategies, and Tools to Successfully Develop Efficient Technology-Based Business Solutions explores many facets of the software development life cycle in a structured and organized format. The purpose of the text is to walk the student through the system development process in the same way a systems analyst would conduct a technology development project. This text also explores the challenges and difficulties that arise during the system development process, drawing a direct correlation to what a systems analyst would encounter in the industry. Highlighting these potential obstacles allows for the development of methods, skills, techniques, tools, and perspectives that mitigate these challenges and result in successful new technology developments.

The primary target audience is undergraduates in a management information systems (MIS) or computer information systems curriculum. This is due to the fact that the information contained in the text will provide both a basic understanding of the system development process and challenge the reader to "think like a systems analyst." The critical thinking component of this text also makes it a viable option for MIS majors in MS and MBA programs as well.

The text does not require an advanced knowledge of technology system design or development. The core concepts, theories, and framework of technology system design are presented from both the business and technology perspectives. This ensures that both business students with a passion for technology and technology students with a passion for business will be equally qualified to take part in the development of a new technology system. Both technology and business material are equally developed to ensure general understanding from the perspective of both concentrations.

Using This Text

This text is intended to be used in systems analysis and design courses. It is designed in such a way as to foster a greater understanding of the software development life cycle by mirroring the tenants of said life cycle in the chapter organization. This allows the instructor to present course material in a more practical, application-based manner.

From the practical application perspective, this text was designed to be complemented by a full semester group project, where the objective is for each group to select an organization, define a problem within the organization's environment, and develop a new technology to resolve the identified issue. The project will develop the selected organization, problem identification, solution development, solution design, and solution implementation. The culmination of the project is a fully developed project plan that is then presented by each group to the class.

To best facilitate this project development, at the end of each chapter, there are identified project activities that depend on the chapter content for successful completion. The compilation of all identified activities will result in a fully formatted project development plan.

CHAPTER 1

What Is Systems Analysis?

Introduction

Image 1.1

"The system is down" is a phrase that has always resulted in feelings of discontent, frustration, and annoyance. However, in recent years, information systems have transformed from a tool in an organization's toolkit used to increase efficiency and operational capabilities to the cornerstone of an organization's ability to conduct business. In every industry, at every level, the need for enhanced technology is rising at an ever-increasing rate. Because of this increased technological reliance, we are now in a position where "the system is down" does not equate to an inconvenience but a potential catastrophe.

Today's business environment depends on technology at all levels of the organization. From an administrative perspective, support services all maintain information systems to meet their responsibilities to the organization. For example, the average human resources department has a human resources management (HRM) system to process payroll, administrate employee benefits, and even conduct employee training. Operational units rely on technology for customer interaction and logistical implementation. As an example, many companies use a customer relationship management system to track leads, record new customer data, and track active customer needs and purchase requirements. Regardless of the industry, business entity size, or scope, technology is firmly implanted in the culture of just about every organization operating at this moment, and with this reliance on technology comes the incorporation of a sometimes frightening concept: change.

The only constant in technology adaptation is change. Think about that sentence for a minute. At first glance, it appears to contradict itself. However, the proof is in the past. Three decades ago, as information systems were beginning to be implemented with more regularity in larger organizations, the expected use life, or life cycle, of a technology system was projected to be 1 to 2 decades. Two decades ago, organizations would budget an information system's life cycle at a decade. Ten years ago, the expected technology life cycles were reduced to 7 to 10 years. Today, many organizations budget technology at a 3- to 5-year life cycle. Why? It's simple, really. The rate of change regarding technology is increasing. Hardware cost decreases, coupled with increases in processing power year over year, facilitate yearly innovation development across the entire spectrum of technology creation, enhancement, and maintenance. All of this results in increased capabilities of newly developed systems as compared to current systems. Additionally, new systems are being produced at a more rapid rate, therefore facilitating organizations making the argument to abandon current systems in favor of new ones more quickly, decade over decade.

This increased rate of technological change is not solely related to system replacement. Organizations with systems in operation today are constantly in need of enhancing and reworking the current system's process. While sometimes these alterations are to increase productivity or reduce costs, other times, the change is driven by a need simply to remain competitive. Within competitive markets, successful technology adaptation can result in increased market share, and late adopters may not be able to compete at all. This never-ending race to incorporate market differentiating technology has resulted in the need for continuous assessment of the current information system scope with the intended result of identifying areas of opportunity within the current system to replace or enhance.

The need for constant change, however, is only half the equation. The other half consists of reliability. While previously, system downtime often equated to inconvenience, today, it equates to panic. The increased reliance on technology adaptation for all aspects of the business environment has created a complete and total reliance on continuous uptime. A system not performing as intended does not slow a business process; in the current business environment, it often breaks it completely. Additionally, as a global society, we grow more and more unforgiving of an incomplete or underperforming technological system. End user expectation is that our daily technology will perform as anticipated each and every time we need to use it. This places a heavy responsibility on those who are tasked with ensuring that organizations have both the correct technology and that said technology is operating at peak performance reliably.

Learning Objectives

1. Describe the systems development life cycle and its phases.
2. Understand the role of the system request.
3. Explain the systems analyst's role in new system development.
4. Explain the necessary traits of a systems analyst.

What Is Systems Analysis?

Image 1.2

At the highest level, systems analysis is the process by which an organization manages the technological needs of the organization through constant assessment of the business and technology relationship within the organization. It requires a keen understanding of the organization's operational requirements, the technologies that are used to facilitate those requirements, and the technologies that are available to be incorporated to enhance that business process/technology relationship.

Many will argue that systems analysis is simply understanding business needs and incorporating new technological developments to meet those needs. However, in today's business environment, this mindset of analyze, identify, and replace is only a segment of the overall requirement. The change and reliability requirements of the business scope require consistent identification, development, and incorporation of incremental change on a current system long before it is overtly replaced. Therefore, the full scope of system analysis is a constant assessment of the current environment, constant assessment of new and emerging technologies, and the modeling of technological change against the current information system design with potential outcomes consisting of do nothing, enhance, insert, or replace as related to the information system or business process being analyzed.

Systems analysis starts with understanding the operational environment of the organization. Defining and clearly recognizing the reason the organization is viable leads to the identification of specific business processes that are conducted and to what degree each process is both necessary and efficient. This leads to an ability to determine where there may be areas of opportunity in which to positively enhance certain processes through either reorganization or the incorporation of technology. That's right, not every aspect of systems analysis requires implementing new technology. In some instances, a business process can be enhanced by simply removing components of the process. For example, a company has implemented a new digital file archive system in which paper files are scanned and stored digitally. The system is also backed up to ensure that if there is ever a system issue, the data will still be safe. A system analysis is conducted a year after the system is implemented, and the process reveals that while paper documents are scanned in, put into the system, and then the paper copy is destroyed, digital documents are printed, scanned in, put into the system and then the printed document is destroyed. The digital documents are already in the format necessary to be put into the system. Therefore, all that is needed to improve the business process is to redirect the end user to simply put the digital documents into the system. The key here is that systems analysis requires an astute understanding of both the business environment and the business processes being conducted within the environment. You cannot enact successful change until you have a baseline understanding.

Systems analysis also has a key requirement of understanding technology development and incorporation. The word technology encompasses a broad range of aspects, and many of these aspects apply to systems analysis. Certainly, there are information systems available for an organization to purchase. For example, in regards to HRM, there are many vendors that offer solutions a company can purchase and implement into their business environment, thereby redefining the current business processes in order to take advantage of the new capabilities contained within the new system. However, that same company could decide to implement multiple vendor solutions, one for each business process, and employees would go to the necessary system to complete the necessary process. A third option would be for the company to implement the same multiple vendor solutions but build an employee portal that would allow employees to go to one place but still access all the necessary business processes. It's also possible for the company to only implement technology on a single business process, such as payroll, and leave the other aspects of the department's current processes as is. Or the company could elect to build its own HRM altogether, tailoring its functionality to the specific needs of the organization. Each one of these decisions uses technology in a different way to reach a desired goal. To make these decisions, you have to be comfortable working with technology in a myriad of ways, including developing, assessing, and implementing, and not always singularly. You may develop some components and implement someone else's development in combination.

Additionally, system analysis is not only contained in the information system itself. In most business environments, a single information system does not work within a vacuum. It requires interaction between other corporate systems and technologies. For example, a company's HRM will maintain all of the master data related to the employee, but portions of that data will be accessed by other systems to facilitate reporting requirements. In the instance of reporting on the cost of an employee to the organization, the payroll data for an employee is pulled from the HRM and is combined with the sales data from the company's accounting software to obtain the desired results. These system interactions are a key component of success for the overall organization and, therefore, are contained within the systems analysis function.

It is also important to understand that the technologies used to connect the information system to both the end user and the data environment are within the purview of systems analysis. The most well-defined system is rendered useless if the end user cannot reliably interact with it. Additionally, as most information systems require connectivity with additional systems, both internal and external, of the organization, the solutions used to maintain this connectivity also require assessment. For example, consider online video gaming; if you try to play on the most basic home Internet service available, will you have the same experience as someone who has a data line that connects directly to the video game server? The answer is no. There are many different architectures used to maintain connectivity to and between information systems, and there are benefits and detractions contained within each architecture. Determining which makes the most sense for a specific use case is necessary.

In summary, systems analysis requires the incorporation of many different aspects of an organization's operation. At the highest level, the organization's reason for being and expected outcomes need to be clearly defined. Operationally, the current state of the business must be explored and defined. This includes all business processes within the scope of analysis and the impact of each step of the current process on the organization as a whole. Additionally, varying aspects of technology need to be fully grasped. From how to develop new technologies to how to successfully implement developed technologies into the business scope, as well as the incorporation of data transport architecture and utilization, systems analysis truly is the melding of business and technology to advance the capabilities of an organization.

The Systems Development Life Cycle

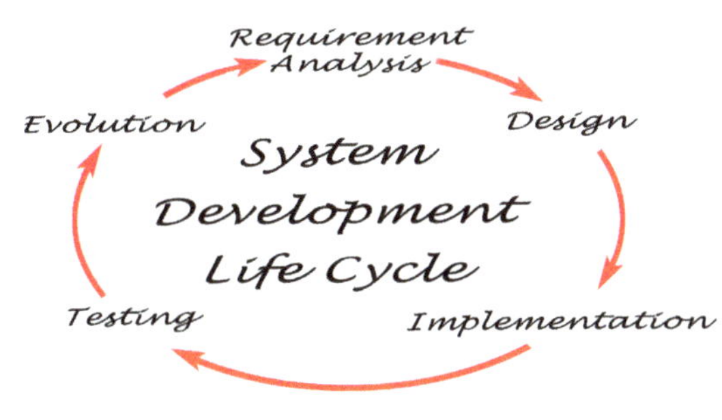

Figure 1.1 The System Development Life Cycle

Whether the goal is to build a new technology system, implement a previously developed system, enhance a business process through implementing specific technology functions, or maintain the functionality of a currently implemented information system, systems analysis is the discipline that will offer the best chance of a successful endeavor. However, the difficulty of these endeavors is not to be understated. It is a big ask of an individual or even a group of individuals to acquire the depth of knowledge required to successfully implement technology, and reports detailing the failure rate of software projects denote this. While varying reports demonstrate variances in software development projects, it is fair to say that even today, 60% to 70% of all software development projects fail. When you think about it, that is an astonishing number. Why would anyone enter into a venture where the chance of failure is greater than the chance of success? Why are these failure rates so high?

To discuss why such a high rate of software development projects fail, let's begin by discussing how system development projects are supposed to be completed. There is no question that information systems are complex developments, and whether you are building one from scratch, enacting changes on a currently developed solution, or even simply implementing a fully developed solution into your environment, there is a structured process that has been proven to provide you the best chance of successfully completing your objective. This process is known as the systems development life cycle (SDLC). The SDLC consists of four stages that progress systems analysis from the identification of an area of opportunity in the current business environment through the implementation of a developed technology-based solution designed to meet those opportunistic needs. These stages consist of planning, analysis, design, and implementation. Let's look at each stage in more detail in order to better understand the overall function of the SDLC.

Stage 1: The Planning Phase

The planning phase is the first step in developing a new software solution. This is where the current business environment is evaluated for areas of opportunity. Oftentimes, potential development projects are brought to the attention of the organization through human resources, specifically departmental management and even end users. These human resources for project identification are perhaps the most important ones because these are the individuals who work within the current business process on the same business tasks each and every day. It would, therefore, make sense that their intimate knowledge of the current process would allow them to identify ways to enhance or even create alternate processes to complete their required work. Even if they are unsure as to how to implement change, they can be the starting point to identifying an issue within the environment. For example, a company's accounts billable clerk, who is responsible for inputting delivery data into the billing system from paper delivery tickets and then recording the entry on three separate spreadsheets, simply complaining about the redundancy of their daily tasks is a primary identifier that technology can most likely be developed and implemented to minimize or even completely remove that redundancy.

However, identification is only the first step in the planning phase. Investigation is also a necessity. Continuing on with our example, the organization must look at the actions of the accounts billable clerk: What are the spreadsheets they are populating being used for? Where is the delivery data they are entering coming from? Is it being printed from another system or being manually created? How is the delivery initiated? Think of the process as a mystery; you must look at the actions of the individual and work through the process backward to the beginning of the process flow and forward to the end in order to determine not only how to assist the individual but also to determine where best to enact change. Assume that the accounts billable clerk is using a printout from a delivery system. Then, the area of opportunity may be building a software system that replicates all of the accounts billable clerk's tasks and is fed the delivery data from the delivery system to begin with. However, if the delivery itself is manual, then the area of opportunity may begin with digitizing the delivery process and then automating the billing. The investigation or analysis of the current process will lead to options on how to proceed forward. These options will lead to further analysis of the positives and negatives of each course of action related to both the potential ability to enhance the current process and the feasibility of the organization to develop the technology solution needed to enact that change. From these options, the goal is to select the solution that has the best chance for success and then push the organization to move forward with the solution's actual construction.

Another aspect of the planning stage that is inherently important is the management of all the potential projects within the organization of the project portfolio. From both a decision-making and labor perspective, it would be convenient if an organization were to identify, develop, construct, and implement only one technology-based solution at a time, essentially completing development projects in a vacuum. However, in today's business environment, that is simply not possible. An organization has multiple managers, and each manager feels the business processes they oversee can be enhanced. Additionally, the goals and strategies are constantly changing. With this change comes changes in priorities for the development of new systems. Change is the only constant in business technology, and that change needs to be managed at the planning phase of the SDLC. For example, if a fuel company has identified that a new dispatch system for their lubricant division is necessary and a new tracking system for their home heating fuel trucks is also warranted, both are feasible, and the return on investment (ROI) to build the dispatch system is twice that of the tracking system, you would conclude that the dispatch system should be developed first. However, if the organization states that they have a potential buyer for the lubricant division and won't know if they are going to sell for at least 6 months, you would then develop the tracking system first. What is most important to remember is that there will always be many potential development projects in an organization, and a determination must be made on which ones are to be done first. However, this decision must be made through analysis of the projects, potential returns, and strategic alignment of the organization.

At this juncture, the organization does not have a development project; they have a development idea. The next step in the planning phase is to formalize the idea into a system request. Essentially, develop a formal document that outlines the business need, benefit to the organization, and reasoning why the endeavor is viable. Not only is this a key component of moving the project forward, but it's the first time the organization as a whole will be exposed to the potential endeavor, and it can result in either the gaining of support for the project or rejection of the idea altogether. The stakes are always high in the development phase, as it's not a tangible solution that is being presented but an idea that must be bought into. System development comes at significant commitment and expense and, therefore, requires continuous buy-in of the organization at all times. At each step of the SDLC, buy-in can be strengthened, weakened, or even lost. Therefore, it is imperative that the proposal of a new project be well thought out, factually documented, and professionally presented.

Assuming that the system request is accepted by the organization, there is one more item that must be developed in the planning phase, and that is the project plan. Most organizations will not allow a development project to be funded or to proceed without an indication of the time, effort, and cost to be undertaken. The project plan outlines the time frame for the project, including key milestones that are to be met. Additionally, it incorporates resource allocation and usage duration of specific internal and external resources. Once completed, the organization will once again review and hopefully approve the project to move forward.

Stage 2: The Analysis Phase

Image 1.3

A project that successfully completes the planning phase will move into the analysis phase. To understand the analysis phase, think of an onion as the business processes being enacted. To successfully develop and propose a system development project, we peeled back the first few layers of the onion to gain enough knowledge to reasonably define our intended objective, course of action, and ultimate goal. Additionally, we made commitments to both the anticipated costs and benefits of the newly developed system, the resources to be used, and even the time the project is going to take. The analysis phase will now peel back all remaining layers of the onion to ensure everything that was stated is actually feasible.

The analysis phase begins with an in-depth study of the existing system and identification of its perceived deficiencies. While it is important to note that analysis of the current business process has already been conducted in the planning phase, the analysis phase will recommit to conducting this analysis at a much more granular level. Many techniques will be used to bring out a comprehensive requirements list that the new system must facilitate to be successful.

The second part of the analysis phase is to analyze the developed requirements and determine specifically how technology is going to be implemented to meet them, as well as to determine if any aspects of the current process scope can simply be eliminated altogether. The ultimate goal is to develop a new system concept that can be modeled, once again, for feasibility. The system concept will be looked at in terms of how the development meets end-user requirements, process requirements, and data requirements to successfully meet the overall project objectives.

Finally, the analysis phase concludes with the development of the system proposal. This development is a formal document that clearly outlines the new system to be constructed and accurately denotes the objectives and corresponding actions that will be completed to meet those objectives. The presentation of this document is yet another chance for the organization to continue to support the intended development or possibly cancel the project.

One of the biggest concerns that is encountered within the analysis phase is how much analysis is adequate. There is a large degree of uncertainty related to system development, and one of the greatest fears is that not enough knowledge has been gained to successfully construct a new technology solution. While there is no hard and fast rule for how much analysis is enough, developed systems analysis methodologies, which we will explore in great detail later, coupled with the experience of systems analysis professionals, are used in combination to ensure that accurate time and effort are expended on these activities. Oftentimes, the analysis phase is the key differentiator between a successful and an unsuccessful project. Knowledge is power in the arena of systems development.

Stage 3: The Design Phase

Successfully completing the objectives of the analysis phase allows an organization to enter the design phase. To reiterate, to get to this point, an organization has successfully identified a challenge in its organizational scope that can be positively enhanced through the development of a technological solution. The current environment has been extensively analyzed. The proposed development was assessed and reaffirmed, and the new system proposal was developed. It is now time to formally develop how the new proposed system will be constructed.

There are many different strategies that can be deployed to build a new technology system. A company can purchase a solution, build its own, or even outsource the development to a third party. Additionally, it is not required that only a single strategy be used. It's possible to purchase a system and then develop enhancements that meet the specific needs of the organization. For example, a company purchases a private payment card system from a vendor but then creates a custom integration that allows that private card to be used as both a payment card and a loyalty card on the organization's point of sale (register) system. The important thing to remember when it comes to choosing a development strategy is that cost is not the only factor. There are actually many factors that come into play when deciding how to proceed with new system construction. Certainly, if the organization does not have system development resources, that will negate your ability to do a custom build, but even if those resources exist, they may not have the knowledge to do the type of technological build necessary for the current project. Additionally, they may already be committed to another project requiring either an outsourcing or purchase strategy to be enacted. The circumstances of the organization at a specific place and time when a project is being implemented will potentially affect which development strategy is selected, and all aspects of the organization must be considered at this phase of the development project.

Once the design strategy is decided upon, the next aspect to be identified and committed to are the design components. A software system is not constructed by programmers alone. There are many architectural aspects to an information system that must be taken into consideration in the design phase. What hardware will the system run on? What does the user interface look like? How is it organized? What are the networking requirements? What data is necessary to be retained, and how will it be stored and accessed? What external systems must be interacted with? How will those interactions be facilitated, and what happens if those systems are unavailable? All of these questions and more must be answered for the system being developed and are done through activities that result in the creation of a system specification document. This document will outline the components that must be used for the system to operate successfully. For example, looking back at the heating fuel truck tracking example, there must be a device that can be installed on the truck, and it must be accessible when the truck is in motion. Therefore, the system specification document would most likely include a cellular data connection requirement for the said device, as well as outline the specific device manufacturer to use for the tracking device itself. In this instance, we are building an information system but sourcing physical hardware that will interact with said system to meet our business requirements.

As with every other phase of the SDLC, the culmination of the design phase will result in the presentation of the system specification document to the organization with an end result consisting of either continued support for the project or potential termination of the project. It is important to analyze the development as it is currently defined against the stated project requirements that were developed at the beginning of the project. How aligned are they still? Are there justifications for any and all alterations between the initial proposal and the current development? How do these alterations affect the overall project cost or time line? Answering these questions ahead of the presentation and anticipating pushback for changes to the original plan can be imperative to keep the project moving forward.

Stage 4: The Implementation Phase

Assuming that the project continues to be supported, the final phase of the SDLC is the implementation phase. There is often some confusion related to the initial tasks of the implementation phase. Those who are new to systems analysis tend to believe that the actual new system is constructed in the design phase, and the first part of the implementation phase is testing the new construction. This is incorrect. The design phase ends with essentially creating the blueprint for the new system. The implementation phase begins with constructing the new system itself. This is a very exciting task. Up until this point, the new system has been a concept brought to life in thought only. Finally, the development project has reached an apex where a tangible item will be developed. For many who are involved in system development, this is the primary reason they entered into this field. Their passion is to bring to life something that did not previously exist, and this is where that creation begins.

However, there are still many tasks that must be completed before the organization has a new operational system. Yes, system construction is the first item to be completed, but it is not the sole task to be completed at this stage. Once the initial build is developed, testing must commence. Even the most well-thought-out and planned system developments will have errors and issues upon construction, and various testing methods will assist in bringing these issues to light. Additionally, testing will not be conducted as a single activity but rather as a series of coordinated activities designed to allow for confidence to be gained in the new system.

Once an appropriate amount of testing has been completed successfully, the next step will be to install the new system in the organization's operational environment. However, the new system will not be migrated immediately. Training must be conducted so that the organization's employees fully understand the changes that are about to be enacted and the alternations they must make to their daily work tasks in order to accommodate these changes. Oftentimes, the old process will remain while the new system completes the same activities side by side. This will allow the employees to be trained on the new system and, therefore, gain experience with their new work tasks while, at the same time, providing a final level of testing to ensure the system is operating as intended.

Once training has been completed, the organization will convert from the old business processes over to the new system. The system will take over the process completion responsibility in totality and hopefully successfully. It is at this time that ongoing system support will be implemented for the new system as well.

It is important to understand that system analysis does not end with the implementation of the new system. The new system has just become the current system. The SDLC is a cycle because it repeats forever, taking new implementations and making them a current component of the organization's overall technology ecosystem and, most importantly, making them an item for future analysis and possibly future action within the planning phase of a new SDLC system development project.

Why Do System Development Projects Fail?

Image 1.4

At face value, the SDLC appears to be a straightforward and well-defined process for identifying, developing, and implementing new information systems. So how can it be that greater than 50% of all system development projects that are attempted end in failure? It doesn't seem viable that such a structured framework would result in such lackluster results.

There is no single answer for the high degree of technology-based project failure. However, there are varying factors that make logical sense as to why failure would occur as a result. Through understanding these factors, we can hopefully minimize them in future system development attempts. It is not the structure of the SDLC that is the issue, but the human component that is using the structure and the actions or sometimes inactions taken at the various stages of the development cycle.

Inadequate Planning

One reason projects fail is due to inadequate planning. The very first phase of the SDLC will often encounter issues. This is concerning in that you can view the planning phase as the foundation of the project. If you build a house on an unstable foundation, there is a good chance that the house will collapse over time. Therefore, it's a reasonable assumption that if you do not complete adequate due diligence in the planning phase of your project, you are creating far greater challenges the further you progress in the endeavor. Primary issues within the planning phase consist of understating the project time frame, resource requirements, and cost. While these underestimates may assist you in getting project approval at the beginning of the project, they are sure to cause your project progression to diverge from your actual development and ensure that there will be contention between the development team and the organization, possibly ending in project termination and greater difficulty getting approval for a future project.

Lack of Clarity in Project Requirements

Another area that contributes to project failure is a lack of clarity in project requirements. Issues in the analysis phase of the SDLC can also lead to disastrous results. Communication is a primary requirement for pulling out requirements for the new system from users of the current system. While communication seems easy, it is often very difficult. Think about it: If I ask you to explain to me how to withdraw money from an ATM, what is the first step you think to tell me? Is it select withdraw? Is it enter an amount? If either of these is your answer, you are part of the problem. However, don't feel bad; you are also thinking like the majority of the population. Individuals tend to provide direction by omitting steps that they believe are universally understood. Therefore, you wouldn't tell me to insert my ATM card into the slot and enter my four-digit PIN because you would assume that everyone who uses an ATM would know how to do that. Now, apply this logic when I ask you to describe the steps you take to complete your daily tasks at work. How much do you leave out because it's ingrained in your daily process and simply second nature? However, I don't do your daily tasks, so the minutia that you leave out becomes missing links to the chain that is required to secure the success of the new development. Communication is hard, and a lack of communication results in a lack of clarity of project requirements and, therefore, less chance of overall project success.

Rushing to Completion

Another main cause of system development failure lies in yet another human tendency in the business environment: rushing project completion. Software development projects are time-consuming and costly. On top of that, there is always the added pressure of beginning new development projects while current projects are in development. The end result is constant pressure to complete the current project at a more rapid rate. Reducing the development time frame often leads to shortcuts and omissions that could prove to be the reason behind missing functionality and sometimes an unusable final solution. The commitment to develop a new information system requires that the time frame identified be the time frame that is accepted by the organization to ensure that the identified system requirements are met in system construction.

Insufficient Testing

While there are many other potential pitfalls when it comes to information system development that we will explore in subsequent chapters, one final issue that bears discussion in the forefront is a lack of testing. Too often, organizations structure testing methods around how the system is intended to function and ignore methods that may bring out unintended consequences of system misuse. For example, looking once again at an ATM. If we were developing a new ATM, we would build testing methods around card authorization, deposit, withdrawal, and balance lookup. We would be less likely to test what would happen if, say, I just randomly started punching numbers on the keypad. Why? Because that is not the intended utilization of the system. However, it just may be that a certain sequence of numbers may cause the machine to dispense funds. If this were the case and someone were to stumble across this bug, it could easily lead to the system costing the company financially or even ultimately bankrupting the company if the bug was exploited to the highest degree. The point is that testing needs to be defined to not only verify intended utilization but also identify potential risks based on unintended utilization of the system. Finally, a lack of testing of intended functionality simply heightens the risk of unintended negative consequences and makes the potential for system failure even greater. Well-thought-out and adequate testing is a high-level requirement for successful new system development.

The Systems Analyst

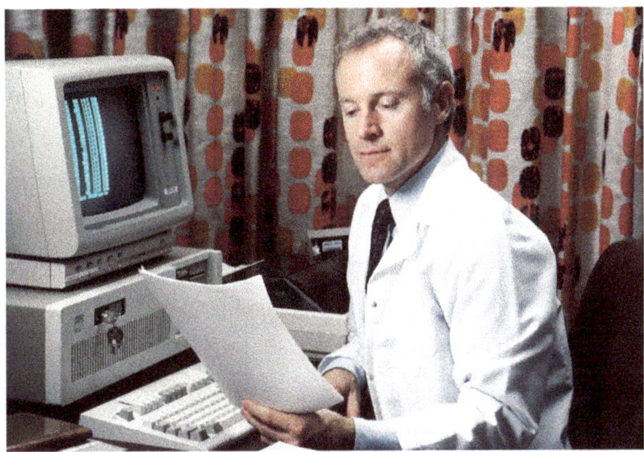

Image 1.5

We have discussed both what systems analysis is and the SDLC that is used to develop a new system incorporating industry best practices. However, there is one more major component that remains to be explored. That would be the professionals who are responsible for enacting the SDLC: systems analysts. I have to make a confession at this point. My father was a systems analyst, and at a young age, I can remember him bringing home boxes of computer printouts and sitting at our kitchen table on weekends, going over them line by line with different colored highlighters arranged beside him, he would highlight segments of code in various colors and wrote notations in the margins. I didn't grasp what he was actually doing, but I can still remember thinking, in no way would I want to do that all day, every day for my career.

What I failed to see at the time, and what I truly couldn't comprehend until I was much older and, yes, as a systems analyst myself, was that what I saw on weekends was a very small, yet necessary, component of my father's overall role. While there are aspects of the systems analyst's responsibilities that can be very detail oriented and even a bit mundane, there are many exciting challenges that make the role both complex and potentially very satisfying. A systems analyst is one who is responsible for the entire system development process and its ultimate success or failure. They guide teams of trained professionals in all the tasks associated with each step of the SDLC. In fact, as the proposed system is not tangible until late in the development process, the systems analyst often becomes the face of the system itself. The decision-makers within the organization often assimilate the individual with the project being proposed, and their response will likely correlate with the degree to which they trust said person to be able to accomplish the system development being proposed. If that seems like a lot of pressure, it is. However, there is no reward without risk, and the level of risk can be minimized with a good process. Ultimately, the systems analyst role is one firmly implanted in providing balance.

The standard definition of a systems analyst is someone who implements information systems requirements by defining and analyzing system problems and designing and testing standards and solutions to solve those problems. While that definition certainly touches on the broad focus of the systems analyst, it fails to convey many requirements of the role.

Business Knowledge

As we have explored the tasks required to create and implement a new system, one aspect that clearly jumps out is the need to understand the business aspect of the organization. The systems analyst is the one who defines how new technology will solve current business needs. However, you can't identify the business need if you are not knowledgeable about general business processes and functions. Therefore, the systems analyst, first and foremost, must be educated in business in general. Understanding operational structure and process flow is paramount in being able to analyze the specific iterations within an organization. However, a broad knowledge of business functions is not sufficient enough to be successful. To gauge the success of a current business process within a specific organization, you must first understand every task within that process. We have already identified that communication can be difficult, and therefore, the systems analyst should be an above-average communicator, well-versed in pulling out requirements through thoughtful questioning and adept listening. However, communication should not be the only way that business process analysis is conducted. The systems analyst must also observe and be able to comprehend those observations. For example, if a systems analyst is trying to define a more effective process for pizza delivery, they must be willing to walk through the current process, certainly talking to employees, but also getting into a delivery vehicle with a driver and viewing firsthand how the process is conducted. Only by immersing yourself in the environment you are trying to enact change in can you fully understand what change is necessary. Successfully completing these activities takes someone with social skills and an understanding of social interaction with a diverse range of personalities. Oftentimes, the efforts of the systems analyst are focused on gaining the support of those around them, and that is not always an easy task.

Employee Perception

One aspect of change as it relates to system development is that change is not solely at the organizational level; it is, most importantly, at the individual level. Through your actions as a systems analyst, you are going to change the daily tasks of the individuals you are interacting with. From one perspective, you are working to make the environment more efficient for the organization. Sometimes, that comes at a cost, like automating a segment or even all of the position requirements of one or more individuals. Therefore, many people will be resistant to change and, therefore, resistant to assisting you in your goal of increasing your understanding of their current business tasks. Even if there is clearly no risk of a person's position being automated, many people take comfort in knowing their day-to-day task requirements, and changing those requirements can be unsettling. They will view it as assisting you in changing or automating the position they are currently in, and that can lead to some very adverse interactions. Each organization has its own strategy and culture when it comes to position automation, but it is exceedingly important for the systems analyst to be cognizant of the perceptions employees may have to change and the resistance they may initially present.

Ethical Implications

There are ethical implications to the systems analyst role. The systems analyst has a powerful role within the organization in that they are able to structure projects that can potentially eliminate headcount. This should never be done for any reason other than necessity. For example, if there is someone within the organization whom the systems analyst has a strong dislike for, it is not acceptable for them to develop and promote a development project with the primary or even secondary priority to eradicate that person's position. It sounds a bit outlandish when you first think about it, but such action is certainly in the realm of possibility. Likewise, pushing for projects that will assist a friend's department within the organization instead of prioritizing ones that are more beneficial to the organization as a whole is not acceptable. As with many leadership positions within the organization, it is important to ensure that decisions are being made to benefit the organization as opposed to satisfying personal fulfillment.

Technology Knowledge

Image 1.6

Just as a firm understanding of business methodology is a key to success, so too is the incorporation of knowledge of technology. In this area, the systems analyst has to be up to date on the newest technologies available, as well as what new technologies have the potential for being developed. Once areas of opportunity are identified in the current business process scope, the systems analyst has to be able to insert potential technologies into the equation to gauge the potential success of integration and thereby meet business needs. However, as technology is constantly changing, the systems analyst must be continually self-educating. In all aspects of technology professions, continuous self-directed learning is the key to success, and this discipline is no different.

Not only is the understanding of available technologies important but so is having in-depth knowledge of the organization's current systems and network. It's not only necessary to analyze how new technology will interact with current business processes but also if and how it will integrate into the organization's current technological environment. While a solution may meet all of the needs of the newly defined business process, if it fails to work within the confines of the other systems currently deployed in the environment, it cannot be initiated.

Personalities

People are at the heart of the majority of the activities conducted by the systems analyst, and it is exceedingly important that they be able to relate to everyone necessary in order to make the project a success. This consists of all aspects of the organization, from ownership to executive management, midlevel management, department heads, administrators, and even entry-level and newly hired personnel. These individuals will have diverse personalities and offer unique challenges throughout the SDLC process.

Not only are individual interactions of concern but so too are group dynamics. Do you feel an entry-level employee is likely to point out inefficiencies in their daily work processes with their supervisor in the same room? What about if an owner were present? It's not likely. So, the systems analyst must always be cognizant of how information is gained through organizational interactions.

It has been well established that the primary focus of the system analyst is to gain and maintain support for the project. This requires interacting with and convincing decision-makers within the organization that they should align with your proposal. This may require including these members in fact-finding initiatives, subject matter expert discussions, and closed-door, information-gathering sessions. While you may not necessarily need their input to make development decisions, pulling them into the project can assist in gaining their support. A productive systems analyst recognizes that there is a degree of "playing politics" to get a worthwhile project off the ground.

Being Detail Oriented

It has been said that success is in the details. This is very true when it comes to the systems analyst. The complexity of both the business environment and technology development results in the potential for a high-risk endeavor. One that results in a greater than 50% chance of failure. One of the greatest combatants to this high-risk environment is amassing as much detail as possible, ensuring that every aspect of the current system is flushed out, documented, and fully understood. Likewise, the proposed new system should be analyzed to ensure that every requirement is met or exceeded; development is in line with a plan from cost, time, and resource perspectives; and system development documentation contains everything necessary to construct the system for intended utilization. That is a massive amount of detail to be organized, structured, and used. It takes a well-organized individual to ensure not only that all the data is compiled but also accessible when necessary. Meeting this requirement will go a long way to minimizing the risks associated with why most technology development projects fail.

The Face of the Project

With all the ways a system development project can go wrong, there needs to be a consistent force within the organization that can assuage fears, reassure, coax, remind, and sometimes simply push back against a sentiment to abandon a project. That is not to say that every project should be seen through to completion. There are times when errors made early on, incorrect assumptions or a changing corporate strategy will dictate the need to abandon a project. However, if all activities have been completed satisfactorily, the operational and strategic corporate environment is static, and the project is tracking to a planned completion from both an effort and cost perspective, pressure to cancel the project can be considered inaccurate, and resistance should be initiated.

You may ask yourself, why would a successful project that was given the green light to proceed be at risk of cancellation prior to successful completion? There are a number of reasons why this may occur. Someone within the organization with enough power to potentially change the outcome of a current project may be aligned with a future project that is waiting to be initiated, and they may be convinced that the benefit of the future outweighs the benefit of the project in development. It is also possible that there is a change in management, and with that change comes a change in the perceived priority of development projects. Or, simply, it may be an oversight or misunderstanding as to where the current project is positioned, and action is being taken based on the misconception.

Regardless of why, it is the responsibility of the systems analyst to ensure that a project does not get canceled for the wrong reason. This may require the systems analyst to go up against someone of greater standing in the organization, which is never a pleasant experience. It is due to these requirements that it can be said that a successful systems analyst cannot simply look at the project as a job. If the system development project is simply a job, it is easy to distance one's self from the endeavor when the job gets tough. To be successful, a good systems analyst must rise to the challenge and push forward through difficult circumstances. Most people do not push to that degree if they are simply going through the motions of the tasks presented to them. There needs to be a passion for the work itself.

The role of a systems analyst is not simply a job. To be successful requires a person to ingrain themselves in the project. Those who succeed truly believe that what they are attempting to do is not only best for the organization, but they also assimilate the project's success with their own professional success and refuse to accept less than victory. They assimilate their contribution to the organization to be the completed working solution, and anything less is their failure. Essentially, a good systems analyst takes on the responsibility for the project's success and stakes their reputation on the future success of the project. You may read this and think it a bit dramatic, but with all the challenges facing a system development, it truly is a positive mindset and an unwillingness to fail that is the difference between project success and failure.

Once an individual is willing to stake their reputation on the development they are overseeing, they become committed to ensuring project support remains within the organization. Again, this is a balancing act. Sometimes, regardless of the level of effort or responsibility you take on, a project will fail, and there is no shame in admitting that mistakes were made. I've always said, "I've never had a failed project. I've had projects that didn't come to fruition, but the information gained through the effort was invaluable to making the next project a success." While project failures can be valuable in gaining additional knowledge to make future projects stronger, there is still no better outcome than to see your final product placed into operation.

There are many instances of immensely successful development projects that altered the course of an organization for the better and would not have been completed were it not for a committed systems analyst. They use their position in the organization and, more importantly, the trust decision-makers have in them to continue to push the project forward. As there is no tangible evidence of the work being completed until late in the SDLC, the systems analyst becomes the embodiment of the project. This allows the organization to buy into and visualize the individual as being the investment they are committing to. A person who can gain and leverage this trust will have an easier time maintaining support through the end of the implementation phase of a system development project.

Team Builder

Image 1.7

A system is not successfully developed by an individual; it takes a team. Not just any team, but one that is compiled from throughout the organization and must include individuals that will contribute to the success of the development. However, this contribution does not always come willingly. For example, when I define a project team, one component I put a lot of thought into is which end users I want to include in the actual project team. I tend to select two types of individuals. One person I look for is someone who is technologically adept and is likely to champion the new development into completion by providing a positive outlook on the development activities, even when issues and challenges are encountered. This would be someone who is pro-change and wants to be a contributing factor in the overall success of the endeavor. The other participant I look for out of the end user group is the individual who is most resistant to the change. Not only are they exceedingly resistant, but they have the ear of a good portion of the end users who are expected to adapt to the changes brought upon by the new system. I begin assessing where their resistance to change is coming from and then consider how I can demonstrate the usefulness of the new system to hopefully change their perception.

Why do I look for such polar opposite views of the project I am trying to complete? Well, in regard to the project-positive individual, they will be an asset throughout the testing phase of the system development. I do not have to be concerned that an error or unanticipated result will scare them away from being a future system user. Their assessment and response will be invaluable for dialing in the system to ensure it meets the end user's needs. The project-resistant individual is all about changing perspective. Think about the remaining end users outside of the project group. There is always at least a segment of the affected users who are resistant to change. If I can take a person who is vocally opposed to the system development I am attempting to complete and make them positive to the system, two things will happen. They will be vocal about their changed perception to the rest of the user group, and it will get the rest of the end users thinking that perhaps the new system is not as scary as initially believed. If this individual sees value, perhaps they should reserve judgment until they experience it as well. The buy-in component of the system analyst's responsibilities is not solely reserved for decision-makers. It also extends to the end users who must willingly adapt to the changes being enacted on them. A new system will never be successful if the ones required to use it refuse to.

It is the responsibility of the systems analyst to put a high level of thought and effort into the selection of each member of the project team. This team will consist of resources throughout the organization. The majority will be selected for their ability to contribute their knowledge to the project tasks. However, some will be selected for their ability to assist in moving the project forward. Others will be selected for their initial resistance and the value they will provide when you are able to convert them from an opponent to a supporter. Notice I said when and not if. A good systems analyst will assess each individual and develop a strategy of how they are going to positively affect the project with each selection; this includes making an educated guess that with the knowledge you obtained, you will be successful in converting a negative opinion to a positive one.

Systems Analyst Summation

The systems analyst must contain diverse aptitudes and skill sets. They must be socially comfortable and willing to not only communicate with many different personalities but also have the ability to direct conversations and pull out information from seemingly mundane interactions. Additionally, this person must be able to assess not only the organization but also the individuals within and make educated inferences on which people will be the greatest assets to include within the development group. Also, they must be able to gain the trust of the decision-makers within the organization and possess an ability to assuage fears and even alter the opinions of those who do not support the development project.

Professionally, this individual needs to be educated in business processes and understand organizational structure as well as strategic planning. While they may not be experts in any aspect of the operational environment, they must have a depth of knowledge sufficient to make change decisions and understand how those changes will impact the operational scope. From a technology perspective, they must be up to speed on the latest technologies. While they may not be able to build a new system themselves, they need to be able to direct the developers and, therefore, must speak their language.

The systems analyst must be structured and organized. They must be able to multitask and think outside the box. It takes skill to be able to look at a problem from a multitude of directions and assess which course is most appropriate. The system analyst does this, not singularly, but across multiple decision points with a keen eye to how one decision may affect other aspects of the development.

Finally, this person must be driven. They must push themselves to succeed and be willing to stake their reputation on the success of the project. They must be willing to fight for what they believe in and not take no for an answer when they are convinced they are heading down the right path.

Image 1.8

Chapter Summary

In conclusion, systems analysis is a complex and difficult discipline. However, it is one that is essential for the continued success of any business in operation today. Technology has become the cornerstone of the vast majority of business entities in existence today or ones planned for initiation in the future. Systems analysis is pivotal in enacting the change consistent with technology adaptation and is, therefore, a primary requirement for business success today and into the future. In the upcoming chapters, we will explore each component of the SDLC, the best practices for how each activity is to be implemented, and how real-world applications provide guidance to successfully navigate the systems development process.

Project Planning Activities

At the end of each chapter, there will be a project planning activities section. The purpose of this section is to have the reader select an organization of their choosing for which they would like to develop a new system. You will then complete activities identified within the chapter content to create a new system development project report for the identified organization. For this chapter's tasks, let's select the organization you would like to work with:

1. Write a brief history and detailed description of the company.
2. Build organizational charts for the executive management structure, as well as the technology department.
3. Identify the system within the organization that you would like to fix or the area of the organization that could use a new technology system altogether.

Image Credits

CHAPTER 2

Selecting and Organizing the Project

Introduction

At the root of each and every successful software development project lies a single commonality: a problem. Problems drive innovation, automation, product enhancement, and process redesign. Problems provide a focus point to generate a new way of completing a task or sometimes removing one altogether. A problem is a powerful motivator.

Take a moment and think about two digital solutions you use regularly:

1. One consistently operates as expected, is intuitive to navigate, and is easy to use.
2. One is cumbersome, unintuitive, and is a challenge to complete even simple tasks.

In a digital society, having regular experience with both types of applications is common. However, which one do you gravitate toward? The one that acts as you would expect, provides value to you as a user, and is simple to navigate seems like the most appropriate choice. So, why are you able to come up with an example of a regularly used yet challenging application? The majority of us would concede that such an application completes a necessary task for us, even though it may create friction in doing so, and therefore, we, as users, push through our discontent out of necessity.

When a user does not have a choice, they will use the digital application that is necessary. However, given a choice, a user will select the application that is more intuitive and easier to use. If you are able to remove friction from a user's interaction, you will gain that user's support. Essentially, fix the problem, and you will gain support.

System development projects begin by assessing the organization itself. Internal and external processes, compliance requirements, safety requirements, and even the strategic goals of the organization are all areas where challenges exist. By researching these challenges and assessing the degree to which a digital system can combat them, the foundation of a development project will begin to take shape. Let's look at some of these areas in greater detail.

Image 2.1

Learning Objectives

1. Explain how organizations identify technology-based development projects.
2. Explain how projects are selected.
3. Be able to create a system request.
4. Explain how to select a project methodology.
5. Describe technical, economic, and organizational feasibility.
6. Be able to perform a feasibility analysis.
7. Become familiar with project estimation.
8. Be familiar with a project work plan.
9. Explain how to manage risk on the project.

Where Do Projects Come From

Business Need

The needs of the business certainly are able to drive new solution development. Oftentimes, when assessing operational processes within an organization, one is likely to hear, "We do it this way because we have always done it this way." While it certainly makes sense that an organization that has found success through consistency would favor that consistency in the future, the replication of historical processes negates the benefit of the incorporation of new advancements in technologies. The only real constant in today's business environment is change, and therefore, this phrase is a clue that some analysis of the current processes should be conducted. It is important to note that problems are uncovered by communicating with the people who interact with the current process being reviewed. Therefore, people are essential for uncovering actual business needs.

The employees within the organization understand the goals of the organization, the reasoning for specific processes, how to complete specific tasks, and overall, what is important to the success of the organization. Customers understand how they interact with the organization, both positively and negatively, and compare their experiences with those they have had with competitors. Even competitors themselves can provide valuable information when it comes to business needs. If they are implementing processes that engage your customers better than your organization, that highlights a need for change. Conversely, if they are attempting to mimic your current process, there is an affirmation that what you are doing is working. You cannot create a project without communicating with the individuals that the project will ultimately affect and analyzing their needs to a larger degree.

USER NEED

In order to best define the importance of user needs, it is important to look at the needs of individuals from various perspectives within the organization. Employees can provide direction for internal process-based system development, while customers and competitors can highlight externally facing system development opportunities. However, it is common that the resulting system will positively affect both internal and external parties, and all people interacting with the organization will play a role in successfully defining the project.

Employees

Organizational employees are a wealth of information when attempting to look for opportunities to fix a problem.

Executive management and owners focus on where the current operational scope of the organization is limiting the organization's ability to complete aspects of the company's strategic plan. They also provide direction when outlining requirements necessary for supporting a new business initiative or strategy or even for the support of a merger or acquisition.

Midlevel managers are able to highlight process limitations, operational inefficiencies, and staffing concerns. They will also often have knowledge of new technologies within their operational scope that they are interested in using.

Departmental managers further expand on both process and efficiency concerns, as well as highlight challenges regarding interdepartmental constraints. These managers will sometimes come up with ideas for altering a current process or even implementing a completely new process.

Departmental staff are often the frontline users of current technology systems or are completing manual tasks that a system could replace. They have a unique ability to communicate not only how they complete their daily tasks but also how the current process contains points of friction.

Customers

Customers are equally valuable when it comes to identifying challenges in an organization's current process or technology. Customers are the reason you have a business, to begin with, and removing friction from the way they interact with your organization goes a long way to ensuring that they will continue to fulfill the role of customer into the future. Your customers will be able to tell you what they perceive you do well and what you can do better. We can all relate to the role of the customer, as we are all customers ourselves.

Think about the businesses you frequent and the technologies they employ. Pick one that you feel does an excellent job of meeting your needs as a customer. Can you think of something they can improve upon? Most often, the answer is yes. Even though we are appreciative of an easy and intuitive interaction with a business, if we analyze every detail of the process, we can usually identify some aspects that could be improved.

Now, take these same steps with a customer who has an issue with a business interaction. They are even more willing to share their opinion as their interaction with the organization contains a degree of friction and, in turn, a negative connotation. Listening to their experience and the feelings it imparts on them can provide a valid reason for new system development.

Competing Organization

An organization's competitor can demonstrate how a like process can be completed differently. If they are leveraging technology that supports a more efficient process, you may lose customer share to them. Conversely, if their process is more ineffective than your own, your organization may gain customer share away from them. Often, it is not an all-or-nothing scenario. Given the scope of a business, a competitor may do some processes better than your organization and some worse. It is important to note that analyzing what your competition does well and where it can improve will assist in assessing where effort should be placed within your organization to best differentiate yourself from your competition.

INFORMATION NEEDS

In business, the phrase "information is power" is not an exaggeration. In a time of artificial intelligence, big data analytics, and cloud computing, data can be the key to success. Data can also be a driver for new system development. Whether an organization is looking to enhance efficiencies, create additional customer value, or simply enhance customer engagement, mining and actioning off of data is increasingly important to maintaining organizational success across industries.

By analyzing how an organization uses its data, gaps where data collection would be beneficial, or even ways that market data can be incorporated to make business decisions, potential software development projects will come to light. As new technologies are constantly being created around data, even current data mining processes are candidates for technological upgrades.

BUSINESS PROCESS MANAGEMENT

Current processes within the organization are always candidates for potential software development projects. Manual processes will often benefit from automation, and digital processes have the potential for enhancement or even leveraging new technologies to combine or eliminate processes altogether. Business process management (BPM) is a methodology used by organizations to continuously improve end-to-end processes and ensure that process agility, industry "best practices," and efficiencies are constantly improving.

BPM consists of four main steps that are enacted on an organization's key operational processes:

1. Define and map the steps in a business process.
2. Create ways to improve steps in the process that add value.
3. Eliminate or consolidate tasks in a process that do not contribute value or hinder productivity.
4. Create or alter digital workflows to match the newly improved process.

BPM ensures that organizational opportunities for technological growth are always available. Additionally, employing this methodology within the organization will ensure that there is a focus on continuous development and assessment of organizational processes and procedures. Not only does the function promote development, but it assists in creating a development culture within the organization.

Figure 2.1 Diagram of Compliance

Compliance Requirements

Meeting compliance requirements is a cornerstone requirement of every organization. Compliance is essentially ensuring that the organization and its employees follow all laws, regulations, and standards as set forth by local, state, and federal regulations, as well as contractually agreed upon between parties that the organization interacts with. This can include suppliers, vendors, contractors, industry regulators, or any entity in which the organization has entered into a legal agreement to operate in a specific way.

More and more, meeting compliance requirements requires the integration of technology and digital processes to complete and maintain defined criteria. These criteria can consist of report submission, data collection and retention, monitoring, notification protocols, and a host of other process-oriented functions to ensure processes are safe and conducted as intended with no adverse consequences. One example would be an organization enacting a cybersecurity policy as required by their credit card processor in order for the company to be able to accept credit card payments for products and services.

Just as business needs drive system development, so too do compliance requirements. More and more compliance requirements not only require new solution development, but as an organization cannot operate without being compliant, these requirements will make this type of solution development a higher priority, even over business process value-added projects.

Finally, it is important to ensure that BPM is used in compliance processes as well. Just because compliance is met with the current process does not mean that it cannot be done more efficiently or that separate processes cannot be combined by leveraging new technology. Just as with operational processes, integration of technology and process automation can result in increased business value for the organization. Therefore, processes should be analyzed regularly.

Project Selection

Now that ways to explore problems within the organization have been identified, how do we initiate an actual software development project? It's simple, really. Identified problems or related groups of problems are the foundation for a potential project. The next step is to define the solution to the problem using technology. It is important to note, and as you will see, that developing a new system is an extremely resource-intensive and detail-oriented process that requires significant effort in researching, analyzing, developing, and implementing the newly created system. It is not possible to conduct research for every problem looking for a solution. However, a systems analyst must do a very high-level analysis of the identified problem to determine if the potential for a technologically driven solution exists.

To make this assessment, the systems analyst will look at the problem from these varying perspectives:

1. Does a technology solution exist that resolves the problem?
2. Can a technology solution be developed to resolve the problem?
3. Does the organization have the ability to implement a technology to resolve the problem?
4. What is the potential value to the organization for implementing a technology solution to the problem?

Potential system development projects exist everywhere. Simply look around the organization and determine if a technology can either be used or created to resolve an issue. Even better, can an entire group of issues be resolved? Then, determine how much value there is for the business if that resolution is actually implemented. If the business value is significant, you have a potential system development project. By maintaining a culture of continuously searching out problems, analyzing for a potential technology-based resolution, and recording those that are deemed actionable, an organization ensures that the potential to enhance the organization through new system development is feasible.

PROJECT PORTFOLIO MANAGEMENT

Assembling all of the organization's potential projects into a central repository will allow the systems analyst to compare the anticipated project scope and value to the organization in order to prioritize which system developments should move forward and in what order. Additionally, as the business environment changes, business needs will also change. The project portfolio will allow for continuous assessment of the continued viability of potential projects within the portfolio. The main benefits of a project portfolio include

1. alignment of organizational objectives and potential system development projects,
2. standardization of project comparison both in scope and potential organizational benefit, and
3. governance and oversight within the project selection process.

When it comes time to select a new development project, the project portfolio will rank potential projects based on the following characteristics:

1. Project cost
2. Project time frame
3. Project ROI
4. Project resource requirements
5. Project risk

By maintaining this information for each potential project in the project portfolio, the systems analyst can determine which project will align with the business needs and resources available, have the highest return on investment for solution development, and move that selection on to the first phase of system development.

The SDLC—The Planning Phase

New system development begins with the planning phase of the SDLC. An organization maintaining an up-to-date project portfolio allows for the selection of the potential project that should have the best chance of being completed successfully by the organization, as well as also having the chance to provide significant benefit. However, just because a potential project is determined to be possible does not mean that it is actually feasible, or even if feasible, this does not mean that completing it is the best use of organizational resources. Although research, analysis, and comparison were all completed in order for the potential project to be inserted into the project portfolio, much more effort must be put into determining the validity of moving forward with project development.

While it is true that the planning phase is technically the initiation of a new project, it is also the initial justification for ensuring that the intended project is feasible and justified from a variety of perspectives. The process is designed to ensure that the following criteria are both met and aligned to a degree that moving forward with investment of time, labor, and financial resources are appropriate:

1. The project has the support of the organization through the identification of a project sponsor.
2. There is enough knowledge of the environment and anticipated development that a system request can be created.
3. Feasibility analysis supports the path forward toward new system development.
4. An appropriate development methodology is able to be selected to support new system development.
5. Project setup tasks are able to be developed, showing a clear course of action toward project development.

By ensuring that all of these aspects are analyzed against the proposed project, the systems analyst has the greatest potential of gaining organizational approval and moving the newly defined project forward toward actual creation. Additionally, it is worth noting that a multitude of project management software is available to provide templates for all necessary documentation development and assist in organizing discovery materials for inclusion into this and all phases of the SDLC.

Project Sponsor

Developing a new system is a daunting task. The vast majority of development projects take considerable time, resources, and effort and must be accomplished in an ever-changing business environment. It is highly likely that a development project will be initiated with strong organizational support, but as time goes on without a fully developed solution, support can easily begin to waiver. It is for this reason that ensuring that the project itself is associated with an individual or group of individuals within the organization who have the ability to campaign for project continuation is often essential for reaching project completion.

One aspect of new system development that is often overlooked is the continuous need for building support for the project. At every step of the SDLC, there is a requirement to push for approval to continue and the potential for the project to be canceled. A project sponsor with a degree of influence over the organization as a whole is a key resource for successfully navigating this requirement.

Finally, it should be noted that the project sponsor is not necessarily skilled at constructing the system itself. They believe in the project, are convinced of its value to the organization, and are willing to align their support to championing organizational support through project completion. This means that their position in the organization, ability to influence, and willingness to enact effort are the characteristics that will make them valuable to the systems analyst.

System Request

In order to begin to build organizational support for a system development project, there needs to be a formal description of the project itself. This allows the project sponsor, as well as the rest of the project team, to more effectively communicate the project intent, benefits, and possible constraints to the group within the organization who collectively decide if the project should proceed. This group is known as the steering committee.

The key components of a system request include the following:

1. Project sponsor identification
2. Business need
3. Business requirements
4. Business value
5. Special issues or constraints

PROJECT SPONSOR IDENTIFICATION

This section of the system request formally names the individual or group who are initiating the project and will act as the primary point of contact for decision-makers throughout the project development process. The project sponsor is important, as this designation needs to have the capability of both appeasing and motivating decision-makers as required. Finally, the project sponsor will be the face of the project and must be willing to provide support from project initiation through project completion.

BUSINESS NEED

This section of the system request clearly communicates the business reason or reasons for constructing the new system. Essentially, this is where the problem that began the process is stated and expanded upon to demonstrate the need for development. These requirements need to be explained at a high level so that the steering committee and project team have a firm grasp of what is expected of the newly developed system.

While a more comprehensive needs assessment will be completed later in the development process, it is important that enough research be conducted to adequately communicate a comprehensive list of all aspects of the problems to be mitigated. If aspects of the business need are omitted, the problem could appear to be understated and, as such, will demonstrate inaccurate valuation to the organization.

BUSINESS REQUIREMENTS

This section of the system request identifies the new capabilities the new system will provide. Again, these requirements need to be explained at a high level so that the steering committee and project team have a firm grasp on how this development will fully meet the identified business need. Therefore, it is important to ensure that the capabilities of the new system align with combating the problems highlighted in the business need section of the system request.

By aligning the new system requirements with all aspects of the identified business need, the steering committee will be assured that the new development will meet all intended objectives. Additionally, this alignment demonstrates a strong understanding of the scope of work by the system analyst.

BUSINESS VALUE

This section of the system request will highlight both the tangible and intangible benefits the new system will create for the organization. The tangible benefits are able to be quantified and easily measured. This is important, as the items stated in this section can be checked against the new system output to ensure what was promised at the beginning of the project was delivered by the new system solution. The intangible benefits are more intuitive and more difficult to measure. For example, increased customer satisfaction is a key driver for system development, but how do you actually measure customer satisfaction? While there are tools such as surveys and questionnaires to obtain a degree of understanding, they will only cover a segment of your total customer population and, because of this, will not provide a fully quantitative result.

SPECIAL ISSUES OR CONSTRAINTS

This section of the system request will contain special considerations that the steering committee must take into account when contemplating approval for new system development. Compliance requirements, time constraints, and external dependencies are all examples of considerations that may increase the importance of moving forward with the development. By incorporating all items that have the potential to affect the project, it emphasizes as much transparency with the steering committee as possible and also demonstrates a keen understanding of the environment by the systems analyst.

Image 2.2

Feasibility Analysis

While the system request is developed in order to more effectively communicate the reasons and perceived value for proceeding forward with development, the feasibility analysis is designed to communicate the organization's ability to successfully complete the project. Feasibility is looked at from three different perspectives to demonstrate this ability:

1. Technical feasibility
2. Economic feasibility
3. Organizational feasibility

All of these feasibility perspectives are organized into a **feasibility study** that will be presented to the steering committee as part of the justification for proceeding forward with the project. However, this development is not to be used simply to gain project approval. It is imperative that project feasibility is reassessed throughout the entire project duration to ensure that the criteria assessed at the beginning of the project are still relevant through the completion of the project.

TECHNICAL FEASIBILITY

This assessment focuses on whether the organization has the technical capability to complete the project, as well as whether the technology required is even possible to acquire or create. An organization's internal resources will have strengths and weaknesses, and it must be determined if the tasks required are within the strengths of these resources. Even when using external resources for solution development, the organization's project team needs to be able to effectively communicate requirements, manage external resources, costs, and time lines, and are ultimately responsible for the developed solution. If these management characteristics are not strengths within the group, the project has a very low chance of success. By comparing the requirements of the development with the capabilities of the project team, the resulting technical feasibility of the project will be more fully understood.

ECONOMIC FEASIBILITY

This assessment focuses on the cost/benefit analysis of the project. Start by compiling all of the costs of the new system, including all aspects of system construction, deployment, and ongoing maintenance. Next, compile all of the financial benefits resulting from the implementation of the developed system. These figures would include organizational cost savings resulting from the replacement of older technologies, automation of human tasks, or increases in efficiency, as well as any increases in revenue directly attributed to the new system itself. Finally, take into account how long the system is anticipated to be used by the organization, which is also referred to as the **life cycle of the system**.

Using these identified financial costs, benefits, and system life cycle, it is now possible to define:

1. ROI—Probability of gaining a return from an investment
2. Hurtle rate—Organization-defined minimum rate of return required on a project
3. Fee cash flow—Cash a company takes in after taking into consideration cash outflows

These metrics will give the organization a better understanding of the potential financial value the development can have for the organization.

ORGANIZATIONAL FEASIBILITY

The operational feasibility assessment determines whether the proposed new system will operate in the way the end user requires. The greatest technological system ever developed can still become a failure if users refuse to adopt it. Additionally, the user base has to be assessed to ensure that they are qualified and experienced enough to successfully work with the newly developed system. This assessment requires further interaction with the intended end users of the proposed system in order to adequately establish these objectives.

It is imperative that the organization's user base is accepting of the newly developed system in order to ensure project success. This assessment focuses on the end user's ability to adapt to the new system and the ability of the new system, as defined, to meet the business need.

Project Methodology

Upon successful completion of the feasibility study, the next aspect of project development to be decided upon is the development methodology. Essentially, there are different methodologies that can be used to construct a new system. Based on the structured phases of the SDLC, the order and constraints placed upon completing one phase and moving on to the next constitute each development methodology. Each one contains strengths and weaknesses and considers aspects of the organization's configuration and culture. The development methodology groups we will be focusing on are as follows:

1. Structured system development
2. Rapid application development
3. Agile system development

Understanding the specifics of each methodology will assist the systems analyst in selecting the one most appropriate for the new system development.

STRUCTURED SYSTEM DEVELOPMENT

Structured system development assumes that the current project phase is completed fully before moving on to the next phase. This structure ensures that there is a high degree of planning prior to actually constructing the new system. This should limit the unknowns when it comes to system requirements and new system-intended functionality. Variations of structured system development include the following:

1. Waterfall development
2. Parallel development
3. V-model development

Figure 2.2 Business man drawing flowchart of the waterfall model

Waterfall Development Methodology

In the waterfall development methodology, all activities of the current phase are completed singularly and in totality before any activity of the next phase can begin. So, all planning activities are completed before any analysis activity begins. Likewise, design activities do not initiate until the analysis activities are concluded. Finally, implementation activities do not begin until all design activities are complete. The emphasis is on ensuring that deliverables from the current phase flow into the task requirements of the next phase. As the majority of research is completed prior to new system construction, estimates of the time needed for each requirement are more accurate, and therefore, development time frames should be more predictable.

Additionally, this methodology allows for compartmentalization and increased control. A schedule can be set with deadlines for each stage of the SDLC and managed at each individual level. This ensures that project oversight is straightforward and quantifiable at every step.

However, there are a number of disadvantages to this methodology as well. Changes are not well received after the planning phase. Therefore, a project with dynamically changing requirements would be at a significant disadvantage. Also, any user requirements not successfully detailed at the beginning of the project will likewise be difficult to incorporate during system construction. If the scope were to change, it could easily result in a cancellation of the project.

Strengths: System requirements identified prior to construction. Requirements are locked in at the beginning of the project.

Weaknesses: Total project time is often inflated. The new system is not tangible until the end of the project.

Parallel Development Methodology

In the parallel development methodology, similar to the waterfall development methodology, all planning and analysis activities are completed singularly. However, once the design phase is initiated, the project is split into separate projects, and design activities are completed for each project in unison, followed by implementation activities being completed for each project in unison.

In more simplistic development projects, modifications are minimal, and conflicts between design entities are few to none. However, in more complex developmental projects, the degree of difficulty involved, necessary modification, or simply the vast amount of communication between groups can cause significant challenges when attempting to combine the separate activities back into a unified system.

Strengths: Overall project time is reduced

Weaknesses: Subprojects may not stay aligned and become difficult or impossible to recompile.

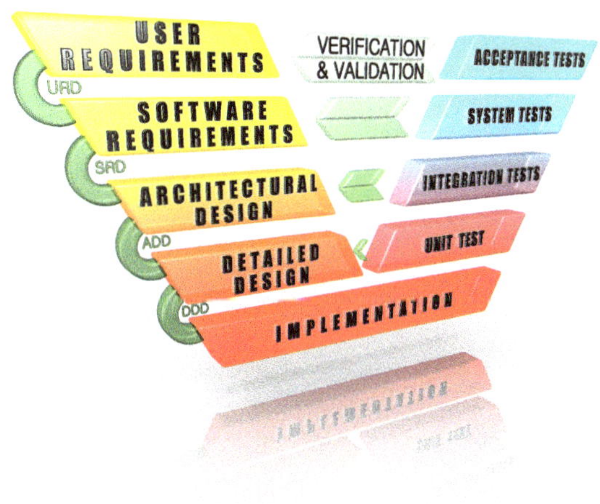

Figure 2.3 Detailed Software Development Life Cycle V-Model: Including Phases, levels, Documentation, Review

V-Model Development Methodology

V-model or the verification and validation model development methodology is based on associating a testing phase for each corresponding development phase:

1. Analysis Phase—Acceptance test design
2. Design phase—System test design, integration test design, unit test design

The system is developed by completing all planning activities, analysis activities, design activities, and, finally, the construction of the new system. However, the next step is to complete unit testing, integration testing, system testing, and finally, acceptance testing. This methodology places emphasis on quality through the development of a testing plan. Because of the stringent nature of this methodology, it is best used in situations where the project length and scope are well-defined, and the new technology being developed or implemented is well-known. This will also allow for enhanced time management, as there will be fewer surprises due to minimized unknown variables.

Strengths: Quality improves through emphasis on testing.

Weaknesses: Rigid.

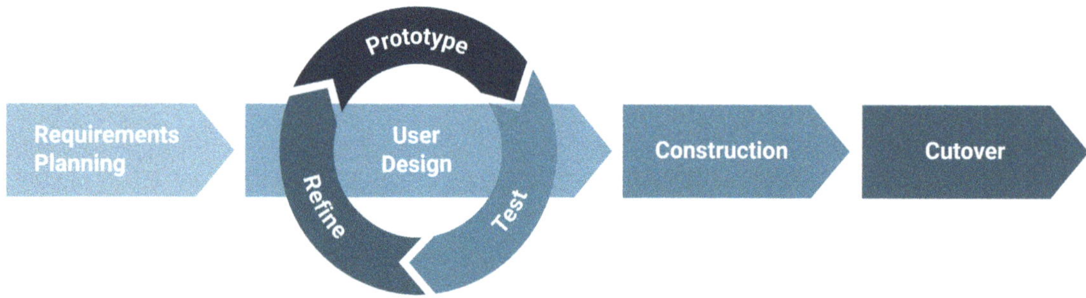

Figure 2.4 Rapid application development RAD software methodology, detailed framework process vector scheme. Requirements planning, User design, Prototype, test and refine loop, construction and cutover.

RAPID APPLICATION DEVELOPMENT

Rapid application development forgoes extensive development and testing cycles in exchange for rapidly developing a tangible system for analysis. One main issue of structured development is that the methodologies put emphasis on locking in design decisions early on in the project. This makes meeting the requirements of a dynamically changing environment difficult during system construction. Rapid application development places less emphasis on fully solidifying system requirements and instead focuses on developing a tangible system model quickly so that it can be used and thereby analyzed. Based on user feedback, changes are developed and implemented, and analysis begins again. Theoretically, this type of development can more easily accept newly defined requirements from a changing environment mid project. There are three main rapid application development methodologies:

1. Iterative development
2. System prototyping
3. Throw-away prototyping

However, rapid application development is not without its challenges as well. Managing customer expectations with each iteration of these methodologies becomes more and more challenging. Once the customer starts seeing something tangible, the system analyst tends to encounter more "What If" requests instead of focusing on the issues that were originally being addressed. The more "What Ifs" that are explored, the more the project scope begins to become unmanageable. The key to the effective utilization of these rapid application development methodologies is a systems analyst who can maintain focus on the original project scope.

Iterative Development Methodology

The iterative development methodology completes the SDLC phases in order but does not look to incorporate all requirements on the first pass. The goal is to quickly get to the first version of a new system and then jump back to the analysis phase to gauge the degree to which the project requirements have been met. The remaining requirements result in the development of a second system version, and the process continues. The development of consecutive system versions continues until all project requirements have been satisfied. Additionally, at each stage, there is the opportunity for user feedback related to the current state and overall new system expectations. This allows for making necessary improvements and new inclusions in line.

One of the main risks associated with this development methodology is that the development team is putting an incomplete system in front of the end user. Based on the aptitude and understanding of the user, this can result in productive feedback or, conversely, could have a negative impact on the project as a whole. Someone who is averse to technology or uncomfortable with new processes may view the missing aspects of the iterative development to be proof that the new system will be a failure. This can often result in challenges related to user adaptation once the final system is fully developed and ready to be implemented.

Aligning a development-capable user base with this methodology is essential for project success. Assuming this is the case, then this methodology has the ability to be very flexible and allow for the incorporation of changing requirements throughout the development of the new system.

Strengths: Users are able to work with the new system quickly.

Weaknesses: Users are working with an incomplete system.

System Prototyping Methodology

The system prototyping methodology acts in much the same way as the iterative development methodology. However, there Is even less focus on incorporating all system requirements and more emphasis on getting a roughly defined system built. This rough system is known as a prototype. The prototype is essentially a model of the system and is used to provide a physical environment that end users can explore to ensure requirements are being met. Once the prototype is in place, continuous user interaction, requirements assessment, and new function incorporation cycles are completed to build the system requirements into the prototype. Once all system functions have been built into the prototype, it is transitioned into the final system.

While this methodology provides the end users with a system very quickly, the initial development is usually missing the required functionality. Based on the user group, this can cause concern or friction. It is important to consider the aptitude and understanding of the user base in regards to being able to work with an incomplete solution in order to further development. Much like iterative development, if this is not the case, the result could be a lack of user acceptance and challenges with user adaptation to the finalized system.

Strengths: Feedback cycles allow users to identify change requirements and refine previously defined requirements.

Weaknesses: Superficial analysis can lead to an incomplete new system. Overlooked features can be difficult to add in later development cycles.

Throw-away Prototyping Methodology

The throw-away prototyping methodology involves creating working models of various aspects of the system at an early stage in the development process. These models are not intended to be used in the final solution development but rather as tools to gain feedback from users to clarify requirements. However, not every model that is created will result in a requirement determination. Many of the developments will be determined to be inaccurate and simply discarded. The risk is that a lot of effort can be wasted if the system requirements are not understood. Once this insight is established, the models are discarded.

Next, a more complete prototype is developed based on the identified requirements and then analyzed against system requirements. If it is determined that user requirements are not fully flushed out, additional models are created to further reign in necessary requirements. While these models are also thrown away, the knowledge gained is incorporated into the working prototype to further advance the development. The inclusion of additional model-based functionality being incorporated into the prototype is continued until all gaps are identified and remediated. Once all requirements are met, the prototype is finalized into the new system.

Strengths: Uncertainty is minimized.

Weaknesses: It may take longer as developments may not be used at all.

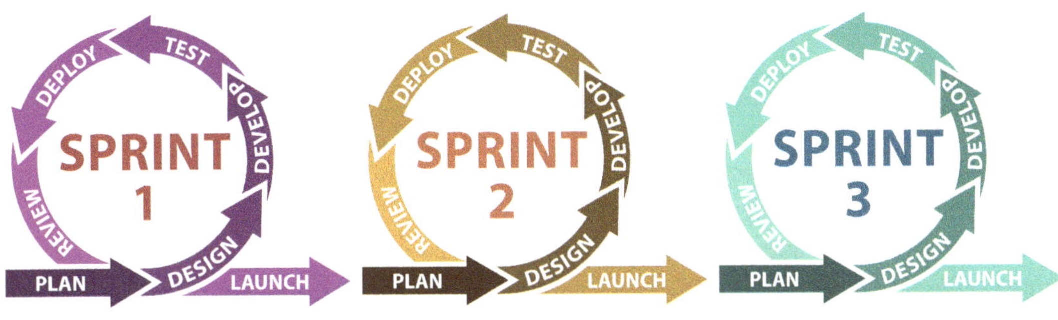

Figure 2.5 Illustration of agile method concept - 3d rendering

AGILE SYSTEM DEVELOPMENT

Agile system development incorporates the need for flexibility in new system design. New system development is facilitated through collaboration and user interaction. Frameworks such as Scrum, Extreme Programming, and Feature-Driven Development are used to quickly develop a solution that can be modeled, manipulated, and experimented with. From these interactions, features are defined and agreed upon. The evolution of feature adaptation results in the new system, which is then compared to defined system requirements. Technology-driven coding allows for almost instantaneous system creation. However, communication and understanding among the development team are imperative to ensure that the developed solution actually meets the needs of the organization.

The Agile methodology is perceived as user-friendly system development. Users have the opportunity to make modifications throughout the SDLC. This means that there is more latitude for a dynamically changing environment throughout the new system development as compared with structured system development. However, operating in a development environment where the project itself is constantly changing can add significant managerial challenges. Therefore, additional layers of management, such as a Scrum master, are often inserted into the project scope to maintain order. In the Scrum example, the Scrum master organizes user requirements and splits them into smaller deliverables or sprints that are produced in a short period of time. These deliverables are then assessed and altered, as necessary, while new sprints are being defined and implemented. The systems analyst will then take the finalized sprints that are deemed useful and add them to the final development.

The key takeaway from Agile development is the quickness with which tangible solutions are produced, altered, and reproduced. This allows for user assessment and communication but also provides many more options and potential inclusions that the project scope can become unmanageable, even with increased managerial resources. Discipline in both the project team and user base is essential for this methodology to be used successfully.

Strengths: Works well when there are undefined or changing project requirements.

Weaknesses: Significant user involvement. High learning curve. Requires discipline.

Project Setup

Once the feasibility of the project has been established, there is still a group of activities that need to be completed prior to having a steering committee approve project continuance and moving on to the analysis phase of the SDLC. It is important that the organization understand the commitment being asked of it, and the only way to communicate the full scope and resource requirement is through the development of a full project plan.

The role of the systems analyst is diverse within the SDLC. One area of responsibility that will often be required is to act as a project manager throughout the development process. Even in organizations with diverse resources incorporating both a project manager and a separate systems analyst, the systems analyst will require project manager competencies to complete requirement determination activities. However, to understand the project manager role, we must first have a comprehension of project management itself.

Project management is the application of processes, methods, skills, knowledge, and experience in order to obtain the successful completion of project objectives. These deliverables are required to meet operational requirements and be developed within time, resource, and budgetary constraints. The project management process is developed through formalized plan development and the execution of tasks to ensure plan milestones are adhered to. Both the project plan and work plan are examples of formalized plan development.

It certainly is challenging to communicate a full project plan when a complete understanding of the inter-workings of the current system or processes has not been fully revealed. This will come from the activities of the analysis phase. However, the system analyst and project team are not without resources to complete these activities. To define the project, a degree of research and analysis has already been completed. If the team is experienced in project development, past experiences can provide a foundation for resource and task estimation. Even an inexperienced team can find guidance in industry and market research of previous successful development projects within the same industry or field of development. The key to successfully organizing a project is using available resources to narrow down the unknowns when it comes to time, effort, and cost within the project plan itself.

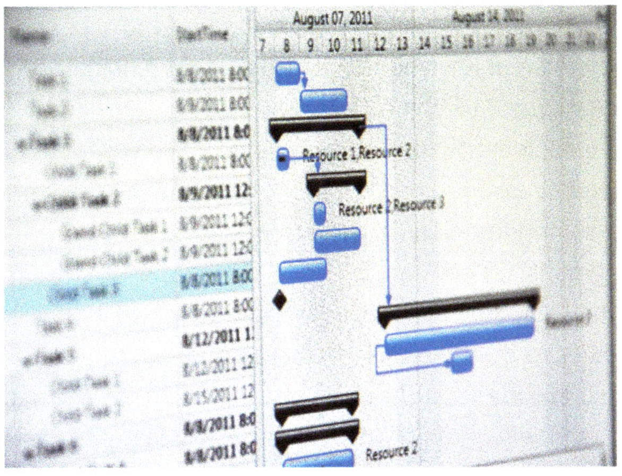

Image 2.3

PROJECT PLAN

Project planning is the process that defines the project scope, objectives, and steps necessary to fully complete the new system development. Developed documentation will act not only as the instruction set for constructing the new system but also as the measuring device to determine to what degree the actual system construction is proceeding to plan. Therefore, the commitments the project team makes within these documents at the very beginning of the project will hold them accountable in every remaining phase of the SDLC.

The project plan communicates all the necessary information in order to demonstrate the full commitment the organization must make if it decides to proceed with the project. Deadlines, key milestones, and task assignments all paint a picture of what will actually be undertaken by executing the project. The work and staffing plans will communicate the length of time and resource commitment the organization must make. Placing financial value on the resource requirements, administrative and internal support overhead, and external entity incorporation provides a platform for highlighting expected project costs.

However, this picture is only as accurate as the team's ability to maintain its guidance through the remainder of the SDLC phases. If estimations are not obtainable, the project approval granted at this phase may be rescinded before the new system is fully developed.

While there are a multitude of reasons why projects fail, this juncture in the system development process is a key contributor to either failure or success. If there is not enough effort placed on defining the project plan as accurately as possible, the criteria the steering committee is basing their approval on is not what the actual development will mirror. This misalignment can have consequences ranging from project setbacks all the way up to corporate mistrust of embarking on future projects. Nobody wants to be associated with failure, and therefore, ensuring that enough time and effort is spent on developing a realistic project plan is essential.

Scope

One of the most straightforward ways to begin building a project plan is to start by defining the scope of the project itself. However, while scope definition may be a straightforward way to begin, it is anything but easy. The amount of research and analysis you have completed up to this point is valuable for formalizing the project scope. However, there are many additional aspects that must be considered as well.

To begin, use the system request to home in on what will be included in the development as well as what will be specifically excluded. Identify the critical functions and the required outputs of the system. Use your technical team to implement assumptions regarding how the new system will actually be developed. From these developmental assumptions, experience with past projects can be used to paint a clearer picture of not only what must be accomplished but how.

The results of the feasibility study will be used to make educated estimations of cost. By incorporating the discovery from the feasibility study, the project team can also begin to align technical requirements with organizational competencies. If experience dictates that certain resource skill sets are required, the feasibility assessment should provide direction regarding whether those skill sets are available within the organization.

It is also worth noting that it is not always possible to ascertain all the information from the system request and feasibility study documents themselves. A systems analyst will sometimes need to communicate with stakeholders and end users in order to clarify requirements and specific task inclusions. The more the systems analyst can reduce the level of unknown regarding what is expected to be accomplished and how the development team intends to accomplish it, the more accurate the resulting project plan will be.

Defining a project scope can be a project in and of itself. However, an inclusive scope will help to ensure that planning project size, project cost, and project time components remain in balance throughout the SDLC process.

Figure 2.6 Hand drawing Time Cost Scope Triangle concept with white chalk on a blackboard.

Balance

To expand on the relationship between size (the amount of work needed to complete the project), cost, and time within a development project, let's look at the **project management triangle**. Consider a triangle where each side consists of each of these constraints. If all three sides are the same length, the triangle is balanced. However, increase one of the sides, and the triangle becomes unbalanced. In order to balance it again, you have to increase one or both of the other sides. For example, if I add three more features halfway through my development, it will reason that either the time frame of the project will also increase, the cost of the project will also increase, or both. You cannot alter one key aspect of the development without impacting one of the other aspects.

Why is balance important? You are making commitments to the organization at the beginning of the project. You are requesting a set amount of resources to complete the intended objective. It is important to maintain an environment that allows you to achieve this goal as close to those projections as possible. Do not forget that project development is a dynamically changing environment, and there will be alterations throughout the SDLC. However, this does not mean that concise project planning is not possible.

The key to success lies in dividing the project into milestones that balance the triangle effectively. This clearly communicates priorities to the development team, as well as provides a gauge of how aligned actual development is to plan throughout the development process. Communication of how well these milestones are being met will allow for adjustment during development to tighten project constraints as close to the plan as possible. Complete the due diligence now, and the benefit will be a successful project later.

Estimation

As previously stated, there are a number of unknowns in all aspects of the upcoming new system development. However, the project plan being developed will hold the project team responsible for what is developed going forward. How do you effectively plan for the unknown? Estimation is a key contributor. When you don't fully understand all the requirements for the task in front of you, you have to increase your knowledge by using the expertise around you. Within system development, this expertise comes from multiple sources, such as the methodology being used, the previous project experience of the organization and project team, and conducting industry analysis.

The methodology being used is a point of reference that allows the systems analyst to begin to build the project plan. Take, for instance, the waterfall methodology. Breaking up your resources into the planning, analysis, design, and implementation phases, based on their professional competencies, will begin to arrange your resource allocation requirements. Gaps in internal resources highlight the need for external support and begin to expand your cost requirements.

Previous project experience is another clear contributor to estimation success. While no two projects are the same, there are many similarities in the cost and effort of projects of similar scope. Therefore, understanding what was required in previous projects can act as a starting point for assigning size, cost, and time estimates on a current project.

Industry analysis can provide a basis for current project estimation as well. External resources, experienced developers, and obtained after-action reporting of completed projects are all examples of inputs that can be used to build a knowledge transfer base to assist in clarifying unknown aspects of the current project. By incorporating the experiences of others, framing the current project becomes less guessing and more estimation.

Tasks

Table 2.1 Work Plan Entry

Task Information	Example
Name of task	Develop project plan
Assigned to	Systems Analyst Bob Jones
Priority	High
Deliverable	Project plan document
Resources needed	Spreadsheet software
Status	Complete
Start date	1/2/2023
End date	1/15/2023
Estimated time	20 hours
Actual time	16 hours

To effectively assign time requirements to the overall project, the tasks needed to be completed have to first be identified. Task identification and planning are significantly simplified by using project management software. Don't forget the SDLC is being used for a reason. It is an organized structure that allows development teams to follow a standardized process when developing a new system. Project management software, while generalized, will start with breaking down the tasks of each phase of the development process. The systems analyst is then able to alter the task heading from general to specific requirements of the current project being worked on.

Task definition, whether manually developed or developed with the assistance of project management software, is intended to break down the project scope into smaller, more manageable deliverables. Additionally, grouping similar tasks together allows for easy identification of individual resources that can complete many tasks. Tasks requiring multiple steps are further broken down into individual activities. Once all the work has been both identified and reduced to its smallest form, we now have all the individual tasks that must be completed to develop the system. The tasks are now sequenced based on what if any, tasks need to be completed prior to the current one being initiated.

Next, it must be determined how much time each task will take to complete. At this phase of the project, the systems analyst will rely on all the estimation techniques in order to start with an educated prediction for each task's time requirement. Based on the complexity of the project, the systems analyst will then add a risk buffer of five to 25% in order to accommodate unforeseen issues, unpredictability of new technology, team conflict, and administrative overhead such as meetings and lost productive hours. The end result will be a duration of time for each task (See Table 2.1) that can be assembled with all the other tasks in order to create a project timeframe.

All these various aspects of task development result in a road map for task completion in terms of number, time, and priority. This organization of task structure is often referred to as the **work plan**.

Staffing Plan

Table 2.2 Staffing Plan

			Estimated			Actual				
Task ID	**Task Name**	**Assigned To**	**Duration (Days)**	**Start Date**	**End Date**	**Start Date**	**End Date**	**Variance**	**Dependency**	**Status**
3	Design Phase		31	3/1/ 2023	3/31/ 2023	3/1/ 2023	3/25/ 2023	−5 Days	1, 2	Closed
3.1	Dev. Database Document	Bob	9	3/1/ 2023	3/10/ 2023	3/1/ 2023	3/8/ 2023	−1 Day		Closed

Just as the work plan is developed from the project scope, the staffing plan (See Table 2.2) is developed from the work plan. The work plan provides you with the tasks that need to be completed, the individual task requirements, and the order of completion necessary. The next step is to assign resources to the tasks in order to complete them. However, there are a few considerations that must be made prior to beginning resource assignment.

The first consideration is does the organization have resources with the capabilities to complete each task. If not, how does the systems analyst fill in the gaps? If internal resources are not applicable, then either external resources or an external entity will need to be sourced in order to meet the requirements.

Once there are adequate resources with the knowledge to complete all tasks, the next consideration is how can the project team complete the tasks the most efficiently. Almost always, there are a number of tasks that do not have any preconditions, meaning other items that must be completed prior to their initiation. By assigning multiple resources to complete these tasks in unison, overall project time is reduced. Therefore, the work plan must be analyzed to evaluate how many tasks can be grouped for completion in unison and what resources are available to meet the demand. If there are gaps, then further analysis must be completed to determine if it is best to have the on-hand resources complete all tasks or if there is enough opportunity to increase the number of resources so that more tasks can be completed in unison, reducing project time. Time and cost factors come into play during this analysis, and the systems analyst needs to understand whether the organization has prioritized an accelerated project schedule or decreased budgetary costs in order to make the most accurate decision.

Once the selection of the most appropriate resources is completed, along with aligning these resources with the most efficient task assignments, the resources are added to the work plan. The end result is a complete project plan that demonstrates each task required, the duration it will take to complete, and the resources required. Not only is the amount of effort the project will take visible to the steering committee, but the actual resource allocation is as well. This makes the cost of the endeavor much clearer.

Risk Assessment

Table 2.3 Risk Assessment

Risk #1:	High app usage results in crashing
Likelihood of risk:	4/10
Potential impact on the project:	Application issues will reduce app usage
Ways to address this risk:	Hire beta testers to define app limitations prior to release

As technological development projects require the incorporation of high levels of knowledge, often coupled with new or emerging technologies, there is an element of risk, which is, at times, significant. Therefore, it is very important to highlight the potential risks of the development project to the steering committee in order to present a realistic picture of what could go wrong within the development process.

So, what exactly is a risk? A risk is a potential problem. Essentially, it is an event or activity that might bring the success of the project into question. As these problems may result in project loss, risk assessment is looking at each possible problem and assessing the probability of it occurring and the amount of potential loss if it does happen.

Not every potential problem within a software development project will result in the cancellation of the project. Some may result in time loss, monetary loss, or even become just a simple inconvenience. It is important to understand what can go wrong, the degree to which it will most likely happen, and the degree to which it will negatively impact the project. To effectively assess potential project risk, systems analysts predominantly look at five main risk impact areas:

1. Organizational
2. User and functional requirements
3. Application and system architecture
4. Performance
5. New, unproven technologies

By brainstorming and listing potential problems that may occur in each of these categories, the project team can further research and discuss each development for both potential and significance.

Just as with the project plan, there are a number of project management software tools available that have risk assessment templates (See Table 2.3) for you to work with. This will provide a structure for both the questions to ask, as well as the rating system of the identified risk. By making use of these toolsets, the systems analyst can ensure that the project team develops a comprehensive risk assessment to further reduce unknown aspects of the development project.

Chapter Summary

The planning phase is a crucial aspect of new system development. These activities solidify the new project, reinforce the need for development, analyze the ability to actually create the desired solution, formalize the plan for constructing the new system itself, and, finally, quantify the potential risk associated with proceeding forward. When you stop and think about it, the design of the planning phase is invaluable. It allows a systems analyst to look at a problem, formulate an idea for a solution, and build that idea all the way into a new development project.

That is not to say that every idea that is brought through the planning phase of the SDLC results in a viable project. Conversely, many who initiate project ideas find more reasons to abandon the project than to continue forward. This is not failure. This is the intent of the process. As long as the project team puts forth sufficient effort, the defined activities are meant to stop poor project choices from continuing while at the same time strengthening good project choices to increase the chance of project success.

It is interesting that a software development project begins with a problem. However, each step of the SDLC is designed to minimize problems when designing the solution itself. Even with all the knowledge that is gained by completing the activities of the planning phase, a project team has only touched the surface of the depth of knowledge required to develop a successful new system. While the project plan at this phase is able to gain support for the project, there is much refining yet to be done to ensure that the risks identified are minimized to every extent possible.

Project Planning Activities

Working from the developments of Chapter 1's planning activities:

1. Identify any problems you encounter with the current system. If no system is present, then identify the problems due to the lack of a technology system in the organization's environment.
2. Develop the objectives of the new system or function you believe will resolve these identified problems.
3. Develop a system request for your example company.
4. Develop a feasibility study for your system request.
5. Develop a project plan for your system request.
6. Develop a risk assessment.

Image Credits

IMG 2.1: Copyright © 2013 Depositphotos/masterart.
Fig. 2.1: Copyright © 2015 Depositphotos/vaeenma.
IMG 2.2: Copyright © 2016 Depositphotos/masterart.
Fig. 2.2: Copyright © 2013 Depositphotos/shawn_hempel.
Fig. 2.3: Copyright © 2012 Depositphotos/dtjs.
Fig. 2.4 : Copyright © 2020 Depositphotos/Litteralis.
Fig. 2.5: Copyright © 2019 Depositphotos/Elnur .
IMG 2.3: Copyright © 2013 Depositphotos/fbatista72.
Fig. 2.6: Copyright © 2015 Depositphotos/ivelin.

CHAPTER 3

Requirements Determination

Introduction

At this point in the project development cycle, the project team has already made some important progress worth notating. They have gained increased knowledge of the organization that allows them to begin to formulate judgments regarding both competencies and gaps needed to be filled when using corporate resources. Additionally, the problem to be resolved has been analyzed to the degree that there is familiarity both with the issue itself and the operational environment impacted by the issue. Also, through the development of the system request and project plan, the project team has an established method for both correcting the identified issue as well as a reasonable expectation that the organization will benefit from the implementation of this new system development. Finally, and perhaps most importantly, the project team has been able to successfully convince the organization that the proposed project should proceed forward, inching closer to actual construction.

However, even with all of the tasks that have been completed, both in document development and immersion into the organization's operation, there are a great number of questions to be answered. While it is true that the compilation of the project plan required a high degree of analysis because of time and resource constraints, the plan construction also incorporated a degree of inference and educated guessing. Should these developed assumptions turn out to be invalid, the likelihood of project success will be drastically reduced. Therefore, it is important to once again minimize the degree of unknown by applying additional resources to gain an even more enhanced understanding of the project to be undertaken.

For all of these reasons, we now enter the analysis phase of the SDLC. The analysis phase is designed to provide a roadmap to increase understanding of the requirements of the new system through the development of documentation of the current system or, in the instance of implementing a brand-new system, the set of manual tasks to be replaced. Additionally, an emphasis on both process and data analysis provides direction on how the new system development will be fully implemented within incorporated into the organization.

Learning Objectives

1. Explain the analysis phase of the SDLC.
2. Describe what a requirement is.
3. Explain the different types of requirements and why they are important.
4. Describe the analysis strategies employed by the systems analyst.
5. Select the appropriate problem analysis techniques to support the analysis strategy.

6. Describe the content and purpose of the requirements definition statement.

Requirements Determination

The system request has provided the system analyst with a number of high-level business requirements. Requirements determination is the process of expanding the analysis of those identified requirements. As the analysis scope is limited in the planning phase, in the analysis phase, greater focus is placed on the requirements of the system as a whole. While the system request is an excellent starting point, the additional effort placed on creating detailed, fully documented requirements will often result in an increase in requirements in both number and depth. While some will view this as an oversight within the planning phase, this is not the case. Where the planning phase of the SDLC is developed in order to make efficient and cost-effective decisions on project potential, the analysis phase is designed to increase resource activity to quantify the degree of potential project success. This increased effort is designed to bring about additional information regarding what the new system must accomplish and allow for additional analysis to ensure that the project remains feasible and justified. Uncovering all requirements and expanding upon them to get a full picture of the objectives that must be met is an essential first step in this process.

It is important to remember that information is the cornerstone of information system effectiveness. Therefore, it is logical that one of the most important aspects of systems analysis is a comprehensive understanding of the information within the organization that is to be created or worked with. A comprehensive understanding of the organization's information will result in the greatest potential for new system success. Conversely, an incomplete understanding of the organization's information will most likely result in project failure. It is for this reason that many believe that accurate determination of system requirements is the cornerstone for the success of all future project steps.

Image 3.1

What Is a Requirement?

In order to successfully identify all necessary system requirements, the system analyst must first comprehend what a requirement is and the full scope of requirements within the new system. A requirement is an essential feature of the new system and includes the creation or manipulation of data, completing business processes, supporting report requirements, and even characteristics of the new system itself.

While many people can easily associate a requirement to a task they expect the new system to complete, they have a more difficult time recognizing that there are requirements that need to be defined for the construction of the system itself. How the system must interact with additional systems, what security measures must be incorporated into the new system, and how fast the new system must process specific data are all examples of system development requirements.

Requirements span all aspects of the organization, current system, and new system to be constructed. In order to comprehensively identify and effectively incorporate all requirements into the new system development, the systems analyst must further break down requirements into specific classifications that can be analyzed using various methods. These classifications will focus the development team on all aspects of requirements determination and provide the best chance for a comprehensive requirements definition.

Types of Requirements

Organizations are complex environments for a multitude of reasons. Business activities are often understood in terms of the output produced, not always by the mechanics that are in place to achieve that output. Individual resources, be it human or technology based, are recognized by their function within the organization. However, analysis of each process, and furthermore, of each step in the process, will often uncover aspects that are known to the resource yet unknown to the organization as a whole. Additionally, the organization itself will often require a new system to be constructed in a specific configuration. For example, if an organization uses software that must interact with the new system, the new system must be developed to successfully interact with the existing software. However, organizational staff may not recognize this interdependency themselves, and therefore, these required interdependencies must also be uncovered through the requirements determination process.

These complexities can make requirements determination daunting, as many will ask the question, if the organization doesn't fully understand how their current processes work or how current systems may have to interact with a new system, how is it even possible to define all of the requirements for a new system? The answer to this is, as always, to minimize the unknown through painstaking analysis and identification of individual requirements.

In order to decrease the feeling that comprehensive requirements determination is difficult or even impossible, the SDLC calls for organizing requirements into manageable segments. These requirement types include:

1. Business requirements—What the business needs
2. User requirements—What the users need
3. Functional requirements—What the new system should accomplish
4. Nonfunctional requirements—The characteristics of the new system

BUSINESS REQUIREMENTS

The business requirements for the new system identify what the business is trying to achieve, why it is important, and what the expected outcome at an organizational level is to be. Business requirements are broad in definition and are meant to incorporate the organization's stakeholders' expectations and business goals.

The activities in the planning stage should directly correlate to the project's business requirements, and the system request should identify the majority of these requirements. However, while the systems analyst should have a strong foundation for assessing business requirements based on the developments of the planning phase of the SDLC, this does not mean that analysis activity should be disregarded.

It is important to review the developed project components defined to date and ensure that what has been developed still matches organizational expectations. Reviewing the project scope document with key organizational members will either reinforce that the project development is well understood and accepted by the organization or highlight the need for additional analysis and development. Additionally, as the focus of an organization, both strategically and operationally, can change over time, it is critical to investigate the organizational fit of the new system development at every opportunity. Analyzing and refining business requirements allows for this opportunity with the organization's stakeholders.

USER REQUIREMENTS

User requirements are the definition of what the user needs to accomplish in order to complete their individual tasks. While it is appropriate to state that user requirements define what a user needs to complete their job, at this stage of project development, the systems analyst needs to be focused on capturing item-level detail within the organization, and therefore, the mindset needs to be focused on capturing information at a microlevel. Therefore, capturing the requirements of each user task will result in the identification of all tasks required to complete a user's job.

Why is this subtle change in user requirements definition important? The answer lies within the potential for project failure based on an inaccurate assessment of requirements. If a systems analyst approaches requirements definition from a broad perspective, I.E., analyzing a user's job, there is a greater chance of brushing over important aspects of the user's individual task completion. Conversely, if the systems analyst approaches the same analysis by looking at the completion of each user task through first task identification and then documentation of each task step, the chance of missing important tasks is minimized. While the change in wording is minimal, the mindset and resulting approach can be significant.

The development team must deconstruct the user's actions into individual steps to understand how best to construct the new system in order to support that task completion. However, it is also important to note that not every task is imperative for success. In fact, through user analysis, it is often discovered that some tasks are unnecessary, and the most appropriate action is to cease completing them altogether. User analysis must identify and focus on tasks that are integral to the business and, at the same time, identify and quantify tasks that can be minimized or even eliminated.

FUNCTIONAL REQUIREMENTS

The functional requirements are the work we are expecting the new system to complete. From the perspective of the organization, these are the operational objectives that are met by incorporating the new system.

Simply put, the functional requirements are the resolutions to the issues identified in the planning phase that the system is intended to overcome.

Functional requirements are solidly tied to user requirements in that these are the requirements defined as necessary to support the user. Whether it be a process performed by the system to support a user task or supporting information supplied to the user in order to complete a necessary task, the end result is that the functional requirements replace or enhance the user requirements to provide operational benefit for the organization.

Functional requirements are aligned with the operational scope of the organization. The goal is to use the newly developed system to fully meet these requirements, thereby providing operational benefit. While these requirements are highlighted at a broad level in the planning phase, additional analysis of the current system, coupled with user analysis, will often uncover additional requirements that have the ability to provide even greater benefit to the organization from an operational perspective.

NONFUNCTIONAL REQUIREMENTS

Nonfunctional requirements are the properties the new system must contain. These are the requirements that are focused on the behavioral aspects of the system. This means that these are the requirements that affect how the system completes the functional requirements from the system perspective.

These requirements are technical in nature and are specific to the configuration of the system itself. Nonfunctional requirements highlight system-specific needs that must be included in the overall system design but do not directly correlate to operational objectives. To put it another way, these requirements are the architectural requirements for the new system.

Nonfunctional requirements can be broken down into four categories:

1. Operational requirements
2. Performance requirements
3. Security requirements
4. Cultural and political requirements

Operational Requirements

Operational nonfunctional requirements define the physical and technical requirements of the organization's technology environment. This includes the new system's integration into the organization's technology landscape. Everything from technology hardware to communications methods plays a factor in how a new system must be developed in order to successfully integrate into a technology topology or layout of the computer network.

Compatibility is the key analytic for assessing operational requirements. Hardware, network configuration, multisystem communication, and external technological environment interaction are all areas within an organization's technology system that provide limiting factors for new system construction. It is imperative that the development team consider the physical environment they are building the new system to work within and include all related requirements within the scope of the requirements determination process.

Operational nonfunctional requirements must consider not only the physical configuration of the technology environment today but also its future trajectory. If necessary technological components are to be altered or replaced within the anticipated life cycle of the new system, then ensuring that the new system not only operates as intended in the current configuration but also can successfully operate in the changed future environment is necessary. Defining requirements for the current physical environment as well as known future configurations are the tasks to be completed when analyzing operational nonfunctional requirements.

Failing to align the new system construction to operate on the physical technology environment will limit or even eliminate the usefulness of the newly constructed system. Operational objectives cannot be met if the system cannot perform physically within the organization's technology architecture.

Performance Requirements

Nonfunctional performance requirements are the requirements related to the speed, capacity, and reliability of the system. Not every system needs to be exceedingly fast or even operational 24 hours a day, 365 days a year. Understanding the operational requirements of the system will assist in determining at least the priority of performance requirement analysis.

The speed of the new system is essentially how fast the system responds to commands. In a transactional system, speed is important, as it is expected to complete commands quickly, often completing multiple transactions at the same time. Conversely, an overnight reporting process may not be expected to provide immediate results, and therefore, speed can be sacrificed to increase other aspects of the system.

The capacity of the new system is essentially the amount of data storage it has available. Ensuring that the system is able to store the amount of data necessary to meet the operational requirements is essential for new system success. Conversely, provisioning the system for too much data storage can take away from increasing other aspects of the system, such as speed.

The reliability of the system is essentially the amount of time the system is able to be used over a set duration of time. Based on the system's operational requirements, increased reliability can be essential for overall system success. For example, you wouldn't want a surgical assistance system to go down in the middle of a surgery. However, a system that only needs to run computations once per month has an increased ability to incorporate regular planned system downtime cycles.

One final aspect of nonfunctional performance requirements that is worth notating is that there is a give-and-take aspect to requirement definition. That is to say, to make a system faster, reliability may suffer. Likewise, in order to increase capacity, speed may have to be sacrificed. Therefore, performance requirements demand an in-depth understanding of functional requirements to be able to assess the prioritization of these requirements.

Security Requirements

Everyone is aware of cybersecurity in today's technological environment. As the need for more technology systems increases universally within the business scope, so too do the efforts to compromise and profit from exploiting incorporated technology. It is, therefore, essential that the development team fully understand the information being used and created within the new system and then develop security requirements to protect said information.

There are new examples every day of a corporate system being used to infiltrate and exploit an organization. However, the same degree of security is not enacted on every system within an organization. The degree to which a new system needs to be secured is directly proportional to the sensitivity of the information it contains, the access it has to other systems in the organization, and the degree to which it can be manipulated to trick the organization into completing a nefarious task or process.

By understanding the potential security risks associated with the implementation of the new system, the development team can construct security requirements that are necessary for minimizing potential risks but not excessive to the extent that they could limit overall system functionality.

Image 3.2

Cultural and Political Requirements

The organization itself is not the only entity that must be analyzed to define all necessary requirements. Societal customs, religions, languages, and governmental requirements are all considerations that must be considered in requirements determination.

The development group needs to factor in not only the cultural and governmental requirements of the organization but also those of all the other geographic regions where the new system may be used. With the increase of global commerce, organizational systems are traversing cultural and political boundaries, and the success of these systems requires these aspects to be taken into consideration and system requirements to be developed as a result.

Additionally, governmental regulation and operational requirements at the local, state, and national levels must be incorporated to ensure system compliance requirements are met. This is necessary for every governing body in which the system will operate. Doing so ensures that the legal liability of the organization is minimized when using the new system.

How to Determine Requirements

Based on the various requirement types that have been identified, it can be stated that requirements determination requires a combination of hardware, software, human, organizational, and environmental (cultural and political) analysis conducted in a group dynamic to achieve a comprehensive requirement analysis. The only way to accomplish these objectives is for the project team to interact with the organization on multiple levels and in multiple ways.

Interacting with the organization's employees is not only helpful but essential to effective requirements determination. Leadership staff will be experts in the operational scope of the organization and can communicate the cultural and governmental considerations necessary for the effective utilization of the new system. Organizational management and end users are able to expand on task-based knowledge and current challenges or perceived opportunities. While it is true that these groups were most likely included in the planning phase of the process, it cannot be assumed that every individual with valuable information was involved. Therefore, increasing both the scope of communication and the depth of conversation will result in bringing to light many requirements.

Corporate documentation is another valuable tool for identifying potential requirements. The current system can be analyzed from the system documentation created while both constructing and maintaining the system. This documentation can contribute not only to an understanding of current limitations but also to nonfunctional requirements applicable then and possibly still applicable today. However, a systems analyst will quickly find that system documentation is constructed based on how the system should be used in best practice scenarios. This is rarely how the system is used in actual production, and therefore, developing requirements through documentation without considering actual user-based system utilization can be dangerous.

Additionally, corporate compliance documentation, as well as corporate policy, can provide direction regarding identified cultural and political requirements. However, it is important to use this documentation as a starting point for increased employee communication. Policies are often outdated and, because of this, may not be representative of all current considerations at the time of new system development.

ANALYSIS STRATEGIES

Understanding the avenues to take in order to gain the knowledge to complete requirements determination activities is important. However, equally important is understanding how to effectively use these resources in order to develop a comprehensive requirements list. The SDLC defines a number of analysis strategies structured to pull out the necessary requirements from within the organization and operational environment. These strategies consist of the following:

1. Problem analysis
2. Root cause analysis
3. Duration analysis
4. Activity analysis
5. Benchmarking analysis
6. Outcome analysis
7. Technology analysis
8. Elimination analysis

Problem Analysis

Remember, a new system starts with a problem, and all the activities completed to date have been focused on developing from that problem identification. It makes perfect sense that the requirements determination process will once again focus on problems encountered by the organization in order to analyze the degree to which the current problem definition is accurate.

By asking users to identify problems they encounter within their daily tasks, assessments can be made as to the degree that the current problem identification aligns with the problems incurred by current system users. Going a step further and asking those same users for potential solutions will demonstrate the degree to which the intended system user views the accuracy of the proposed development.

As this analysis is conducted at the user task level, unidentified items tend to be small and incremental, resulting in individual improvements that, in and of themselves, do not support significant business value enhancement. However, the degree to which the new system proposal aligns with the identified problems at the user level assists in determining if the intended development overall has the ability to meet the end user's perceived problem resolution.

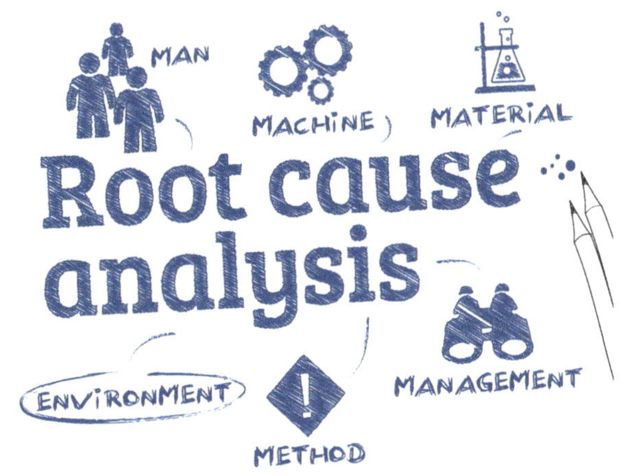

Figure 3.1 Root cause analysis. Chart with keywords and icons

Root Cause

Root Cause Analysis

Not every problem identified through problem analysis is an issue worth resolving. That is to say, not every problem is the result of the root cause of an issue. Some problems are simply a symptom related to a larger issue. Therefore, root cause analysis looks at the cause and effect of all identified problems to better understand the actual item behind the problem at hand.

Sometimes, a problem will be determined to occur due to a specific reason. Resolving the reason resolves the problem. However, other times, it will be determined that the problem is simply a by-product of a completely different problem. Resolving the problem being analyzed does not resolve the problem that is the actual or root cause. Additionally, often, by setting aside the problem being analyzed and instead working to fix the problem that is the actual root cause, both problems will ultimately be corrected.

Root cause analysis challenges assumptions as to why problems exist and emphasizes the importance of tracing problem symptoms to their actual cause to determine the primary problem that needs to be corrected. This is an important analytical strategy, as it builds efficiency into the requirements definition. Instead of listing each and every problem identified, root cause analysis pairs down problems to those that need to be addressed and those that will be remediated by addressing other problems.

Duration Analysis

Duration analysis consists of analyzing the time required to complete each step in a process. The primary reason for the comparison is to look for idiosyncrasies between each step's time requirement as compared to both the other steps in the process, as well as the overall time required for completing the entire process. Large time differences point to tasks that may contain problems to be resolved.

Time-based task problems are often able to be resolved by integrating tasks together or possibly completing tasks in parallel. This will reduce the time completion for individual tasks, as well as reduce the time for process completion as a whole. Implementation of these requirements will enhance the efficiency of the system and can result in moderate gains in relation to positively affecting the overall project.

It is important to note that not all tasks with a longer completion time are problems. Some tasks may have already been reduced to their most efficient method of completing a required activity. In these instances, analysis will result in leaving the process as is and simply incorporating the tasks as defined.

Activity Analysis

Activity analysis is conducted in much the same way as duration analysis. However, instead of time being the guiding factor, cost is. Each task is analyzed based on the cost associated with its completion. Each process is also notated from a cost perspective. Processes with a higher cost are given priority for analysis, at which point individual higher cost tasks are reviewed.

The goal, as with duration analysis, is to integrate or eliminate steps that are more costly to reduce expense. The ability to do so lowers operational costs and demonstrates the increased value of the new system.

However, just as with duration analysis, not every process or task that is more expensive can be reduced, combined, or eliminated. Critical processes and tasks may already be as efficient as possible, and therefore, the cost associated must simply be incurred in order to complete the necessary functions.

Benchmarking Analysis

Benchmarking analysis, also known as informal benchmarking, analyzes the organization's processes and tasks as compared to similar processes and tasks in other successful organizations. This form of analysis looks to incorporate more effective processes or task configurations proven to be successful in other organizations as a method for enhancing the internal organization's environment.

The thought process is that there is no need to reinvent the process. If there is evidence that an organization is more effectively completing required tasks, then simply incorporating that method adds value to the new system. Based on the degree to which efficiency is enhanced, or cost is reduced, there can be significant gains to the overall value of the system development for the organization.

Benchmarking analysis requires a degree of transparency in the process of the organization being compared. Without a good understanding of all steps of their process, a true comparison cannot be made. While there are many methods of acquiring this information, often industry groups and even positive competitor relationships will provide a basis for organizations to share this level of information.

Outcome Analysis

Outcome analysis focuses on seeing the organization in a new light. Instead of looking at how the organization completes processes and tasks today, the project group focuses on new ways to significantly impact the organization through a radical redesign of complete business processes.

Outcome analysis defines new desirable outcomes from the customer's perspective. Essentially, the project group will start by defining what new outcomes would provide significant benefit to the organization's customer base and thereby greatly enhance the value of the organization itself. They then work backward to determine how to restructure the process and task completion to meet these intended outcomes.

Leveraging technology is a core component of redefining the current processes to meet the newly defined outcomes. Due to this, feasibility factors must be incorporated into the newly defined process and task development completed in outcome analysis. However, effectively doing this type of requirement analysis can result in a newly defined system that has the potential for a massive positive impact on the organization as a whole.

Technology Analysis

Technology analysis is complementary to outcome analysis in that outcome analysis must often leverage technology to accomplish effective process redesign, and technology analysis focuses on analyzing new technologies available to the organization. The project group will begin by listing new, important, and interesting technologies.

Operational staff will often also be brought into technology analysis, as they will have an awareness of important technologies that have the potential to positively impact their environment. Collectively, these technologies will be assessed by the group as a whole and identify how each one could be applied to the organization and to what potential benefit of the organization.

When coupled with outcome analysis, this level of requirements determination analysis has the power to change the face of the organization as a whole. Completely changing how the organization operates is not out of the question in regard to greatly enhancing the customer experience and, thereby, the value of the organization itself.

It should further be noted that the incorporation of new technology may completely alter the development plan to date, and therefore, all feasibility assessments will need to be completed again to ensure the new system is still viable with the incorporation of the new technology.

Elimination Analysis

There are times when the biggest benefit to an organization is achieved by eliminating tasks or even entire processes. Any organization that has been in operation for a period of years most likely has processes in place that, when analyzed, will result in staff stating that they are being completed "because we have always done this process." It is not uncommon to see business requirements change, but long-standing processes remain in effect, even if there is a divergence between the new business requirement and the current process. With enough divergence, new processes will be enacted to meet the new business need and the long-standing process may now be completed for little to no reason at all.

Therefore, elimination analysis investigates what happens when each organizational process is eliminated from the operational scope. Even processes that are deemed essential to the success of the organization are removed to analyze the actual impact on the operation as a whole. The goal is to try and accomplish an intended result without the utilization of a specific process. If the intended result can still be accomplished, the necessity of the removal process is brought into question.

However, it is not simply an all-or-nothing analysis. Even removed processes that are deemed to be necessary are not simply added back in. Each step of the process is analyzed and attempted to be removed in order to ascertain if individual tasks can be eliminated, making the overall process more efficient.

Elimination analysis is an excellent way to break an organization of that "we've always done it this way" mentality. Instead, it focuses the organization on creating more enhanced requirements determination, thereby facilitating a more comprehensive new system development.

ANALYSIS TECHNIQUES

Analysis strategies provide solid methods for approaching the elicitation of requirements from both the organization as well as the external environment interacting with the organization. However, it is important to recognize that along with these analytical strategies also come analytical techniques that provide the best chance of implementing said strategies.

Every interaction within the organization is an opportunity for the project team to gain requirements-based knowledge. However, structuring interactions in specific ways will greatly enhance the degree to which this knowledge is both obtained and able to be applied. Regardless of the analytical strategy being implemented, the analytical techniques outlined in this section will assist in successfully completing the intended objective of acquiring all the necessary requirements to comprehensively define the new system to be developed.

While each technique is described singularly, it is important to note that comprehensive requirements determination will require the utilization of multiple techniques in combination throughout this section of the SDLC. Understanding the nuances of the following techniques will prepare the systems analyst for determining when to use each method when interacting with the organization as a whole. These analysis techniques consist of the following:

1. Observation
2. Interviews
3. Questionnaires
4. Surveys
5. Joint application development
6. Document analysis

The majority of these techniques require interaction with individuals both internal to the organization as well as external. Parties ranging from the organization's customers, vendors, and sometimes even competitors will fall into the analytical scope, and the analytical efforts as a whole will only be strengthened by their willingness to participate. Due to this, please remember to always be respectful of people's time and be considerate of the efforts they are making to assist in the overall success of the project.

Additionally, ensure that there is careful consideration being made to select participants for appropriate techniques being used. Some techniques will burden the participant to a larger degree. These techniques should be used when a participant has significant knowledge to transfer to the development team. That is to say, keep the level of burden on the participant equal to the depth of knowledge they have to provide. Aligning effort and the perceived value of the interaction will ensure that time and effort are not wasted both on the part of the project team and the participant.

Finally, keep in mind that every interaction is an opportunity to garner interest, support, and enthusiasm for the project. This is especially helpful with the organization's internal participants, as they are the ones who must be accepting of the new system when it is finally implemented. The value to the organization's customers cannot be overlooked. A customer who has an issue with your current process may not be a customer for long. Identifying why you are including them in the requirements determination process may just convince them to remain a customer, as the current customer interactions will eventually be enhanced.

Observation

Observation is an analysis technique where the analyst will actually watch people perform their daily activities to gain knowledge of the system and how it functions. This is a very powerful technique, as it places the analyst directly in the operational environment and, through assimilation of the participant being viewed, makes the analyst a member of the operational scope itself. Gaining knowledge of process and task completion through actually viewing the tasks being completed ensures that the analyst has every opportunity to fully understand each component of the current process. While other methods may lead to a misunderstanding of what is being communicated, viewing the tasks with your own eyes ensures that the analyst comprehends every aspect of the process scope.

If there is confusion on aspects of a task or overall process completion, the analyst has the ability to ask questions and clarify on the spot. Additionally, communicating with the user at the time of task completion provides an ability to get the problem and potential resolution perspective from the user in real time and with direct application to the task immediately performed.

However, while observation is a very powerful analytical technique, it is not without potential drawbacks. Observation is time and effort intensive for both the analyst and participant. Most people would agree that their daily professional tasks are difficult enough to complete without having to explain each action to a third party. Likewise, the analyst must dedicate significant time to mirroring the participant as opposed to completing other analytical activities. Also, the analyst is limited to viewing the tasks being completed during the observation period. Not every task is completed daily in most instances. Therefore, periodic tasks may be missed and will not be able to be considered when defining requirements.

Because of the level of effort that must be enacted to complete observation activities, this technique is best reserved for times when the validity of data collected using other techniques is in question or when the complexity of the process or task scope cannot be effectively communicated. Additionally, if the current technology being used by the organization is unfamiliar to the analyst, this technique would be warranted. However, as you will see, other techniques will allot for information gathering that is less burdensome for both the analyst and participant. This is especially useful where a large degree of knowledge transfer is not necessary and will be a more appropriate choice in regards to being sensitive to the use of the participant's time and efforts.

Image 3.3

Interviews

Interviews are one of the most powerful and widely used techniques for requirements determination. Being able to interact with a variety of organizational staff in either a group or one-on-one setting has the ability to promote extensive knowledge transfer in a relatively short amount of time. While it does not provide for the visual representation of each individual task completion that observation does, the same objectives can be met through clear, concise communication. Additionally, multiple resources from various aspects of the organization can be assembled and incorporated into a group interview dynamic. This has the potential to provide value through varying perspectives, knowledge bases, and responsibility scopes, especially when researching issues that are cross-positional or even cross-departmental.

Interviews have the ability to be extremely powerful as they provide a strong base for structured and focused collaboration from the individuals who are most intimate with the current environment. This means that these individuals are also most intimate with the issues within that environment and will oftentimes have valuable opinions on how the business can operate more effectively. Tapping into this wealth of knowledge can certainly lead to very efficient requirements determination interactions and, from that, a comprehensive list of new system requirements. However, the degree of success often rests solidly on the analyst's ability and awareness surrounding those being interviewed and the dynamics of the organization.

Successful interviewing requires strategy and a degree in psychology. Simply asking questions and recording responses will often lead to an incomplete or inaccurate description of processes and tasks and is very often a large contributing factor to incomplete requirements determination activities. A systems analyst quickly learns that even the most educated and experienced corporate resource can be challenged when tasked with explaining their task contributions within the organization. At first glance, this seems incorrect. How can someone who does the same tasks every day have trouble explaining those tasks to an analyst? The answer actually lies within the resource's comfortability with their job tasks. They unconsciously omit steps that seem obvious to them, as they do those steps every single day. However, as the analyst does not have the same experience with these processes, the omitted tasks are not clear, and therefore, the recorded process is not complete.

Another challenge to successful interviewing, specifically in the group interview dynamic, is having organizational resources from various levels of the organization in the same room. An employee who is sitting across from their supervisor is less likely to speak freely and provide their complete opinion or expand on issues within the current process, especially if their discussion is at odds with their supervisor or even management in general. Group dynamics are imperative to understand going into the organization of interview activities, and resource configurations should attempt to minimize friction within the discussion.

Additionally, every individual has their own personality, comforts, and discomforts. Even in a one-on-one interview, not every person is going to be comfortable discussing their job tasks for the potential issues within the organization. Even when a resource is willing to discuss certain aspects of their thoughts and feelings, they may hold back certain information. One of the reasons interviews are so powerful is that the analyst has the ability not only to listen to the resource but also to read their reactions and expressions. Therefore, it is important for the analyst to be aware of not only verbal responses but visual responses as well and search out additional information where required.

Working with interviewees can be challenging, but structuring interviews in a specific order can be very effective at ensuring success with this technique. The analyst should interview managers and corporate decision-makers early on to get a broad understanding of both the organization and its operational scope. Staff and end users should be interviewed afterward to provide details and specifics or even to identify a disconnect between management and operational staff on process completion activities. Finally, it is worth noting that there are individuals who may need to be interviewed for political reasons. While their input may not be required to build the actual requirements determination document, they may have influence in terms of ensuring that the organization commits to the development project, and this is an opportunity to gain or reinforce their support of the project through activity inclusion.

While structuring the types of employees is important to interview success, so too is the structuring of the interviews themselves. There are two main types of interview structures that are employed. These would be as follows:

1. Top-Down—Questions begin broad and become more specific through the interview session.
2. Bottom-Up—Questions begin very specific and become broader through the interview session.

Top-down is the most common interview structure used, as it allows the analyst to lead interviewees to more specific information as necessary. However, bottom-up interviewing allows for a greater focus on individual details and can be useful when analyzing complex processes or tasks.

Also, the questions themselves can be constructed in various forms to pull out requirements throughout the interview. The main types of questions employed in interviews are as follows:

1. Open-Ended—Allows for undirected responses from the interviewee.
2. Closed-Ended—Knowledge transfer of facts and details or confirmation of assumptions.

3. Probing—Follow-up to broader responses or to clarify a point or perspective.

It is most common to see all of these question types used in a single interview session. The key is for the analyst to know when to deploy each type.

Finally, it is important to effectively communicate before, during, and after the interview. The analyst must ensure that they prepare for each interview by creating focus and questions that are best suited to the strengths of the interviewee. Additionally, the analyst wants to ensure that they take notes throughout the interview, ask for clarification where necessary, read nonverbal cues from the interviewee, and question any response that is unclear or appears to be incorrect. Finally, it is important to create a formal written interview summary after the conclusion of the interview and share it with the interviewee to ensure that what was perceived by the analyst was actually what was being communicated by the interviewee.

Interviews are a powerful technique used to pull requirements from the organization. They allow those who are most closely associated with the system being constructed to provide knowledge and insight while at the same time allowing the analyst to pull additional information in an effort to close knowledge gaps. However, this technique is also very time-consuming and requires the support of both the organization as a whole and the individuals who must be interviewed. The analyst needs to have strong interpersonal skills as well as analytical skills in order to be effective in completing this technique.

Questionnaires

Questionnaires are an analysis technique that enables the analyst to quickly collect information from larger groups of resources. This technique is mindful of the resource's time as they are able to fill it out and return it at their leisure. Many times, this technique will be used to obtain directed responses from customers as it is one of the least evasive requirements elicitation techniques. This technique also allows for the mass distribution of the developed questions, resulting in a mass collection of data that can be helpful in generating requirements.

There are two primary methods for developing questionnaires:

1. Fixed-Format Questions—Questions contain pre-developed responses that resources select.
2. Free-Format Questions—Allow resources to respond in written format with no constraints placed on the response.

Each of these methods has strengths and weaknesses that should be noted. Fixed-format questions are easily tabulated and reported on in comparison to all responses within the group. However, the only information that is able to be provided by the resource is what is defined on the questionnaire. Therefore, there may be resource knowledge that does not get communicated as a result. Conversely, free-format questions allow for the resource to provide an unscripted response that has the potential to increase knowledge of the topic being questioned. However, these responses can also be unpredictable and are not easy to tabulate and compare against the entirety of the group responses.

Questionnaires are a viable requirements elicitation technique and are often used in combination with other techniques. Additionally, many questionnaires are crafted using both fixed and free-format questions.

This allows the analyst to home in on specific information while at the same time providing the resource the ability to expand on information where necessary.

Surveys

Many people believe that questionnaires and surveys are the same. However, this is not the case. Surveys are research methods that use questionnaires in a specific way to gather information from a specific group in a structured way, evaluate the data collected, and draw conclusions. Predominantly, surveys are used to generalize results in order to facilitate statistical analysis of the area of focus.

Essentially, questionnaires are sets of questions, while surveys are strategic structures that are focused on specific data-gathering methodologies to gain specific predefined insights. It is also accurate that a questionnaire isn't always a survey, but a survey always contains a questionnaire. Regarding requirements determination, surveys have the ability to focus more heavily on the response pool to a predefined response set, allowing for greater response comparison. This technique is effective when clarification of specific aspects or details related to the project requires directed and measurable response management.

Joint Application Development

Joint application development (JAD) takes group interview strategies to the next level. Essentially, this technique involves all aspects of the organization that can add value to the requirements determination process and places them all into a group environment where the goal is not to emerge until all of the requirements are clearly defined. This group will contain the systems analyst, project team, project sponsor, relevant management, important users, and representatives from any other aspect of the organization who are able to assist in analyzing and participating in the identification of requirements across the entire requirement scope.

This strategy is perhaps both the most invasive and the most resource intensive of all the requirement elicitation techniques. A full requirements list, even for projects of a smaller scope, is not developed in a matter of hours. Significant time and effort will be required of the assembled analysis group. Often, a remote facility with accommodations will be selected to make the group as comfortable as possible. These accommodations are due to the fact that the extended term of the engagement, coupled with intensive group work, will often drain participants. This can easily lead to negative results. By putting effort into maintaining a comfortable environment, the analysis group is being positioned for the best chance of remaining positive and focused on the intended objectives.

Consider all of the potential concerns related to interviewing. All aspects of those potential pitfalls are not only a concern in JAD but elevated in many ways. Personality conflicts are a primary concern, along with an inability for all members of the analysis group to feel as though they can contribute equally. When you have a group consisting of shareholders down to entry-level employees, certain group dynamics are going to impede progress. That is why this type of structure requires a trained facilitator who has the ability to level-set group dynamics and maintain positive group objectives throughout the engagement. Failure to set a tone of inclusivity at the beginning of the engagement will most likely lead to failure.

Group facilitation alone is not always enough to combat detractors from complete group participation. Therefore, electronic JAD facilitation methods, often called electronic JAD, facilitate the anonymous contribution of information or participant opinions without the fear of retaliation. While we would all like to think that every business environment would welcome differences of opinion and perspective in new system development, this is not always the case. The goal is to complete activities successfully and further the system development project. A degree of anonymity can go a long way to overcoming group dynamic issues.

JAD is a technique that is best used when there is strong managerial support for the project, as the resource commitment will be substantial. Additionally, member selection should be well thought out both from a knowledge and contribution perspective, as well as an aptitude for working positively in a group environment. Even with positioning both organizational support and participation as positively as possible, this process is one that requires focus, commitment, and constant reiteration of the intended objectives in order to have the best chance of successfully completing the full requirements determination.

Document Analysis

Document analysis makes use of existing documentation within the organization to better understand the current environment and to uncover potential issues leading to developed issue resolution. This strategy relies on many different types of documents, not simply the documentation of the current system. Everything from organizational structure, change history, previous system studies, business studies, and even completed competitor analysis are areas that can provide direction and focus for developing requirements.

However, rarely is documentation maintained consistently within an organization. Therefore, it is important to analyze not only the document content but also its applicability to current times. Additionally, especially when it comes to system documentation, documentation is often written from a best practices perspective. This is rarely how systems are actually used, so there will often be a divestiture from how the document says the system should be used and how it is actually used by the organization.

Document analysis can be a valuable strategy for increasing knowledge on both the organization and the environment to be changed. However, it should not be the only method used in requirements determination.

Requirements Definition

The main goal of using a combination of requirements analysis strategies and techniques is to compile a comprehensive requirements definition document for the development project. The requirements definition document defines all of the functional, nonfunctional, and technical requirements of the new system.

This document is intended to be used by the project team, organizational staff, steering committee, or corporate decision-makers who need to either approve furthering the project or provide input into the validity or completeness of the currently developed requirements list. Not only will the requirements definition provide increased visibility into all requirements of the project, but it will also highlight all areas that were analyzed throughout the requirements determination process. The end result should be a comprehensive document that provides guidance on how to develop the system in order to maximize positive impact on the organization by meeting all identified organizational needs.

HOW TO CREATE A REQUIREMENTS DEFINITION STATEMENT

Creating the requirements definition statement begins by analyzing all of the requirements defined through the requirement elicitation activities. The systems analyst and project team need to begin by analyzing each defined requirement for appropriate fit in regard to the intended project. It is possible that some developed requirements are only loosely associated or may even not be associated at all with the defined project scope. While this may seem odd, when dealing with multiple requirement elicitation techniques spread across multiple analytical groups, this is not uncommon. Analyzing each requirement again for project fit is a way to both refamiliarize the group with each requirement definition as well as to ensure that only relevant requirements are to be acted on.

Each identified requirement will fit into one of the following categories:

1. Functional requirement
2. Nonfunctional requirement
3. Out of scope—potential future enhancement
4. Out of scope—does not meet a need

Verified functional requirements are listed in the functional requirement section of the requirements definition statement. Likewise, verified nonfunctional requirements are listed in the nonfunctional requirement section of the requirements definition statement. Out-of-scope requirements that have the potential to be future enhancements are also recorded as potential future enhancements. Inaccurate requirements are discarded.

When creating the requirements determination statement, there are a couple of additional considerations that the development team must consider. Requirements need to be prioritized in order to communicate what items are nonnegotiable and what ones may be altered if the development process requires. Scope creep is a real concern, as the requirements determination process will often bring to light new requirements or considerations or even a whole new project scope at times. Ensuring that changes within the project scope are tracked, communicated, and approved by the steering committee is the only way to truly ensure that the project that continues after the requirement analysis has been completed has the continued approval and support of the organization.

ISSUES WITH REQUIREMENTS DETERMINATION

Even with extensive requirement elicitation activities and significant analytical effort placed on the development of the requirements definition statement, there are still considerations that the development team must consider when moving forward with the project. Verifying and validating requirements can be difficult to impossible. Therefore, there is always a chance that a developed requirement may not actually be required for project success. Conversely, some requirements may not come to light until further on in the development process, being completely missed in the requirements determination phase. Finally, the analyst may not have access to all of the most educated and informed resources within the organization. This lack of access can result in an incomplete requirements definition that may cause difficulties in later stages of development.

Chapter Summary

Requirements definition is the first step in the analytical phase of the SDLC. It is also one of the most critical steps to complete comprehensively and accurately. Comprehensive requirements definition will minimize unknown factors that can negatively impact project progression. Additionally, it will allow for efficient and effective new system development that not only meets the intended objectives but often exceeds them.

However, it is important to note that there are also difficulties associated with analytics. Often, there is no definitive way to identify that all requirements have been completely and correctly defined. There is always a chance that an aspect of the current system or environment has been missed. The goal is to minimize this possibility as much as possible but also to expect that there will be challenges throughout the system development process. The SDLC does a good job of aligning appropriate structure and strategy to provide a strong basis for comprehensive system development and a chance to analyze development at each step to ascertain if the current effort has exposed new or missed aspects of the design.

By clearly understanding both the developed analytical strategies and techniques, as well as the necessary aptitudes and characteristics of the analyst, your team will have the best chance of effectively mitigating requirement determination tasks and developing a requirements definition statement that can lead to the development of an effective new system.

Project Planning Activities

1. List the functional requirements of the system.
2. List the Nonfunctional requirements of the system.
3. Create the requirements definition statement.

Image Credits

CHAPTER 4

Use Case Analysis

Introduction

Image 4.1

During the analysis phase of the SDLC, we often find that manual processes are being completed in conjunction with system processes. Why is this the case? Shouldn't the system have been developed to handle these manual tasks as well? Manual task incorporation happens for a variety of reasons. The system may not have been designed to correctly complete all required tasks, new task requirements may have been introduced since system construction, or even a combination of both of these scenarios are examples. Therefore, the creation of the new system allows an opportunity to not only meet current system needs but also incorporate functional requirements that were previously not included.

Due to the importance of incorporating both system and manual tasks into the new system development, a comprehensive understanding of functional requirements is essential. As the functional requirements dictate the processes the new system will complete, disregarding even a single requirement can easily result in an underperforming or even nonfunctional system. While requirements determination provides a solid basis for defining functional requirements, the importance of ensuring that this list is both complete and each requirement well-defined requires even further in-depth analysis than what was previously conducted during requirements determination activities. The need for an increased level of process analysis has led to the development of an activity for validating both the completeness and correctness of the functional requirements of the use case.

Use cases serve a number of critical roles in the analysis phase of the SDLC. Not only do they highlight the interaction of the user and the system from the user's perspective, but they also are able to uncover additional manual processes that can be incorporated into the new system development. In some instances, use cases will uncover development opportunities that were missed in previous tasks completed to date. In other instances, they will simply reaffirm the completeness of the development team's understanding of the business environment and current system from both the functional requirements and system user perspective. In either case, the end result is to ensure that the most comprehensive new system development possible is being completed.

Learning Objectives

1. Describe the purpose of use cases.
2. Explain why the use case is used in the analysis phase of the SDLC.
3. Describe the various parts of a use case.
4. Explain how each part of the use case contributes to the functional requirements.
5. Explain how to create a use case.

What Is a Use Case?

A use case is a formal document development designed to increase clarity regarding the interactions between the user and the current system. It is created by analyzing and documenting the steps taken to complete a core process of the current system from the user's perspective. It requires the analysis of the following:

The user's interactions with the system

The environmental conditions that must be true for the user to be able to begin the process

The initial action that starts the process

The information inputted into the system

The steps to complete the process by the user

The information outputted from the system when a process completes successfully

The environmental conditions that are true when the process completes successfully

Possible alternatives based on a user's choices when completing process tasks

The outcome(s) when a process does not complete successfully

Any manual process that is being completed in combination with the system process

By analyzing and documenting all of these aspects of a current system's process, the use case becomes a text-based document that users are easily able to understand and contains a wealth of information that can express and clarify user requirements. This provides a solid foundation for ensuring that all functional requirements are uncovered, understood, and incorporated into the final new system design.

It is important to emphasize that a single use case is not developed for all processes within a current system but rather a single use case is developed for each core process. Additionally, the current system process is not simply the current automated or digitized processes the users are completing. Manual tasks and activities must also be brought into the use case development process in order to identify areas of opportunity for enhancing system utilization. Use cases are powerful, as their creation depends on in-depth interaction and assessment of end users and their interactions and utilizations of the current system.

Some of the key competencies that must be used by the development team to successfully complete comprehensive use cases include the following:

1. Observation
2. Interviews
3. JAD sessions

The only way to successfully build a use case is through the comprehensive assessment of user interactions with both the system and the business environment. The degree to which the systems analyst and their team are able to pull every piece of information required from the user will largely depend on their ability to use these techniques.

Use Case Characteristics

A use case is built from a goal-oriented perspective of the user's interaction with the system. That is to say that the use case is meant to identify not only what the user is doing but what they intend to accomplish by completing the process within the system. This results in a goal-focused sequence of events that are able to be tabulated and presented in such a way that is easy for users and developers to follow, as information related to each task is described in great detail. Therefore, the core components of a use case include the following:

1. The conditions that must be met to begin the process or the **preconditions**
2. The user or the **entity**
3. An event that initiates the process or **trigger**

4. The steps of the process or the **normal course**
5. A goal or goals that are accomplished when the process completes successfully or the **postconditions**

By identifying and analyzing each one of these use case components, the development of a comprehensive explanation from the user's perspective is now possible. This allows for even the most complex system interactions to be broken down into individual steps so that the project team can analyze the necessity of each action.

In a use case, there is additional consideration that must be given to the recording of the tasks themselves. The tasks completed by the user are not always singular in regard to decision-making. This means that every process step that allows the user to make a choice results in a different action taken on the data within the system also described as a different **process path**. Since decision logic can create different process paths, it also stands to reason that this can result in different process outcomes. Therefore, it is not sufficient for the use case to note a single set of steps for a process but rather all of the potential paths, also known as **flows,** that may occur in the process.

Use cases also contain a hierarchy for recording the potential process flow of a system process. The primary process flow is identified as the one in which the process steps are all completed as intended, and the process outcome is the expected result. This is the process flow known as the **normal course,** which is documented as the expected steps within the use case, with each individual step fully described. Process flows that change steps and result in other outcomes are documented as **alternative outcomes** based on the outcome demonstrated by the change in the step. The end result is a document that provides a detailed description of the primary process, as well as a listing of possible alternative outcomes related to that process. For example, a use case developed to document the steps to purchase a product would describe each step from initialization to product purchase as the primary flow. However, if the product was unavailable, that would change the outcome, as the product cannot be purchased, and therefore, the unavailability of the product would result in an alternative flow.

In summary, a use case displays the following characteristics:

1. Organizes functional requirements
2. Identifies system users
3. Records process flows from the initiation event to the process goal
4. Describes the main process flow as well as identifies alternative process flows

The Usefulness of Use Cases

Image 4.2

Use cases serve a variety of functions related to building the most comprehensive and all-encompassing new system development possible. This begins with the benefits related to the creation of the use case itself and extends to the utilization of each finalized use case document. Each step of the process is a chance to reevaluate previous analysis, capture additional processes that were potentially missed, and ensure that there is a good understanding of each process previously identified and assessed. Essentially, use cases benefit both the development team and the developers themselves.

The systems analyst and development team gain many benefits throughout the use case development process. The user interactions required to pull out all the details contained within the use case improve communication methods among the development team. The collaborative efforts required to describe business processes effectively and efficiently result in an in-depth discussion regarding individual steps in each system process. This discussion brings forth various perspectives and contributions assisting in ensuring that the analysis of each system process is comprehensive. Likewise, the finalization of the use case document is only accomplished through the development team consensus that the process description is accurate, which ensures that there is group agreement on the functional system requirements at the end of the process.

The process of working with end users and analyzing process completion from their perspective also allows the development team to reevaluate the current process and potentially identify process alternatives. The more comprehensive the project team is involved with the user-system interaction, the more plausible it is to utilize varying team perspectives to reevaluate the most appropriate way to complete necessary processes in the new system. Additionally, this analysis provides the ability to expose process steps that may have, to date, been incorrectly described or even unknown to the project team. Also, there may be alternative paths that are identified or exceptions if the process path is not completed correctly. There may even be aspects of the current process that are not even in the current project scope and need to be removed in order to meet other agreed-upon project constraints. Conversely, these same activities can identify manual processes that can be incorporated into the project scope in order to automate a currently manual activity.

The software developers also rely on use cases for new system construction, especially in situations where the developers are not employees of the organization. There may be a lack of understanding of the business and business functions. The use case documents will provide clarity regarding the business processes that the new system is intended to function within. The identified alternative paths and exceptions will assist in ensuring they are correctly handled in the software logic.

The use case documents will allow software developers to identify similarities in process structure that can be translated into singular software objects to be deployed for multiple uses. In short, use cases provide transparency regarding process steps, which can be used to group software development requirements and streamline software development. Identification of the conditions that need to be met prior to the process starting, as well as conditions that are facilitated by process completion, are also used by the developers to ensure that software logic contains the correct checks and balances.

Once the new system is operational, software developers will also refer to the use case documents as a way of doing an initial user test on the new system. The new processes developed will be interacted with, and the use case referred to in order to ensure that all aspects of the use case are accounted for and correctly handled. Essentially, the use case is used to develop user testing test scripts.

Use Cases and Functional Requirements

It is impossible to discuss use cases without relating them to the functional requirements of the system. That is because the development of use cases focuses on what the user expects the system to do. However, with that being said, there is an important distinction that needs to be made. The use case is created from the user's point of view. Therefore, while a use case will act as a tool to clarify user requirements, it is up to the system analyst to turn the items identified in the use cases into functional requirements to be used by the software developers.

Essentially, a use case will bring out functional requirements. However, this is done by analyzing the use case steps and outcomes in order to decode what each functional requirement actually is. This is done by the system analyst, who will formally list each additional functional requirement that was identified through the use case process within the functional requirements documents previously created.

Elements of a Use Case

As a use case (See Table 4.1) is a formal document, its development requires standardized components. Each use case must consist of the following information:

1. Name
2. Number
3. Description
4. Priority
5. Actor
6. Trigger
7. Preconditions
8. Postconditions
9. Assumptions
10. Normal process flow

11. Alternative process flows

Table 4.1 Use Case Format

Use Case Name:	Schedule an appointment	ID:	UC-3	Priority:	High
Actor:	Scheduler				
Description:	The scheduler opens the appointment calendar, selects an open time slot for an available lawn care team, and assigns the customer account.				
Trigger:	The scheduler needs to schedule a customer appointment.				
Trigger Type:	☒External ☐ Temporal				
Preconditions:	1. The scheduler is authenticated in the system. 2. The scheduler has security access to the appointment calendar.				
Normal Course:	1. Schedule an appointment in the system scheduler. a. The scheduler specifies the customer account number and the date range requested for the appointment. b. The system brings up a calendar view showing currently available open time slots and the name of the corresponding available lawn care team. c. The Scheduler selects the desired open appointment. d. The system notifies the selected lawn care team of the newly assigned job. e. The system notifies the customer of the upcoming appointment. f. The system stores the appointment in the appointment data store.				
Exceptions:	E1: No open appointments for the selected time frame. 1. The system displays the message: "No appointments available; please select another date range." E2: Two schedulers select the same appointment at the same time. 1. The first scheduler processed by the system will retain the appointment. 2. The system displays the message: "A scheduling error occurred; please select another appointment" to the second scheduler.				
Postconditions:	1. The appointment is scheduled in the lawn care management system. 2. The lawn care team is notified on their handheld of the new appointment. 3. The customer appointment notification is produced and sent to the customer.				

Name

Table 4.2 Use Case Name

Use Case Name:	Schedule an appointment

The use case name (See Table 4.2) identifies the use case. As such, a name should be chosen that clearly depicts what the purpose of the use case is. Therefore, a verb/noun combination is generally used.

Number

Table 4.3 Use Case Number

ID:	UC-3

A use case is given a number (See Table 4.3) to allow for the organization of all use cases for future use, as well as for use in future analytical tasks such as process analysis. The number also acts as a reference to tie additional analytical development back to the use case.

Description

Table 4.4 Use Case Description

Description:	The scheduler opens the appointment calendar, selects an open time slot for an available lawn care team, and assigns the customer account.

While the use case name provides a general understanding of the intent of the use case, the description (See Table 4.4) provides more detail on the process being analyzed. This allows for clarification when use cases are referenced by various parties later in the development process.

Actor

Table 4.5 Actor

Actor:	Scheduler

The actor (See Table 4.5) identifies the main individual(s) and systems that will be involved in the process. Any individual or system that is used in the use case's process flow must be included.

Trigger

Table 4.6 Trigger

Trigger:	Scheduler needs to schedule a customer appointment.
Trigger Type:	☒External ☐ Temporal

The trigger (See Table 4.6) is the vent that causes the use case to begin. There are two types of triggers:

1. External—This is an action that is completed by an actor.
2. Temporal—This is a time-based action.

Preconditions

Table 4.7 Preconditions

Preconditions:	1. The scheduler is authenticated in the system. 2. The scheduler has security access to the appointment calendar.

The preconditions (See Table 4.7) are the aspects of the environment that must be met in order for the process to be able to be initiated. Essentially, they are tests that must prove true before the process is allowed to proceed. Oftentimes, preconditions are checked within the process and, therefore, will also show up as a step in the use case.

Postconditions

Table 4.8 Postconditions

Postconditions:	1. The appointment is scheduled in the lawn care management system. 2. The lawn care team is notified on their handheld of the new appointment. 3. The customer appointment notification is produced and sent to the customer.

The postconditions (See Table 4.8) are the aspects of the environment that should be met when the process ends. These are the items that the process must handle prior to terminating. For example, recording a transaction in a journal file prior to initiating a new transaction.

Assumptions

Each use case is only one process of a total system. Therefore, it is possible that another process will satisfy a precondition prior to the initiation of the current use case. There is no need to incorporate that already completed step in the current use case as well. Therefore, the requirement will be listed as an assumption, denoting that it is handled in another use case.

Normal Process Flow

Table 4.9 Normal Course

Normal Course:	1. Schedule an appointment in the system scheduler. a. The scheduler specifies the customer account number and the date range requested for the appointment. b. The system brings up a calendar view showing currently available open time slots and the name of the corresponding available lawn care team. c. The scheduler selects the desired open appointment. d. The system notifies the selected lawn care team of the newly assigned job. e. The system notifies the customer of the upcoming appointment. f. The system stores the appointment in the appointment data store.

The normal process flow (See Table 4.9) is the expected steps the user will take to get to a successful result. In other words, the normal process flow contains the steps identified as the correct actions for every step of the process, with the end result being the expected system result.

Alternative Process Flows

When a process step is reached, that includes a decision point, making an alternative decision to the one made in the normal process flow will create an alternative process flow. For each decision point, each potential alternative choice must be made and documented as a separate alternative process flow. Additionally, for any exception that is notated, initiating the process without observing the rules of the exception must be completed and documented as an alternative process flow. Alternative process flows begin at the step in which the decision is made. That is to say that these process flows will not always start at the initial process trigger, but the decision point becomes the trigger for the alternative process flow. Additionally, alternative process flows will often result in postconditions that are different from those identified in the normal process flow.

Use Case Formats

There is not one specific way to write a use case regarding the level of detail that is required. It is important to remember that a use case is meant to clarify information. If there is already clarity regarding a specific process, then less description is required. However, regardless of how detailed the description of each use case component is, the completeness of the development is always imperative. For example, each process step must be documented. Even if the project team is fully aware of specific steps, it cannot be eliminated from the use case. The level of explanation can be adjusted, but not the inclusion of all required information. Therefore, at the initiation of use case development, it is important to determine just how much description is required and align to one of three use case development methodologies:

1. Brief
2. Casual
3. Fully dressed

Along with the level of detail developed in the use case component explanation, there are also two distinct writing styles that use case development can be approached. These styles are defined as follows:

1. Conversational form
2. Narrative form

Brief Use Case Format

A brief use case format is developed with the intent to summarize as much as possible. This type of use case development format will identify the entity, pre- and postconditions, and trigger but summarize the process itself. Instead of documenting each step of the process, the process itself is explained in one or two sentences. While this can be useful early on in the use case development process, a brief will need to be further expanded in order to capture each process step. However, the value of brief use case development is such that it allows for quick creation and organization of the actual use cases within a system.

Casual Use Case Format

A casual use case format expands on the development of a brief by including the process steps. However, the steps themselves are developed through description without being formally numbered. While the reader will be able to progress through the process on a step-by-step level, clarification regarding what specific number each step is in the process will not be glaringly apparent. System Analysts will allow a casual use case format development on projects where there is a very high degree of knowledge and comfortability with both the current system as well as the organization and processes being enacted.

Fully Dressed Use Case Format

A fully dressed use case is one that includes the highest level of detail related to the process being analyzed. The fully dressed use case will contain all attributes of the brief and casual use case combined, as well as more formally representing each process step. Each process step will be numbered, and representative of not only the normal process flow but also alternative process flows. This means that the viewer will know exactly what steps result in decisions and what the outcome process steps of each decision will be. Additionally, the level of detail of each use case component will be greater in order to provide additional clarification to development parties who are less familiar with the organization, system, or specific process being documented. Based on all of this, a fully dressed use case will contain the following additional items:

1. Alternative process flows
2. Inputs for steps
3. Outputs for steps
4. Summary inputs
5. Summary outputs

ALTERNATIVE PROCESS FLOWS

Alternative process flows are most often initiated by the choices the user makes within the process. The steps resulting from a specific decision are accurate when that decision is made. However, the converse decision will normally result in a series of different steps. Singularly, the inclusion of alternative process flows seems very straightforward. However, when you start to consider a process with multiple decision points, the number of alternative process flows will grow exponentially as the number of alternatives requiring documentation increases. This can lead to use cases that are large and contain significant amounts of information. Ensuring that each alternative process flow is developed helps to assure that a user will always traverse the process fully, leading to an associated postcondition that makes sense.

INPUTS AND OUTPUTS FOR STEPS

In order to gain clarification on complex processes, it is often helpful to ensure an understanding of the input being entered into the process at each process step, as well as the output being developed by the process step. In a fully dressed use case format, both the input and output of a given process step are formally written to supply such clarification. This will ensure that the project team fully understands what the expected user interactions with the system look like, as well as the intended results from the system.

SUMMARY INPUTS

The summary inputs section lists all the process inputs that were defined at the process step level. This section provides a clear picture of all information being fed into the system during process completion.

SUMMARY OUTPUTS

The summary outputs section lists all of the process outputs that were defined at the process step level. This section provides a clear picture of all the information being returned from the system during process completion.

Conversational Form Writing Style

Conversational form, as you might expect, is a descriptive format that feels like a conversation between the user and the system. Traditionally, conversational form is written in a two-column format where one column documents the user steps and the second column documents the associated system response. This form is also known as the **dialog form**. This format works best when focused on a single user and system set of interactions. Adding additional users can make it difficult to follow which user is interacting with the system for a given step and, therefore, result in a less clear picture of the overall user-system interactions.

Narrative Form Writing Style

The narrative form is written in a single-column format. Each step is described in one or two sentence descriptions and organized by individual user interaction. This provides a clearly described and ordered process flow with differentiation between different users. Therefore, this style is preferred when working with processes that incorporate multiple user interactions with the system.

Create a Use Case

Image 4.3

Now that there is a clear understanding of each of the components of a successful use case, the next course of action is to define how these components are arranged to actually create the use case itself. As previously stated, there is no universal right or wrong answer as to how a use case must be constructed. The amount of information required will vary from project to project, as will the need to include or exclude a certain level of detail within each process description.

As there are so many variables to use case construction, many questions must be asked prior to defining the use case format itself. How well does the project team know the organization and the system? How much internal knowledge is there of the current processes and individual process steps? How much information will the developers need in order to successfully construct the new system? How many decision points are contained in the associated process, and how radically does decision-making alter the expected outcomes? How many exceptions are possible as related to the normal course, and what impact do they have on the associated process as a whole?

Answering these questions leads the systems analyst to a decision point regarding what level of detail is required in the development of the use case. If there is a high degree of background knowledge by the project team coupled with many single user and system interactions, a casual use case development incorporating a conversational form writing style may be appropriate. A lack of internal knowledge regarding organization or process, or a process that requires the interaction of multiple users, will often result in a fully dressed use case format written in narrative form.

Once the level of development detail is decided upon, the next task is to determine what the actual use cases are for the system. Remember, use cases are developed for core system processes. These are processes that are essential to adequate system utilization and individually require multiple steps to complete. From this list, individual use cases will be developed and confirmed and finally result in the revision of the functional requirements, if warranted.

Event-Response List

At a most basic level, system processes are nothing more than events and responses. Whether it be an external trigger or a temporal trigger, an action initiates a response from the system. Therefore, when attempting to identify the main processes within a system, analysis of the external and temporal events the system is responding to is an excellent way to initiate this investigation.

Starting with the data collected through the requirements determination activity, the systems analyst will focus on user interactions with the system and record what event is taking place and what the system response to the event is. Each event will be tabulated into a list, with the event order of action being replicated within the list itself. For example, if the user enters a username, the system then prompts for a password, the user enters the password, and the system then brings them to a home screen; events will be recorded in series as follows:

1. Event: User enters user name Response: System prompts for password
2. Event: User enters password Response: System presents home screen

The project team can then review the event-response list and group logically connected events and responses. This will begin to demonstrate the processes that make up the system and, therefore, the use cases that must be developed.

Just as with every other aspect of use case development, the level of detail regarding the development of the event-response list will be correlated to the knowledge of the system and environment. If there is a good understanding of both, not every event will be recorded, but rather, a group of events will be defined. For example:

1. Event: User log on Response: System presents home screen

All of the individual events are contained within the event group and will be decompiled in the actual use case form creation.

The development of the event-response lists provides clarity of user interaction from an action and reaction perspective. This will align with the previously defined functional requirements, as these are the steps to meet those requirements and may even bring to light some that were previously unidentified. Grouping the events into core system functions allows for the identification of the actual use case scope, and the use cases can then be formally documented.

Use Case Form

Now that the main processes have been identified, the actual use case can formally be constructed. The use case itself will be arranged in a standard format so that specific information will always be in the same location. The systems analyst will begin by naming the use case and providing it with a unique ID and a priority in relation to its importance to the system. Next, the description will provide details on the process being completed and documented within the use case. This will be followed by the identification of the actor in the process, followed by the trigger, which initiates the process, and further clarifying whether this trigger is an external event or temporal in nature. The preconditions will next be listed to demonstrate what must be satisfied for the process to be able to actually begin.

The next section of the use case will be composed of the development of the normal course. This section details the **major steps** of the process in written form and numbered chronologically by order of completion. A detailed description of each step will narrate what action is being performed on the system, as well as the associated system response, and allow for identifying the **inputs and outputs** of the process. Whether you are developing a conversational or narrative use case will determine if these descriptions are created with multiple columns or in a linear format where a response immediately follows an event. If your event-response list is highly detailed, it will often translate into the individual normal course steps being detailed.

Following the normal course section, the exceptions section is developed next. The format is very similar to the normal course in that each exception is listed, and then system interactions resulting from the initiation of the exception are listed and described. This is repeated for every identified exception contained within the process.

Finally, the postconditions are listed. This demonstrates what will be accomplished by the completion of the process. This provides a basis for **use case confirmation**, ensuring that what is accomplished by the process is the intended and necessary result.

MAJOR STEPS

The major steps are the identified actions and responses within the process being documented. Essentially, each user event and associated system response encountered by the user when completing the process make up the major steps of the process. By recording the steps sequentially, you define a step through description of how the process is completed. The major steps demonstrate the actions of both the user and the system from the user's perspective. That is to say, the response is the result the system presents, not necessarily the steps within the system to get to that result.

INPUTS AND OUTPUTS

The inputs and outputs are really just the events and the responses. Each event is an input, and the associated response is an output. Therefore, it can be said that the major steps are comprised of documenting the inputs made by the user and the associated outputs made by the system. It must be noted that inputs can be either external, such as user action, or temporal.

USE CASE CONFIRMATION

Once a use case is developed, it is important to confirm the correctness of the development. As previously stated, analysis of the postconditions will assist in determining if the process result is aligned with the functional requirements that have been defined for the system. Additionally, having the user(s) role-play and walk through the normal course and exception developments will assist in confirming that all steps are accounted for and correctly developed. Once the use case is determined to be accurate, if it cannot be aligned to a currently defined functional requirement, it may be that it represents additional functional requirements that were not previously defined and now must be.

Functional Requirement Revision

For instances where the user confirms the accuracy of a use case, but a currently defined functional requirement cannot be aligned, it is possible that a new functional requirement has just been identified. This is one of the primary reasons use case analysis is conducted and must not be ignored in order to get the most benefit from the activity. If new functional requirements are defined, they must be added to the functional requirement list in order to ensure they are incorporated into the development going forward. Additionally, the associated use case can be used to provide increased clarity to the project team and highlight the area that was originally missed.

Chapter Summary

Use case development is a very important tool for ensuring successful new system development. When done correctly and comprehensively, use cases fully represent the functionality of the system. Not only do use cases identify the core processes but also the actors responsible for completing those processes. Additionally, use cases highlight the expected course of action to complete each process, as well as the outcome if errors are encountered during the process. All of this empowers both the project team and, in the future, the development team to gain a much greater understanding of the user's needs and expectations for the system.

The analytical phase is structured to gain the most understanding possible of the current system and what needs to be accomplished to make the new system successful. However, it is important to understand that use cases in and of themselves will not accomplish this. This tool is meant to focus on user interaction and system utilization from the user's perspective. The clarification and advanced knowledge will be valuable but must also be incorporated into additional system analysis to gain a more holistic picture of how the current system fully functions. That said, ensuring that the user interactions are wholly represented will greatly assist in the development of the system-side analysis that comes next.

Project Planning Activities

1. Develop an event-response list.
2. For each event, complete the following:
    a. Identify the major steps.
    b. Identify the inputs and outputs for each step.

3. Create a use case form for each complex event.
4. Role-play each use case to confirm correctness.
5. Revise functional requirements developed in Chapter 3, if necessary.

Image Credits

CHAPTER 5

Process Modeling

Introduction

After the project team gains a better understanding of the user interaction with the system by completing the use case development, the next logical area of focus is on the system itself. Process modeling attempts to provide an accurate graphical representation of system function. This is accomplished by mapping out each primary business process and how the data flows as the process is completed.

Data flow diagrams (DFDs) are a popular technique used for developing system process models. By understanding the core components of DFDs, how to create them, and how the project team is able to benefit from them, the true value of process modeling activities can be more clearly understood. Additionally, the development of the DFDs for the system will also begin to expose more of the data utilization that is required for system functionality. This will be an important takeaway as the project team transitions to future analysis phase activities.

Learning Objectives

1. Describe the rules for developing data flow diagrams (DFDs).
2. Describe the style guidelines for developing DFDs.
3. Describe the process used to create DFDs.
4. Create DFDs.

Image 5.1

Process Models

Process modeling is a process management technique that visually depicts the organization's internal system processes to assist in identifying potential areas of improvement. The goal of process models is to depict the current state of each system process as the system exists today, identify areas of change that will enhance the process completion for the organization, and develop the new process.

Process modeling is a core component of developing process automation in a new system. Process models graphically depict business processes with an emphasis on the entities interacting with the process, the steps required to complete the process, and the data flowing through the process. These components of the process model, when assembled, allow the project team to better visualize the current process in order to facilitate a better understanding of internal business procedures and more easily identify areas of opportunity for enhancement. By being able to look at a graphical representation, tasks are not only defined but highlighted. This can allow for much easier identification of unnecessary repetition of effort or even where effort is being expended unnecessarily altogether.

It is important to note that process models are not solely created to depict current system functions. Any manual process that is currently being conducted in combination with system utilization should be included in process modeling. This will highlight areas where manual effort can potentially be automated or possibly even eliminated. Process modeling needs to be comprehensive to facilitate clarification of the current system scope, as well as the total amount of effort being enacted by system users.

Process modeling is a strategy. No strategy will be successful unless it is aligned with overall company goals and objectives. Therefore, the systems analyst must ensure that the project team clearly defines these aspects of the organization. This will allow the team to question why each task is performed within a process and evaluate whether the task is required and, if so, to see if it is possible to complete the task in a more effective way.

Process modeling is intended to provide multiple benefits to the project team. Some of these benefits include the following:

1. Efficiency improvement
2. Increase transparency
3. Emphasize best practice
4. Enhance understanding
5. Increase coordination

Efficiency Improvement

By highlighting areas of redundancy, inefficiency, and unnecessary task requirements, process modeling acts as a tool to provide the project team with areas of opportunity. These identified process inefficiencies can be reviewed, and the process reworked to become more efficient.

Additionally, representing each task step by step allows the project team to evaluate areas where resources can be optimized. If multiple processes require similar task completion, resource alignment is potentially able to increase task completion rates with fewer overall resources required. The visualization of these process steps makes identifying these similarities easier.

Increase Transparency

The activity of identifying the processes to be mapped allows for a better understanding of the main processes contained within the system. The activity of mapping out each process can validate that the processes are correctly organized or highlight that some identified processes are really the combination of multiple unique processes.

The overall activity of process model development will provide greater transparency into how the system completes its required objectives. This will allow for enhanced analysis of what the new system must also be able to accomplish.

Emphasize Best Practice

Process modeling will assist in consistency and standardization of development throughout the system. By creating a set definition of how process models are to be designed, the systems analyst is able to employ multiple segments of the project team to construct process models in unison. This will save time overall and ensure that the results of each group are aligned with the developments of every other group.

Enhance Understanding

Graphically representing complex processes or processes that the project team does not have a clear understanding of allows for a much more simplistic view of the complex combination of process steps. Oftentimes, this form of process depiction will allow the project team to clarify areas of uncertainty. Additionally, by looking at the models of multiple system processes side by side, the project team will be able to more easily pick out similarities in steps between processes. This can provide insight to the development team on areas of focus where system functions can be combined or even reused.

Additionally, process modeling will clearly identify the start and end points of a given process. This can be important in order to differentiate system functions and, therefore, development requirements.

Increase Coordination

Process models bring together the people, system tasks, and data that are being used in the current system. By depicting how each of these organizational components interact in each process and allowing for comparison between processes, it is possible for the project team to evaluate the degree to which the coordination of activities is as efficient and effective as possible.

When there are areas of opportunity, alteration of the process steps, process priorities, or even human interactions with the system, it can allow for more coordinated efforts and ultimately enhance overall system performance.

Types of Process Models

Image 5.2

Functional process modeling develops an outline of what the system needs to do by focusing on the steps the system completes in order to complete the overall process. These process models do not evaluate how the processes utilize the data they interact with but rather focus on where the data originates, how it flows through the process, and where it is distributed at the completion of the process. Functional process modeling will focus on the process data relationship from multiple perspectives.

In new system design, there are predominantly two types of process models that are developed to assist in gaining an increased understanding of the current system processes. These models are similar in construction as they both focus on the system's unique processes, the steps required to complete them, and the data flow throughout the process completion. However, areas of focus are also slightly different for each type of process model development. These two unique process model types include the following:

1. Logical process models
2. Physical process models

Logical Process Models

The logical process model is focused on the business process and looks at the process flow from the perspective of the business activities that are completed from process initiation through completion. Each process action is described as follows:

1. Gathering data
2. Delivering data to a task

3. Controlling access to data
4. Determining which task to complete based on criteria
5. Determining if the task completes successfully

From this list of activities, the systems analyst can describe all the steps in even the most complex process by breaking the process down into these steps and ordering them based on process order. Additionally, some tasks may occur sequentially, while others are completed in parallel, and based on successful task completion, some tasks may become cyclical until a successful result is achieved.

Now that the concepts behind logical process model creation are clear, the logical process model can be developed. The systems analyst will focus on the movement of data and the decisions made that control the path of the data as it flows through the process in order to develop the logical data model. The processes themselves will be limited to only business activities being completed with at least some assistance of the system and will be described using business terminology, not technical terms. The process descriptions must also be comprehensive and incorporate all tasks necessary to complete the process being evaluated.

Additionally, it is important to note that when evaluating the current system, a systems analyst must not only analyze each individual process but also the interdependence of processes. System dependency evaluation from a process perspective will allow the project team to better understand what processes are truly core to system performance and which ones have the potential to be reduced or even removed. While understanding which steps in the process are truly required, understanding what processes impact other processes is equally important in the analysis phase of system development.

Logical process modeling methods take the organization of these components and format them in ways that are easily understood. Whether descriptive or graphically, the intent is to demonstrate the logical flow of data through the process being evaluated. These models do not provide details on how decisions are made or the technical inclusion of how process tasks are completed by the system. Logical process models also do not take into account system limitations or technical requirements. Some examples of logical process models include the following:

1. DFDs
2. Flow charts
3. Functional dependency diagrams
4. Function hierarchies
5. Written description

The focus of the logical process model is on each process as a representation of the set of activities being completed from a business perspective. This type of modeling is meant to provide many benefits for the project team. Some of these benefits include the following:

1. Knowledge of data required at each step of the process
2. Knowledge of data access requirements at each step of the process
3. Understanding what is required for consistent process execution
4. Understanding of where adjustments may allow for current process enhancement

5. Understanding of data security requirements at each step of the process

Physical Process Models

Physical process models build on the logical process model development. This means that the systems analyst and his or her team will first focus on logical process model development and then utilize that development in order to define the system's physical process models. However, that is not to say that both logical and physical data models will look the same. This is often not the case. The physical process models will focus on the topology, data, roles, and rules of the process and, therefore, will incorporate aspects of the system that the logical process model does not.

The physical process model will focus on individual tasks, data, and order of task execution, just like the logical process model, but will add to these components the following:

1. The rules used for decision-making in routing the data through the process
2. Roles and permissions of process participants
3. Highlighting how exceptions are handled by the process

Data Flow Diagrams

While there are many ways to represent logical and physical process diagrams, the data flow diagram (DFD) is one of the most popular methods used by system development project teams. A DFD maps the flow of data through a system or process by using defined symbols such as rectangles, squares, circles, lozenges or rectangles with rounded corners, and arrows in combination with text labels that clarify data inputs, data outputs, data storage, and the routes between each item.

DFDs are able to be used to create multilevel diagrams that deconstruct the system from the perspective of how data interacts with the system. The DFD components will be structured to show how the system interacts with the external environment. Then, in decompiled layers, additional diagrams will be developed in order to show the system in terms of core processes and, eventually, the tasks completed within each process. This is an important aspect of how DFDs are used by the systems analyst because it highlights the development of multiple diagrams. Most systems are too complex to be adequately depicted by the development of a single DFD. Therefore, many diagrams will be developed during the completion of process analysis.

Perhaps the most powerful aspect of the DFD is the diagrams themselves. Each development has the ability to provide information about the process that is often difficult to describe in words. Additionally, these diagrams will have value for both technical and nontechnical audiences, which makes their development multiuse. Also, while the focus of the analysis phase is the assessment of the current system, DFDs are useful for modeling both currently deployed systems and proposed new ones yet to be developed.

Elements

The elements of the DFD have already been alluded to by the identification of the symbols contained within the developed diagrams. If you suspected that each symbol is related to a corresponding DFD element, you would be correct. However, as there is no universally accepted standard for element and symbol correlation, it is important that the systems analyst ensure the project team is consistent in their utilization of symbols representing the same element for all DFD development during the project.

While the element/symbol relationship may vary from project team to project team, the guidelines for DFD creation call for the consistent depiction of four elements to accurately create DFDs. These elements consist of the following:

1. Process
2. External entity
3. Data flow
4. Data store

PROCESS

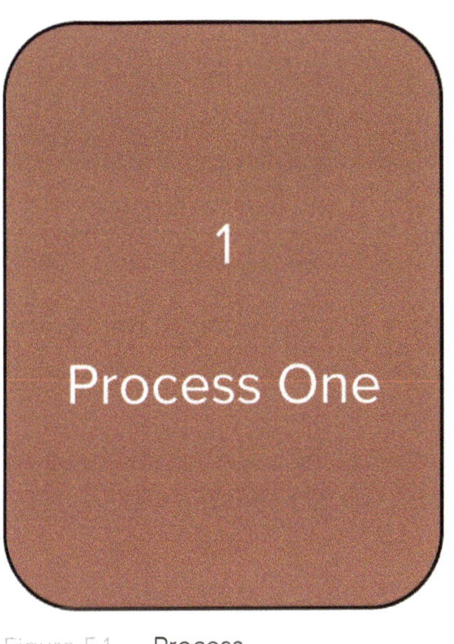

Figure 5.1 Process

A process element (See Figure 5.1) is any associated set of tasks that changes the data to produce an output. The change requirement is important, as there may be processes in a system that simply move data from one location to another. These non-data-changing processes are not included in logical DFD development.

Another way of looking at a process element is that it is an activity or function performed for a specific business reason. Processes that change data will do one of the following:

1. Perform computations
2. Sort, filter, or summarize data based on logic
3. Use stored data to create, read, update, or delete a record
4. Organize data, such as report creation
5. Trigger another process
6. Alter data flow based on business rules

Essentially, a process that alters the data in any way becomes a process element in the logical DFD. Not only will this element be identified by a symbol such as a circle, but it will also contain a short label that describes the process the symbol represents.

EXTERNAL ENTITY

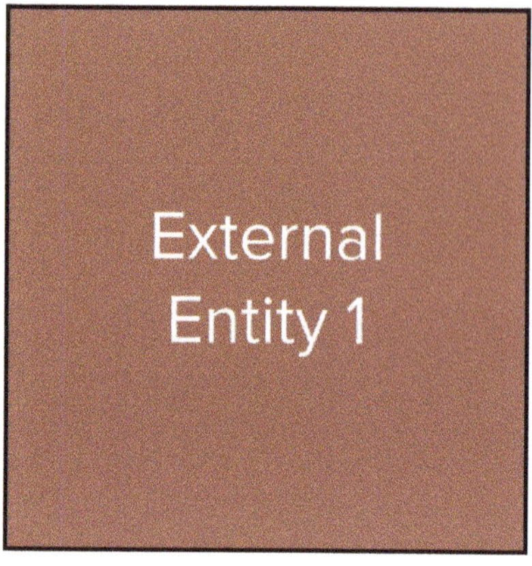

Figure 5.2 External Entity

An external entity element (See Figure 5.2) is any actor on the system that is external to the system itself. These actors will either input data to the system or receive data from the system and can consist of an individual, organization, or even another system.

Each external entity will be represented by a symbol, such as a square. This element will also be made up of a short label that contains both the entity name and a short description of what the entity represents.

DATA FLOW

Figure 5.3 Data Flow

The data flow element (See Figure 5.3) is the graphical representation of the data moving through the system. These movements can be between the eternal entities, data stores, and processes. Additionally, as processes are deconstructed, data flows will represent the data movement through the process itself. The data itself may be a single piece of data or a logical collection of data. Think of a data flow as data in motion.

In a DFD, a data flow always starts or ends at a process. While this may seem inaccurate at first, it is important to remember that the DFD's main responsibility is to clarify system processes. Without the process being an integral part of each development, the project team is missing the intent of the activity.

Data flow elements are almost always represented by an arrow, which identifies which way the data is flowing in the system. Additionally, the element will contain a short label that has both a name and description that describes the data being represented. Whether it is a single piece of data or a collection of data, the label should clearly demonstrate what data is being represented.

DATA STORE

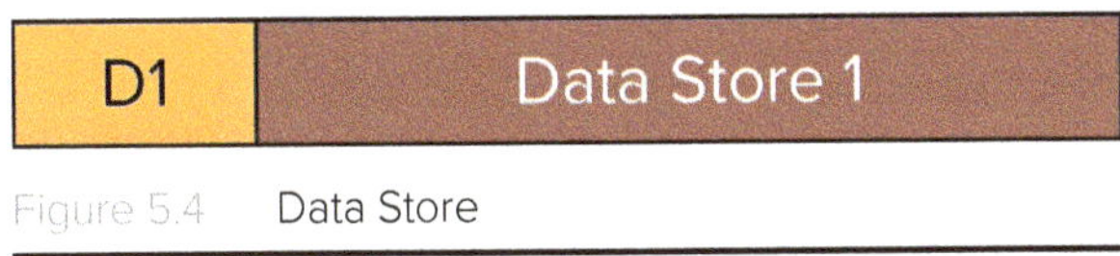

Figure 5.4 Data Store

A data store element (See Figure 5.4) represents a repository that holds data for later use. These repositories can consist of files, database tables, or any other data collection method currently used in the process. Keep in mind that there may be manual aspects to current processes, so anywhere data is retained, even manually, such as a notebook, must be taken into account as a data store. Think of a data store as data at rest.

Data flows entering the data store; input data flows consist of updates or new data being added. Data flows leaving the data store, output data flows, are data retrievals. However, for a data store to be included in a DFD, it must contain at least one or more input data flows and at least one or more output data flows represented somewhere in the process modeling. This is because a data store can only be effective if data is being used by the system. If data cannot be both accessed and altered by the system, the data store is either not necessary or not correctly implemented.

Data store elements are represented by a symbol, such as a rectangle. These elements are also labeled with a name and a description, both of which describe the data contained in the data store at a very high level.

Mapping Business Processes

As already established, the DFD is an excellent way to graphically represent complex business processes. However, it must be emphasized that a single DFD will not have the depth of scope necessary to effectively map all the business processes contained within even a small system. Therefore, it is important to establish a **hierarchy** of development in which the systems analyst and project team will begin by looking at the system at a high level with a single DFD development. Through the process of **decomposition**, the project team will focus on the system processes more and more granularly by developing a series of complimentary DFDs. Just like an onion, the project team will begin to peel back the layers of the system configuration to accurately identify every process and, eventually, every step of every process.

The efforts expended in the process modeling tasks will result in a number of DFDs that can be compared, contrasted, and authenticated not just among themselves but also against the use cases that were previously developed. At this juncture in the analytical phase of the SDLC, there not only needs to be symmetry within the hierarchy of DFDs created but also reflected in the processes that are related to the user external entities incorporated in the use cases. It can get confusing as to how these symmetries both exist and are to be verified, so for clarification, we must look not only at the DFD development hierarchy and actual creation but also at how to **balance** the use cases and DFDs once created.

Hierarchy

The decomposition method of the DFD development process will take the project team through multiple iterations of DFD development. With the first level highlighting the system's interaction with the external environment, an additional level of development will deconstruct the system into a series of core processes. These processes will each be further deconstructed to identify the actions required to be taken in each process. The actions will be deconstructed into individual steps taken.

The process analysis activities will be completed when enough DFDs have been finished to graphically identify every process step needed to be executed for every core process in the system. The hierarchy itself has defined levels of deconstruction that each has set definitions of what information should be clarified by the DFD created at that level. The hierarchy of DFD creation consists of the following:

1. Context diagram
2. Level 0 diagram
3. Level 1 diagrams
4. Additional level diagrams

CONTEXT DIAGRAM

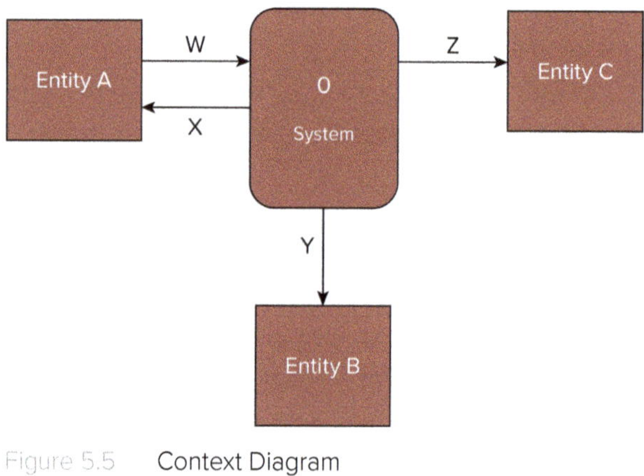

Figure 5.5 Context Diagram

The context diagram (See Figure 5.5) is the top-level diagram of every process model. The purpose of this diagram is to show in what context the system fits in the external environment. That is to say, the context diagram denotes the system as a single process identified as process zero. This diagram then depicts the external entities that receive information from or contribute information to the system. Finally, the context diagram adds data flows that highlight what data is flowing between the external entity and the system with arrows to represent which way the data is actually flowing.

Once completed, the context diagram will give the project team a visualization of how the system interacts with the external environment. It will identify all the external actors, as well as not only the type of data being traded between the actor and system but also whether that data is being provided by or to the system. Even at this level, the information graphically presented can assist the development team in better understanding the intent of the system.

LEVEL 0 DIAGRAM

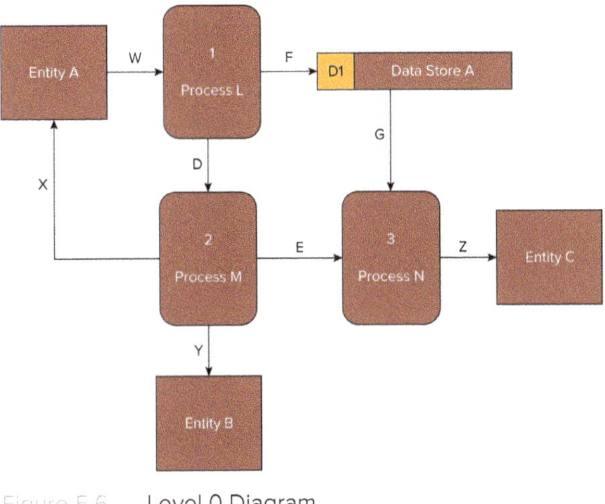

Figure 5.6 Level 0 Diagram

The level zero diagram (See Figure 5.6) is the next level DFD to be developed. It also contains all the external entities and process flows developed in the context diagram. However, the level zero diagram removes the process zero representation of the system and replaces it with all the major processes that the system is composed of.

Each process is numbered with a whole number, and the data flows between processes are added. These additional data flows demonstrate how the processes are interrelated. Additionally, the data flows to the external entities are drawn to the actual associated processes. This clearly demonstrates which process or processes are related to which external entity or entities.

Finally, the data that is stored by the system is added at this level as data stores. These data stores are connected to their associated processes by data flows. This demonstrates not only the interaction of processes with stored data but also highlights whether the process is accessing data, changing data, or both.

LEVEL 1 DIAGRAMS

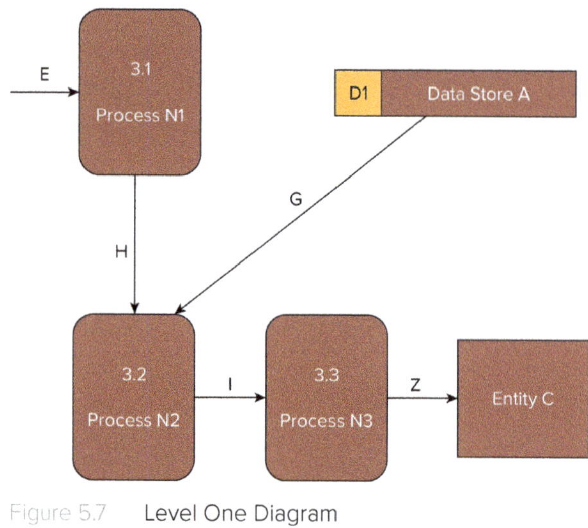

Figure 5.7 Level One Diagram

A level one DFD (See Figure 5.7) is created for every process identified in the level zero DFD. This diagram deconstructs the process into a set of internal processes that need to be completed in order to complete the overall process. Each internal process is drawn and numbered. The numbering methodology used for a level one process is to retain the whole number of the associated process from the level zero DFD. Each internal process is then given a number as a 10th. So the first process would be x.1, the second process would be x.2, the third process would be x.3, etc.

Data flows are then drawn to show how the data moves between the internal processes. Any associated external entities or data stores are also redrawn in the level one DFD to demonstrate which internal process is interacting with the associated external entity or data store.

The level one DFD will provide a graphical representation of the steps required to complete a core process. These diagrams can be compared in order to find similarities in requirements for completing each core process.

ADDITIONAL LEVEL DIAGRAMS

As the goal of the process analysis is to identify every step required to complete a process, every level one process that requires more than one step must continue to be deconstructed. Therefore, level two DFDs will be created for any level one DFD that requires two or more steps to complete. Level three DFDs will be created for any level two DFD that requires two or more steps to complete, and so on. For each level that is created, the project team will add a .x numbering system. So, for a level two process of process one, subprocess one, the numbering would look like 1.1.1 for the first process and 1.1.2 for the second process. For level three of the first process, for the first process in level two, the numbering would look like 1.1.1.1, and for the second process in level two, the number would look like 1.1.1.2.

Additional levels are only required for processes in the level above that require more than one step to be completed for the process to be complete. Once each process is represented as single steps, no additional levels are required. Additionally, only the multiple-step processes need to be decompiled into an additional level. That is to say that if there are three processes in a level one DFD and only one process is multistep, only one level two DFD needs to be created.

Additional levels of DFD development must also carry forward the requirements of the level one DFD creation. That is to say, external entities and data stores must be represented if the process segment being drawn interacts with them. Additionally, process flows must be depicted at all levels as well.

Diagram Numbering

The semantics of the numbering strategy have been demonstrated in the explanation of each level of hierarchy development. However, it is important to understand why this numbering system is so important. The main benefit of the standardization of the numbering system is to assist the user in understanding where a given DFD development fits in the overall hierarchy of the process analysis activity. The larger and more complex the system, the more DFDs will be created. Even smaller, simple systems will consist of many DFD developments. Maintaining a structured numbering methodology will allow everyone on the project team to quickly identify just where in the overall process analysis a given DFD fits.

To reiterate the numbering structure to be used for DFD development:

1. The context diagram process is always process zero
2. Level zero processes are numbered as whole numbers
3. Each subsequent level has a parent-child relationship. The parent process is identified by the whole number; a dot precedes the process number for the current level. Therefore, for level one, there would be one dot; for level two, there would be two dots; for level three, there would be three dots, and so on. The numbers preceding the final dot will always be carried down from the associated process that is being deconstructed at the current level.

The purpose of DFD creation is to promote clarification of the processes that comprise a system. Accurate diagram numbering being incorporated into the DFD creations will only help to enhance the level of clarification provided by these activities.

Alternative Data Flows

One aspect of DFD creation that is worth highlighting is alternative data flows (See Figure 5.8). While it is apparent in process analysis that decisions will be made within the process that will affect the future flow of the data, it is important to understand how to handle these scenarios in DFD creation. Viewing a DFD should allow for an easy identification of where decision logic is contained within a process, and it does. A process containing decision logic will be denoted by having multiple data flows flowing away from the process.

In these instances, the project team will use the process description to explain why there are alternative data flows exiting the process. This will accomplish two items. The drawing rules will allow for easy identification of decision-based process steps as well, and the descriptions will provide clarification on the decisions to be made. While logical DFDs do not focus on the technical aspects of the system, physical DFDs do, and therefore, methods need to be in place to accommodate technical clarifications, such as decision logic contained within the process. Process descriptions are a tool that can accommodate this requirement.

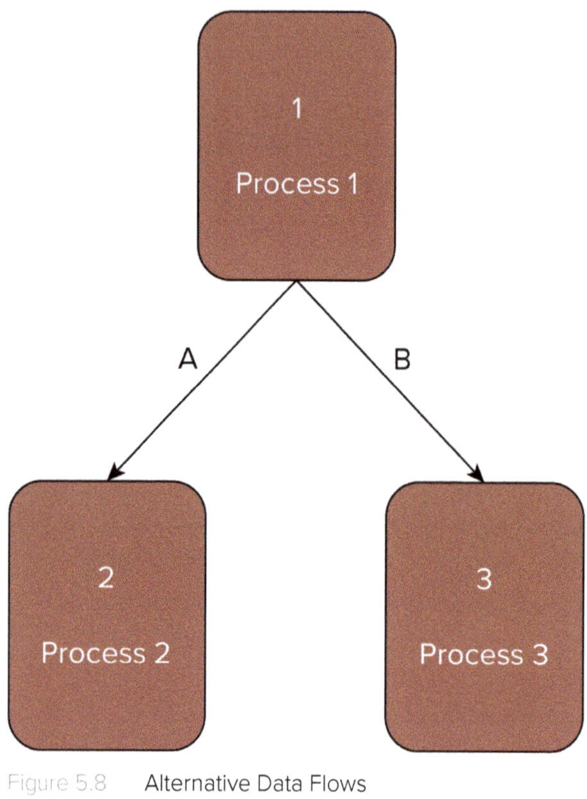

Figure 5.8 Alternative Data Flows

Process Descriptions

While process descriptions are highlighted throughout the DFD design process, the importance of what information is contained within the description is great enough that clarification should be provided. The process description is a text-based development that is intended to provide more information about a given process than can be demonstrated in the DFD by itself.

These descriptions act to clarify logic in the associated process that may be complex or contain aspects that are not well-known to the project team. Process descriptions can provide more detail in the form of structured English or even decision trees or table developments. The purpose of using this feature is clarification, but descriptions should only be developed where appropriate clarification is required.

Balancing

Balancing the hierarchy of DFD development is essential for process analysis. Balancing refers to the process of assessing and asserting that the relationships depicted between entities, processes, data stores, and data flow at a given level of the DFD are accurately represented at all levels of the DFD. This means that relationships depicted on the parent diagram are carried forward to the child diagram. The child diagram will then add new processes and data flows to the already-established relationships of the parent diagram.

Balancing ensures that the deconstruction of the system is fully understood and represented in all DFDs created by the project team. This is important as different project resources may use only some of the DFDs for clarification or educational purposes. Discrepancies in DFDs at various stages can cause a lack of understanding or even a wrong representation of the system processes. Any development initiated from an incorrect depiction of the system will most likely result in negative consequences for the system development project.

Creating Data Flow Diagrams

Image 5.3

Creating the DFDs that accurately represent the system takes a lot of thought and effort. Leveraging the developments of the project team created to this point can assist in accurately identifying the external entities, their relationship to the system, and even the core processes of the system itself. All of these aspects of the system's processes are essential to understand and organize in order for effective process mapping to take place. The deconstruction method of the DFD creation hierarchy will assist in reasoning through the identification of all these components; however, thought and analysis should be conducted at each step to ensure that nothing has been missed.

There are also correlations to the DFD from the requirements determination and use case development activities that have previously been completed. While these activities have different focuses, they incorporate aspects of process development that can be used to ensure that comprehensive process development is completed by the completion of the DFDs.

The hierarchy of DFD creation becomes the general outline for system DFD creation:

1. Build the context diagram first.

2. Identify the major processes of the system.
3. Create the level zero diagram.
4. Create the level one diagram.
5. Create additional levels of diagrams as required.

Start With the Context Diagram

The context diagram is the logical start to system DFD creation. This diagram focuses on the external environment as it relates to the system. Analyzing the system's external relationship will allow the project team to begin to search out not only the external interactions of the system but also begin to familiarize the team with core processes that facilitate these external interactions.

The context diagram also facilitates the introduction of data incorporation into the analytical process. While this level is primarily focused on data flow, it does allow the project team to begin to assess what type of data is being used by the system and can assist in establishing some relationship between the core process and associated data.

By the time the context diagram is completed, the project team has already established some key information regarding system processes. The developed diagram provides a basis for system interaction and, therefore, high-level process identification.

Identify All the Major Processes

Before additional DFDs can be created, the process team must next agree on what the major processes are that constitute the system itself. The developed use cases can be highly effective for assisting in this process. Each use case represents a primary event that the system is responsible for. It is, therefore, reasonable to assume that each of these events is completed by a process. Therefore, there should be a correlation between the use cases developed and the core processes of the system itself.

In fact, the correlation of use cases to system processes is one to one. Assuming that the use cases were comprehensively developed, each use case represents a core system process. While it is not best practice to simply turn developed use cases into processes, the project team can use this as a starting point and create additional analysis activities to ensure that no processes are unaccounted for.

A worthwhile activity when assessing use cases as a basis for core process identification is to create DFD mini-diagrams for each use case event. The external entities and data stores are then added to the associated DFD mini-diagram. If accurate, these mini-diagrams will both assert the core processes of the system and ultimately act as the process representation of the level zero DFD diagram. Additionally, the steps defined in the use case will become the internal processes defined in the level one DFD diagram. These can also be developed into mini-diagrams with data flows drawn to show the progression of one mini-diagram to the next as the project team walks through the use case.

Create the Level 0 Diagram

Once the development team is in firm agreement that all core processes have been correctly identified, the next step is to create the level zero diagram. The mini-diagrams developed to represent each use case are organized, and process flows are used to connect interacting processes. External entities and data stores are also connected to interacting processes using data flows. The end result is the continuation of the data flows, and external entity development in the context diagram, but with the additional information of which core process or processes each external entity interacts with.

The clarity of data utilization is enhanced at level zero, and data stores are also introduced into the diagram. This provides the viewer with an understanding of not just how the data is flowing through the system but where it is being kept as well. Additionally, which processes require which data is also made clearer by the level zero DFD.

Create the Level 1 Diagrams

Now that each core process is identified in the level zero DFD, the next step is to create a level one diagram for each process. As previously stated, the internal processes of each core process will be highlighted in the identified steps of the associated use case. This will assist the project team in drawing each internal process as well as correctly assigning data flows between each internal process. The associated external entities and data stores are also redrawn, and data flows are mirrored, depicting which internal process step is associated with these items.

It is important for the project team to ensure that a level one diagram is completed for every core process identified in the level zero DFD. The project team will need to assess all internal processes for every core process, and this can only be completed if a corresponding level one DFD has been created.

Create Additional Levels of Diagrams as Required

Additional levels of DFDs will only need to be created for any process segment that requires more than one step to complete. These levels will be organized, as all levels of DFDs are, by accurate numbering of each process. Once all process segments are represented as a single step, the DFDs required to be developed for system process representation are complete, and analysis of the current system processes can begin in earnest.

Balancing Use Cases and Data Flow Diagrams

As can be seen in the development of a system's DFDs, the use cases are intimately tied to process analysis. This is because no aspect of the analysis phase is developed without a dependency on all other aspects. DFDs start with system events, which are captured in the use cases. The requirements definition for the system, also leveraged by the use cases, reflect the need for the processes themselves. With all these interactions between analytical developments, it is important to ensure that there is comparison between them to ensure balance.

The use cases being compared to the DFDs are essential to ensure that the project team is completing developments that complement each other. As we have seen, the DFDs flow directly from the use cases, and as such, the following should be true:

1. Names of use cases become names of major processes in the level zero diagram

2. Steps in the use case become processes in the level one diagram
3. Use case inputs and outputs become data flows starting at the level one diagram

With all the interdependency between use cases and DFDs, there is an opportunity for the project team to assess the completeness of each deliverable. Especially in instances when the use cases were not directly used to create the DFDs, the degree to which the developments align can assert or negate the correctness and completeness of each development.

In instances where there are marked differences between the use case and associated DFDs, the project team needs to assess the differences and the reasons behind them. Either the use cases will need to be adjusted or the DFDs, but differences cannot remain if the developments of the analysis phase of the SDLC are going to be used to their greatest potential.

Common Design Flow Diagram Mistakes

While there has been a lot of emphasis placed on the appropriate way to develop DFDs, there must also be an understanding of errors that are commonly made when developing DFDs. Knowing what the common pitfalls are allows the project team to be on the lookout for these mistakes and hopefully will result in any errors being caught early on in the process. The DFD errors that are commonly made fall into one of two categories:

1. Syntax errors
2. Semantics errors

Syntax Errors

Syntax errors are errors that can be considered as violating drawing rules. That is to say that there are identified criteria that must be met when creating DFDs. By knowing these criteria and reviewing DFD developments to ensure the criteria exist, the project team can better assert the validity of the development. When it comes to syntax, three criteria must be met:

1. Every data flow must connect to a process
2. Every data flow must have at least one inflow and one outflow
3. Every data store must have at least one inflow and one outflow

Semantics Errors

Semantics errors can be a little more difficult to identify as they are not simply identified by how the DFD is drawn. Semantics errors are errors in the meaning of the diagrams. They represent the misunderstanding of system processes and how they are completed. In order to identify these errors, actions must be taken throughout the DFD development process. These actions include the following:

1. Have users walk through DFDs to assess accuracy.
2. Check for consistent use of terminology.

3. Check for consistent levels of decomposition.
4. Verify that the inputs are actually able to produce the outputs represented in the DFDs.

Chapter Summary

Design flow diagramming can be essential to the project team's comprehensive understanding of the processes that the system is composed of. Especially in complex systems, processes can be very difficult or even impossible to explain verbally. DFDs take complex descriptions and simplify them through graphical representation. Furthermore, the standardization of the DFD process assists in ensuring that all developments can be equally understood by all resources reviewing them.

However, in order to ensure that the diagrams developed in the process analysis phase of the SDLC can be used to their greatest potential, it is imperative that the systems analyst guide their team to not only create the diagrams but also put in the effort to validate the developments. Not only should the DFDs be compared to each other, but they should also be assessed against the created use cases and requirements definitions for the system. In the analysis phase, all developments are interrelated and, as such, should be compared for consistency.

Project Planning Activities

1. Develop the entity diagram
2. Develop the Level 0 DFDs
3. Develop the Level 1 DFDs
4. Develop the Level 2 DFDs (if necessary)

Image Credits

IMG 5.1: Copyright © 2018 Pexels/Christina Morillo.
IMG 5.2: Copyright © 2018 Pexels/Christina Morillo.
IMG 5.3: Copyright © 2020 Pexels/Anna Shvets.

CHAPTER 6

Data Modeling

Introduction

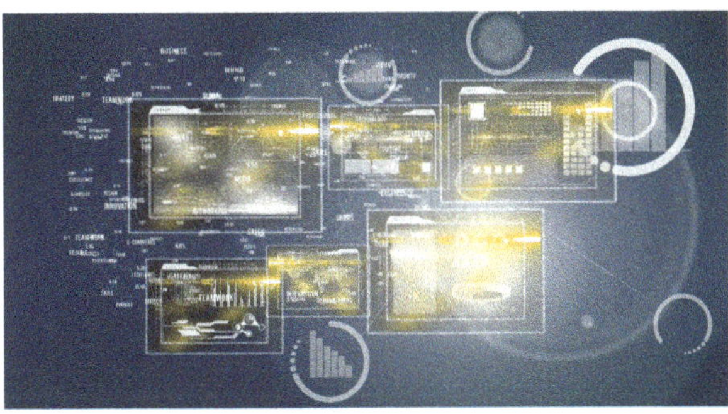

Image 6.1

In process analysis, the project team begins to assess the data within the system from a high level. As this is a critical component of any system, it is no surprise that the final activity of the analysis phase is to build from the understanding of the data that was initiated by modeling the processes and continue to enhance that understanding by modeling the data itself.

Data modeling will provide many of the same advantages for the project team as process modeling. The key difference is that the focus switches from how the data flows and is stored at a high level to developing models that provide a more granular understanding of how the data is organized and used by the system.

In order to fully understand the tasks associated with modeling the data, the project team must first be educated on the various ways data is configured within a system. Therefore, data storage formats will be explored first, followed by data modeling and the specific data modeling format used in SDLC system development.

Learning Objectives

1. Become familiar with file and database formats.
2. Describe the goals of data storage.
3. Understand the differences between the logical and physical data models.
4. Describe the rules for developing entity-relationship diagrams (ERDs).
5. Describe the style guidelines for creating ERDs.
6. Describe the process for creating ERDs.

7. Create an ERD.
8. Explain balancing.
9. Explain normalization.
10. Describe the process for creating a CRUD matrix.
11. Create a CRUD matrix.

Data Storage Formats

The understanding of the various ways data can be stored in a system is essential for the systems analyst and his or her team to effectively model the data itself. Data storage is the method chosen to both store and handle data for the applications that run the system. As each system has varying levels of both functional and nonfunctional requirements, there are a number of data storage formats that have been developed over time to meet specific system requirement demands.

New data storage formats are continuously being developed to meet the demands for increasing levels of data required by new systems being constructed. As the data is perhaps the most critical component of the system itself, developers are constantly working on methods to more effectively store and access data. The diverse requirements for both the amount of data and the speed at which it is accessible result in various strategies for data storage construction. Some strategies focus on the efficient use of system resources while leveraging system resources to develop a less efficient but sometimes more effective data storage strategy.

It is clear that there are a diverse amount of data storage structures used by project teams. However, with all of the unique versions of developments in use today, there are still two primary structures of data storage that these various developments can be classified under. These data storage structures consist of the following:

1. Files
2. Databases

Files

File structures used to store data are not only one of the earlier data storage methodologies but are still viable for many applications today. Files are essentially electronic lists of data that are grouped based on specific criteria. A system may use a single file for data storage or a myriad of files that are organized in specific ways.

Files are somewhat easily understood as they mimic lists and organizational practices used by people from grade school through adulthood. The file itself represents a list. Individual files are stored in folders much like hard copy documents are stored in a filing cabinet. The digital organization and utilization of system files can easily mimic the manual storage and utilization functions of hard copy records. The similarities between manual file storage and the design of data file structures make digital file structures more easily understood by system users. This was a key driver to the success of file structure data storage, as well as why it is still widely used today.

When a file data storage format is used within a system, most often, each row within the file will contain a specific data record. These records may consist of multiple pieces of data separated by a unique character, such as a comma or even a blank space. For each row, the same type of data will be stored in the same order. For example, if a row of data contains a customer's first name, last name, address, and customer number in that order, every row will contain that information in that specific order. That way, the application can be developed to always know what piece of data is in what location for every record in the file.

Additionally, files will usually contain a piece of data in each row, which is known as a **pointer**. This pointer is a piece of data that will link the data from one file to data in another file. These connected files are also known as **linked lists**. With the inclusion of pointers and linked lists, file-based data storage can be comprised of multiple files grouped by similar information that can all be linked together to store a significant amount of data for a specific entity.

Files developed for utilization for a system will often be grouped by specific function. The types of file groups that are commonly found in file-based data storage development consist of the following:

1. Master files
2. Look-up files
3. Transaction files
4. Audit files
5. Historical files

MASTER FILES

Master files store the most important data that is critical to application success. By developing a master file grouping, system developers are able to develop access methods that prioritize the location of these files, making them the most easily accessible to the system. This is important when items like processing speed are an important consideration.

LOOK-UP FILES

Look-up files are files that contain data that will always remain static. These files are used for reference and will be read frequently but written infrequently. This designation again allows system developers to take advantage of file location and data access strategies that enhance the overall operation of the system based on the way these files are used by the system.

TRANSACTION FILES

Transaction files store results of processes that can be either used for reference by system users or even used to update information contained within master files. The purpose of this file type is to create a record of process completion while at the same time facilitating more efficient methods of making updated, pertinent data available to the system when it is most critically required.

AUDIT FILES

Audit files record data before and after it is altered by the system. For data that is critical to system success, audit files can be invaluable. If a process errors out and the data is corrupted, these files act as a fail-safe. Additionally, if a process creates an unanticipated change in data, these files act as a point of reference that can be used to analyze where incorrect changes to data occurred.

HISTORICAL FILES

Historical files or archive files store completed process data just as transaction files do. However, there is no expectation that these files will be referenced with any frequency. These files are often developed with the least efficient access methods within the system, as they are intended to be referenced infrequently.

Databases

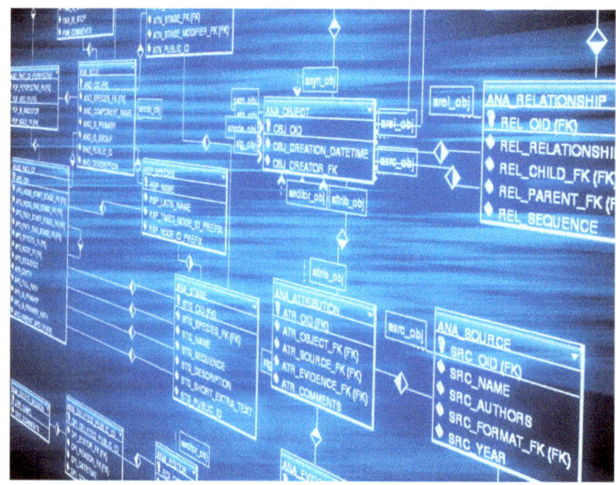

Image 6.2

Databases store data in more complex ways than can be achieved by file data storage methods. A database methodology will look to define a structure and design on both the data environment and data itself in order to be able to store different data entities with unifying information that associates the data across the database. This allows for a system to make use of a vastly greater amount of information in a single data environment.

Information is arranged in a database in a table format. These tables contain columns and rows and are arranged to identify like pieces of data as well as unique data entries. In some database formats, the columns represent the types of data being stored, and the rows represent the unique entities. Reverting back to our file data storage example, the first column would store the customer number, the second column would store the customer's first name, the third column would store the customer's last name, and the fourth column would store the customer address. Each row would be a unique customer record. In other databases, the rows represent the data being stored, and the columns represent the unique entities.

The table structure of databases is chosen for their ease of use characteristics. Additional tables of data can easily be added to the database. Data itself can easily be accessed and modified. Additionally, tables requiring efficient access to data records can be **indexed**. Indexing is a form of record sorting that adds a sorted data field that can be quickly referenced in order to find individual data records as efficiently as possible.

Relational databases are most commonly accessed by Structured Query Language or **SQL** data access developments. SQL is the primary language that data queries are constructed from for the purpose of interacting with the data in the data tables.

Just as there are multiple types of data storage files, so too are there many different types of databases. Some of the most commonly used databases consist of the following:

1. Relational databases
2. Multidimensional databases
3. NoSQL databases

RELATIONAL DATABASES

Relational databases are one of the more mature and still widely used forms of database structure. This database methodology is developed by using a collection of data tables. Each row in a given table is a data record, which contains a unique piece of data called the table's **primary key**. The primary key ensures that every row of data in the data table is both unique and, therefore, uniquely identifiable. The primary key constitutes one column of the data table, with the remaining columns consisting of attributes of the data being retained in the table.

Data attributes are the pieces of information that the system needs to retain. These attributes are grouped in a specific data table based on some form of organization or commonality. One remaining column is reserved for the **foreign key**. The foreign key is the primary key of a related data table. The primary key/foreign key relationship relates the data of different data tables, allowing for the system to retain and use extensive data on individual entities.

Relational databases support **referential integrity**, essentially ensuring that the values linking the tables are both valid and accurately synchronized. Referential integrity's ability to link disparate tables to each other provides a basis for data expansion that is seemingly limitless. In fact, the amount of data able to be stored and, therefore, used by the system is only limited by the physical system storage, communication, and processing limitations of the system itself.

MULTIDIMENSIONAL DATABASES

Image 6.3

With the growth of big data analytics comes the requirement to more quickly and efficiently process very large amounts of data. While the structure of the relational database in and of itself can be limiting when looking at the massive scope of data big data analytics requires, it can be leveraged to a more effective result.

Multidimensional databases take the two-axis methodology of the relational database and add minimally a third axis to the structure. The addition of the third axis allows for greater reference of individual data points in the data storage design. What this means is that the application can be developed to more efficiently get to a specific data point when a vastly larger data set is being worked with.

As the amount of data being leveraged by newly developed systems increases, so too can the number of axis' defined to reference individual data points. However, increasing the number of axes does not come without a cost. The greater the dimensions of the database, the more processing power required to traverse the data. Therefore, this database structure is often combined with large amounts of physical system processing and physical data storage resources.

NOSQL DATABASES

More recently, as systems are being developed where not only the increase in data requirements is vastly increased, but so too the user load, even multidimensional databases are being seen as too limiting. For these types of systems, a complete divergence from relational tables has been developed in the form of NoSQL databases. These database structures leverage rapid processing provided by replicated cloud-based database servers. By leveraging massive computing power, **document**, **wide column**, and **graph** database structures have been developed.

All of these variations of NoSQL databases disregard the need for refraining from data duplication, the primary strength of relational databases, and instead leverage reduced cost physical data storage and increased physical processing power to store and query huge amounts of unstructured data. The ability to process data not only efficiently but also infinitely more quickly allows for data duplication to be adequately managed by the system processes and, therefore, not required to be handled by the data storage design at all.

The end result is data storage structures that focus on data collection structures as opposed to organized and uniquely identifiable storage design principles. The reduced cost of storage and processing power allows for the implementation of less costly and less structured data storage methods.

Storage Format Selection

When analyzing the three database methodologies presented, it is apparent that each has strengths and weaknesses. Relational databases are highly organized and enforce the uniqueness of each stored record. The format is expandable but becomes exponentially more complex the more data sets are added to the system. The end result can be a lengthy and costly data storage development initiative.

Multidimensional databases are effective for big data analytics and data warehousing activities. However, they require larger amounts of both physical data storage and physical processing power to be effective. Additionally, the more axes that are added to the data storage design, the more complex the application development becomes for accurately storing and accessing system data.

NoSQL databases allow for even more rapid processing of even greater amounts of data. Additionally, less time needs to be spent on data structure design as inefficiencies are handled by the massive physical data storage and processing power structures that go hand in hand with these types of database formats. However, those two physical requirements can be a detraction to this methodology in and of themselves. If the complexity of the data does not warrant such extensive physical data storage and processing, then essentially, the project team has a costly and inefficient data storage structure.

Therefore, when attempting to determine which database method is most appropriate for the system being developed, focus on the following:

1. The organization's existing physical data storage and system processing structures.
2. The organization's existing data storage formats.
3. The data types being used by the system.
4. The type of application being developed.
5. Future data storage requirements.

Data Models

Image 6.4

Now that there is a clearer understanding of how data is stored in an information system, the concept of data modeling can be better understood. A data model is a visual representation of a technology system's data elements and the connections between these elements. These visualizations allow for collaboration between business and technical resources to better understand not only how data is grouped and how those groupings of data are organized within a system but also gain further understanding of the actual data components being stored within each data group.

Data models simplify complex data structures into more easily readable graphical models. By being able to focus specifically on the data alone, the project team is better able to ensure that all required data components not only exist but do so in such a way that related data is able to be combined by the system when necessary. This is why data models focus not only on the data groups and individual data components of each group but also on the connections between the data groups as well.

When developing and analyzing data models, it is important to remember that data is a shared resource that is most effective when it is available to as many processes as necessary for the system to operate as expected. Organization of the data within a system must, therefore, be flexible and adaptable to business requirements, both known and sometimes unanticipated. This can be challenging for project teams as the data properties and defined data structures of a system are some of the most permanent aspects of a technology system. This is due to the fact that the data is the cornerstone of the system, and therefore, all other aspects of the system are built around the data. While many of these aspects, such as processes or hardware selection, have some ability for change, once the data structures are defined, they are often extremely difficult or even impossible to change.

Due to both the importance of data within the system and, hence, correctly structuring the data, as well as ensuring that all the necessary data points are included, data modeling is a critical activity for not only assessing current systems but also developing new ones. Therefore, data modeling will usually occur in two phases of the SDLC. **Logical data models** will be developed during the analytical phase of the SDLC. This is to both create a better understanding of the current system and to identify areas of opportunity for adjustment to both the data structure and data points to facilitate more comprehensive or efficient system processes.

As data structures and data properties are often very similar in both the existing system and the new system developed as a replacement, physical data models are developed during the design phase of the SDLC. This will allow for the integration of the conceptualized data requirements into the development of the actual system data structures and data components.

Logical Data Models

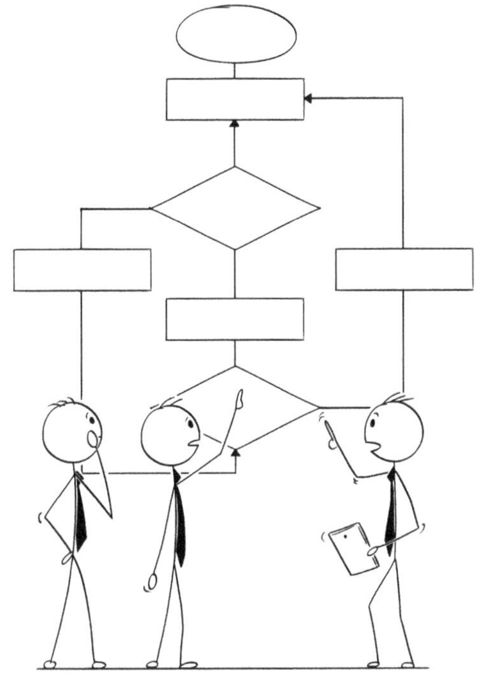

Image 6.5

Logical data models show how data is organized in a system. This type of model will focus on the data groups or data objects and the relationships between them. From a graphical perspective, each data object is drawn as an object, such as a rectangle, and given a name that highlights the commonality of each piece of data or data point contained within the group. The data object is then populated with the names of the data points contained within the data object. Finally, connections between data objects are denoted to show what data is related.

Data models enable data analysis in much the same ways that process models enable process analysis. These models provide clarification and identification of opportunities when analyzing a system's data. By focusing on the data itself, the data model allows for collaborative assessment of whether the correct data is included in the system, what potential oversights may have been made that may hinder system operation, and whether the organization of the data is able to facilitate efficient and effective use of the data by the system.

Logical data models focus on the following:

1. Data objects
2. Connections between data objects
3. Specific data points

Physical Data Models

Physical data models are built from the logical data model. The development of the data objects, data points, and data object connections are converted to database or file structures. This models how the data will actually be developed in the new system.

For the current system analysis, the physical data model will be developed on the data storage strategy already implemented in the current system. However, for new system data modeling, in order for the project team to convert a logical data model to a physical data model, they must first determine what data structure will be used for the new system build. Only when that decision is made is it possible to develop the physical data model detail.

Physical data models will focus on the following:

1. Convert logical data object names to data tables or file names.
2. Convert data point names to system field names.
3. Add system information for each system field.
4. Denote what system fields enforce the relationship between related data tables or files.

Entity-Relationship Diagram

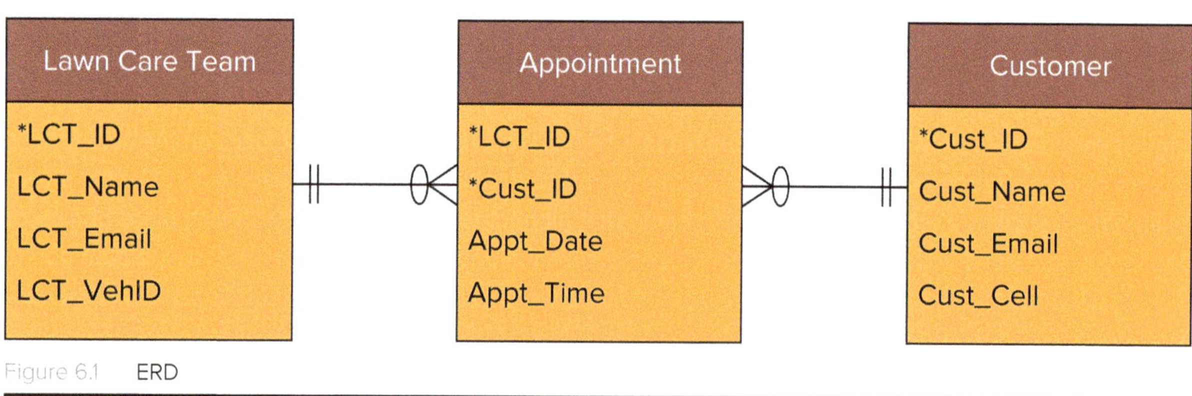

Figure 6.1 ERD

An entity-relationship diagram (ERD) (See Figure 6.1) is a common flowchart created as the process model in the SDLC process. In this model, the data objects are called **entities**, the data points are called **attributes**, and **relationships** are used to not only show the connection between entities but also give a verb name that explains how the entities are related.

The ERD not only shows the relationships between data contained within the system, but it also highlights the business rules for the system. The business rules are the constraints that are followed when the system is functioning. These constraints can include having an instance of one entity being required in order for an instance of another entity to exist. Additionally, there can be business rules that require one instance of an entity can only be related to only one instance of another entity. Finally, business rules may dictate that one instance of an entity can be related to many instances of another entity.

Entities

Lawn Care Team

Figure 6.2 Entity

The entity (See Figure 6.2) represents the people, objects, or concepts of the system. Essentially, the entities are the groupings of data that are required for the system to function as required. Calling these grouping entities is not without purpose. Just as the process models highlight the entities that interact with the system, the data model entities are the data representation of these system actors. When you think about the data a system stores and uses, the DFD process entities are always represented in the data of the system, and therefore, this design ensures that aspect is incorporated in the ERD development. An entity is drawn on the ERD as a symbol. While the chosen symbol can be one of many, such as a rectangle, diamond, or oval, once a symbol is selected, every entity on the ERD will be that same symbol.

In order for an entity to exist in a system, there must be multiple occurrences of the entity. That is to say, for there to be a data grouping, more than one instance of that data group must exist.

Attributes

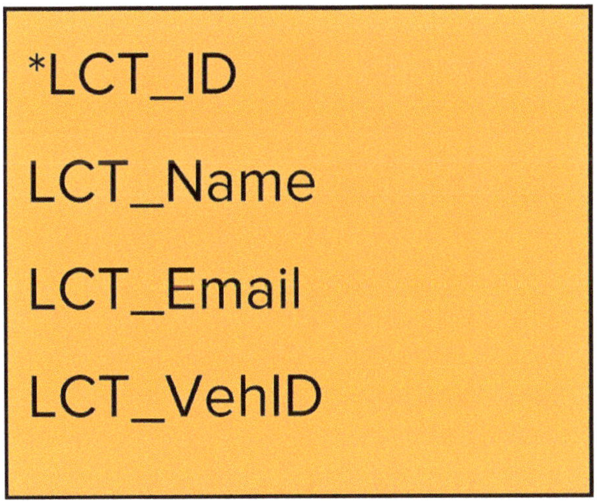

*LCT_ID

LCT_Name

LCT_Email

LCT_VehID

Figure 6.3 Attributes

An attribute (See Figure 6.3) is a property or characteristic of an entity. Essentially, these are the identification of the individual pieces of information the system must retain about the entity. An entity can have a number of attributes defined for it. For example, a student entity may have the following attributes:

1. Student ID
2. First name
3. Last name
4. Birth date
5. Major
6. Grade point average (GPA)
7. Phone number
8. Address

When you review the list, you will see that the names of the attributes are all nouns. However, the attributes themselves are of different types. Student ID, first name, last name, birth date, and phone number are all versions of a **simple attribute**. This means that the attribute will only have one value. The major attribute is a **multivalued attribute,** as a student may have more than one major. The address attribute is a **composite attribute,** as an address is composed of a street number, street name, city, state, and zip code, simple attributes. Finally, the GPA attribute is a **derived attribute,** as it is calculated from other values found in the system data.

As relational database structures need to ensure that uniqueness is maintained throughout the data structure, ERDs of this data architecture will also include identification of the **primary key** and **foreign key** attributes for each entity. However, while this information may or may not be contained in the logical ERD, it will always be present in the physical ERD.

PRIMARY KEY

Figure 6.4 Primary Key

The primary key (See Figure 6.4) is the identifier for an entity, which ensures that every instance of that entity will be uniquely identifiable. A primary key can be a single identifier or a concatenated identifier. A concatenated identifier is a combination of attributes that, used together, create the identifier. This identifier can be a primary attribute for the entity that is guaranteed to be unique, such as a person's social security number. This identifier can also be an artificial attribute, such as a student ID number, added to the entity for the explicit purpose of guaranteeing that each instance of the entity will be unique.

The primary key is essential to relational database structure, as the effectiveness of this architecture depends on ensuring that the records contained within the data structures are all unique. The primary key is the component of each entity that enforces this requirement.

FOREIGN KEY

The foreign key is established in order to promote the relationships defined by the lines in the ERD. The foreign key of an entity is simply the inclusion of the primary key of the associated entity as an attribute. So, for example, if student ID is a primary key of entity A, and entity A is related to entity B, then student ID would be placed as an attribute in entity B. This would make student ID the foreign key for entity B.

Another aspect of foreign keys that must be noted and is directly related to the relationships between entities is that the foreign key is always placed on the child entity of the relationship and matched to the parent entity in the relationship. The parent/child relationship will be further explained in the "Relationships" section.

Relationships

Table 6.1 Relationships

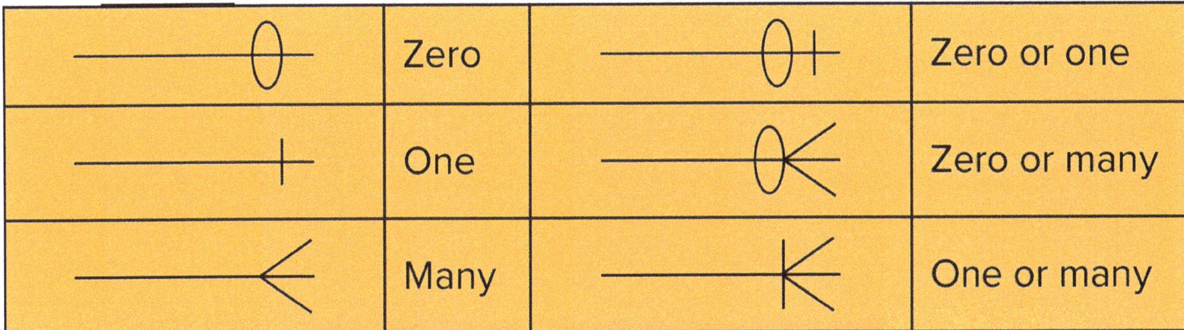

Symbol	Meaning	Symbol	Meaning
	Zero		Zero or one
	One		Zero or many
	Many		One or many

The demonstration of the relationship between associated entities in the ERD is developed to quantify the association. As such, a line is drawn between associated entities and given an active verb name that describes the relationship. This active verb name will also assist in denoting which entity is the **parent entity** and which is the **child entity** in the relationship. Additionally, symbols are placed on the line to assert both the **cardinality** and **modality** of the relationship (See Table 6.1).

PARENT

Parent entities are entities whose attributes will be extended to the associated entity. This means that the parent entity contains pertinent information that the system will use whenever interacting with the parent entity directly or the associated entity. The parent entity will have a primary key that will be used as an attribute in the associated entity and act as the foreign key for that entity. For example, a product line and product relationship would make the product line entity the parent, as it will contain many products.

CHILD

The child entity is the associated entity to a parent entity. This entity is dependent on the parent entity. That is to say that the child entity inherits all the attributes of the parent entity. This is highlighted by the requirement of the foreign key. As a foreign key is the primary key of the associated instance of the parent entity, the parent entity is asserted on the child entity. The primary key/foreign key relationship emphasizes dependence in entity relationships. Looking again at the product line and product relationship, the product would be the child, as it is the dependent entity of the product line.

CARDINALITY

Cardinality refers to the number of times instances of one entity can be related to instances of another entity. There are three types of cardinality found in ERDs. These cardinality types are represented as follows:

1. 1:1 (One to One)—One instance in an entity refers to one and only one instance in the related entity. An example of this would be mailboxes to apartments. Each apartment will only have one mailbox, and each mailbox will only be for one apartment.
2. 1:N (One to Many)—One instance in an entity refers to one or more instances in the related entity. An example of this would be invoices to line items. An invoice can have many line items, but a line item will only be assigned to a single invoice.
3. M:N (Many to Many)—One or more instances in an entity refer to one or more instances in the related entity. An example of this would be students to classroom seats. A student can sit in many classroom seats, and a classroom seat will have many students sitting on it. The instance of this cardinality is an issue for data storage development, as it does not enforce **referential integrity**. Referential integrity ensures that each record in a relational database is unique and therefore presents incorrect records from being added, deleted, or modified. A M:N relationship will need to be adjusted to ensure referential integrity is enforced.

MODALITY

Modality refers to whether or not an instance of a child entity can exist without a related instance of the parent entity. Not every associated entity relationship requires instances in both entities; some, however, do. Modality is meant to identify whether or not instances are required in both entities.

For example, if you look at the entity's invoice and line item, an invoice cannot be created without at least one line item, so for every instance of an invoice, there must be at least one instance of a line item. Now, take, for example, a musical artist and song. A musical artist can exist who has never written a song. Therefore, an instance of the song does not need to exist in order for an instance of a musical artist to exist. Modality is defined in one of two ways:

Not Null—An instance in the related entity must exist for an instance in another entity to be valid.

Null—No instance in the related entity is necessary for an instance in another entity to be valid.

Create the Entity-Relationship Diagram

While there are a finite number of components that comprise the ERD, the process of building ERDs can be complex. While the project team has had some exposure to the data requirements of the system and has already worked out what they believe the data stores will need to be, there is still considerable work to be done to fully define every data component the system will require.

To fully define not only the data components of the system but also appropriate relationships between the data entities, drawing ERDs is a process of trial and error in which the project team will progress through an iterative process. ERDs will be drawn and assessed, alterations will be determined, and then redrawn, and the process will begin again. However, just as with every other model in the analysis phase of the SDLC, the ERDs themselves will simplify the complex nature of data within the system and provide a basis for discussion and analysis that will drive both greater understanding and, with that, the ability to enhance the overall system environment.

The steps to build an ERD consist of the following:

1. Identify the entities.
2. Add appropriate attributes for each entity.
3. Draw the relationships that connect associated entities.

Identify the Entities

The first step in the ERD development process is to identify the entities themselves. The entities are really the major categories of information that the system is working with. This process does not need to be completed from scratch. Both the use cases and process models will be beneficial for assisting in defining the system entities.

Oftentimes, the major inputs and outputs of each use case will signify a potential data entity. Analyzing these use case components will drive conversation among the project team to determine if this is the case. Any input or output that is perceived to be an entity will be recorded.

The DFDs are another quality source of entity information. The data stores defined on the DFDs become entities. The external entities from the DFDs can be analyzed to determine if data retention is required. Any external entity that meets the data retention requirement will become an entity in the ERD as well.

Previous analytical phase developments will start the project team in the right direction regarding collaborating on necessary data entity development. However, it is also important to review each potential entity to ensure the system will require more than a single instance of the identified entity. If only one instance is ever used by the system, then the group of information is not actually an ERD entity and should be omitted from the model. Once the project team is in agreement on all defined entities, they will move on to the next step in the development process.

Add Appropriate Attributes for Each Entity

The next step in the process is to identify the required attributes of the entity that are required by the system in order to support successful system utilization. Attribute candidates can be numerous, so it is important that the project team retain a process for ensuring that potential attributes are analyzed for actually being necessary for system process requirements. Again, previously developed system models, as well as other previous system analysis activities, can assist in not only attribute identification but also justification for attribute inclusion within the entity definition.

The DFD data stores and data flows will provide clues to potential attributes that should be included in the ERD. Additionally, the requirements definition itself will list data requirements. These data requirements translate to required entity attributes and will be included. The project team will need to put thought into the organization of the data requirements into associated entities. However, this activity can also assist in identifying if one or more required entities were missed and, therefore, need to be included.

Reviewing document analysis activities, especially focusing on forms and reports, will provide insight into what attributes are essential to the system. The data contained in these documents need to exist in the system in order for the system to be able to create them. Again, these activities will support ensuring that the appropriate amount of entities have been defined as well.

As with many other activities related to the SDLC, user interviews are yet another method that will assist in uncovering attributes. The users are knowledgeable about the data they need to complete their daily tasks. Having these users review attribute developments will both assert that a comprehensive attribute list has been developed or demonstrate that more data attributes are required.

Once all the attributes have been defined for each entity, it is important for the project team to review each entity and attempt to determine the primary key attribute or attribute grouping. While this is not always possible in the analysis phase and may need to wait for the design phase, the activity should still be attempted. Where it is possible to define the primary keys, this will assist not only in a better understanding of how the entities will be implemented as data files or data tables but also will assist in the development and analysis of relationship construction.

Draw the Relationships That Connect Associated Entities

The project team will begin by drawing an entity and listing all the associated attributes within the entity drawing. They will then review the remaining entities and determine which entities share relationships with the drawn entity. These related entities will be drawn next. A line will be drawn between the related entities and labeled with a verb phrase that describes the relationship. Finally, the business rules that incorporate the verb phrase of the entity relationship will be reviewed to determine the cardinality and modality of the relationship. Once determined, the appropriate symbols will be added to the relationship line to denote both the cardinality and modality of the entity relationship.

This process will be completed for all remaining entity relationships within the system. Once all the entity relationships have been drawn, the ERD is nearly complete. The final step in ERD creation is to review the cardinality of each entity relationship and ensure that no many-to-many relationships exist. If a many-to-many relationship does exist, an **intersection entity** must be created to alter the many-to-many relationship down to two one-to-many relationships to assert referential integrity within the system.

Intersection Entities

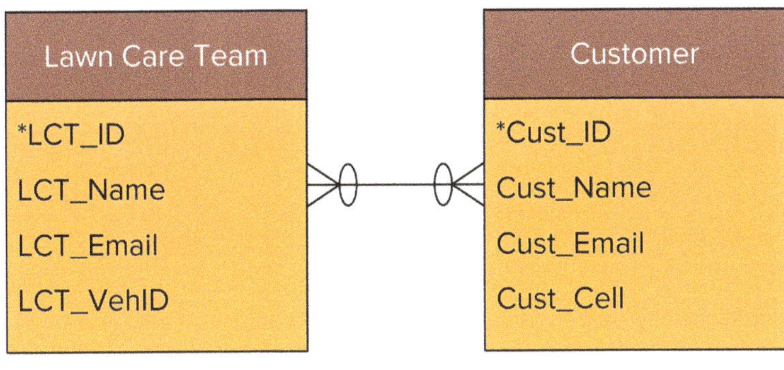

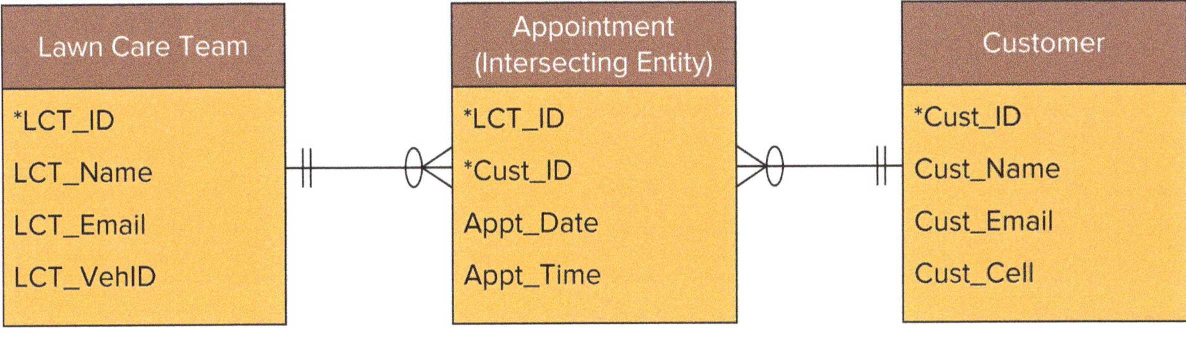

Figure 6.5 Intersection Entities

An intersection entity is essentially a brand-new entity that is created simply to remove many-to-many entity relationships. When a many-to-many relationship exists, the system cannot enforce the uniqueness of data instances. Therefore, an intersection entity will be created to contain developed attributes that will turn the many-to-many relationship into two one-to-many relationships with the intersection entity. In order to accomplish this, the systems analyst will do the following:

1. Remove the many-to-many relationship between the two entities and insert a new entity between them.
2. Create two one-to-many relationships. Each of the original entities will be the parent entities, and the new entity will be the child entity of both.
3. Migrate the primary keys of both parents to the new entity as foreign keys. This will ensure the two one-to-many relationships required.
4. Name the intersection entity with a name that represents the combination of the attributes from both parent entities. (See Figure 6.5)

By ensuring that all many-to-many relationships are removed from the logical ERDs, the systems analyst will be assisting in assuring that the physical ERDs constructed in the design phase will provide a strong basis for data structure development that enforces referential integrity across the entire data scope of the new system.

Validating an Entity-Relationship Diagram

As this is an iterative process, it is rare that the data analysis activity is done with the completion of the first iteration of the ERD drawing. The next step in the process, therefore, is to validate the ERD that was just developed. When it comes to ERD validation, there are many aspects within the ERD to be looked at and analyzed.

ERD validation should be a process of best practice, not rigidly defined rules. That is to say, ERDs are not universally valid. The validity of the ERD development is tied to aspects of the system they are developed for. Therefore, the drawing rules must be compared to system requirements and business rules, as well as assessing the drawing rules of ERDs.

As previously noted, entities must have more than one instance in order to be valid. This is often one of the first checks the project team will complete. Regarding entity assessment, the entities will also be reviewed to ensure that no unnecessary attributes are included, all required attributes are included, and, finally, labels clearly identify the purpose of the entity. Additionally, the attributes will be reviewed per attribute type, and composite attributes will be broken down into the lowest level required for understanding all data required.

Relationships will next be analyzed. The related entities will be reviewed to ensure the relationship actually exists. Next, the relationship symbols will be assessed to ensure that cardinality and modality are both reflected and accurate. Again, labels will be reviewed for accuracy in describing the relationship they are identifying.

Once all the ERD components have been reviewed and determined to be accurate, the ERD will be further assessed in two additional areas. These assessment areas consist of the following:

1. Balancing
2. Normalization

Balancing

Just as balancing was conducted for DFDs, so too will the project team conduct balancing activities for the ERD. The ERD needs to be compared to the DFDs to ensure that DFDs data stores are reflected in the ERD. Each data store should be shown as an entity in the ERD, with the associated data elements of the data store being reflected as attributes in the entity.

Ensuring that the data stored in the DFDs completely match associated entities in the ERD will assist the project team in assessing the degree to which the data is understood both from a process perspective and a data design perspective. This is imperative if the new system is to have the data necessary to function as intended.

Normalization

Once an ERD is determined to be balanced with the other analytical models, it is important to also ensure that it is normalized. Normalization is a technique used in relational model design with the goal being to remove attribute redundancy between data entities. The reason for this is primarily that the logical data model will be converted to a physical data model.

Redundant data storage in a system makes data manipulation more difficult or sometimes even impossible. Therefore, to increase the efficiency of data manipulation within the relational database structure, normalization will isolate data so that additions, deletions, and modifications of an attribute will only need to be completed in one place. That data is then used across the entire system wherever needed.

Essentially, the process of normalization works to ensure that for every data attribute, there is only one physical location for that attribute within the entire system. Any process that needs to interact with the attribute will be directed to that single location, and any changes to the attribute will update that same location. This will ensure that all actions on a data attribute will always be reflected across every process contained within the system.

Normalization is completed by starting with an entity in an **un-normalized form** and then enacting three normalization rules on the entity in order to ensure normalization is achieved. These three normalization rules consist of the following:

1. First normal form
2. Second normal form
3. Third normal form

UN-NORMALIZED FORM

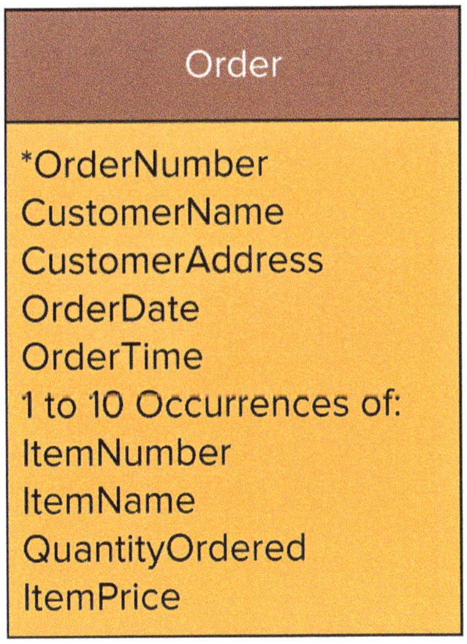

Order
*OrderNumber
CustomerName
CustomerAddress
OrderDate
OrderTime
1 to 10 Occurrences of:
ItemNumber
ItemName
QuantityOrdered
ItemPrice

Figure 6.6 Un-normalized

To determine if an entity is in an un-normalized form, the systems analyst will review each attribute and determine if any attribute, or group of attributes, occurs more than once for a single occurrence of the entity. If this answer is yes, the entity is in an un-normalized form (See Figure 6.6), and the normalization rules must be applied to the entity.

FIRST NORMAL FORM

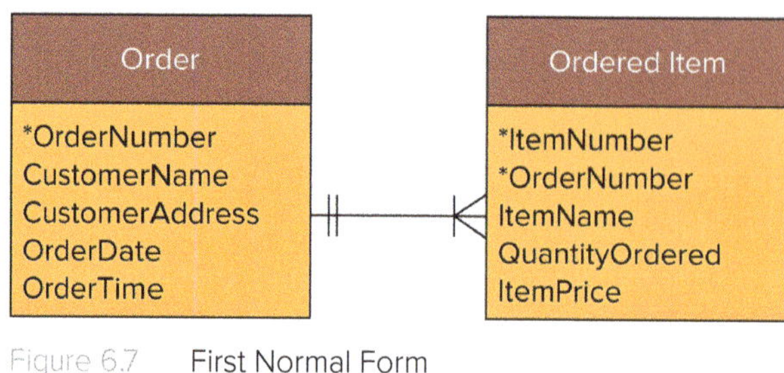

Figure 6.7 First Normal Form

Once it is determined that an attribute or group of attributes occur more than once for a single instance of the entity, the first normal form rule states that these attributes need to be removed from the entity and placed in a newly created entity developed specifically for them.

Once the formation of the new entity is completed, the relationship between the original entity and the newly formed entity is drawn (See Figure 6.7), and the resulting ERD is reviewed. To determine if there are any anomalies that exist in the new development, the following questions are asked:

1. Can you insert a new value into every attribute?
2. Can you delete an instance of every attribute?
3. Can you update an instance of every attribute?

If the answer to any of these questions is no, the entity is not yet normalized, and the second normal form rule must be applied.

SECOND NORMAL FORM

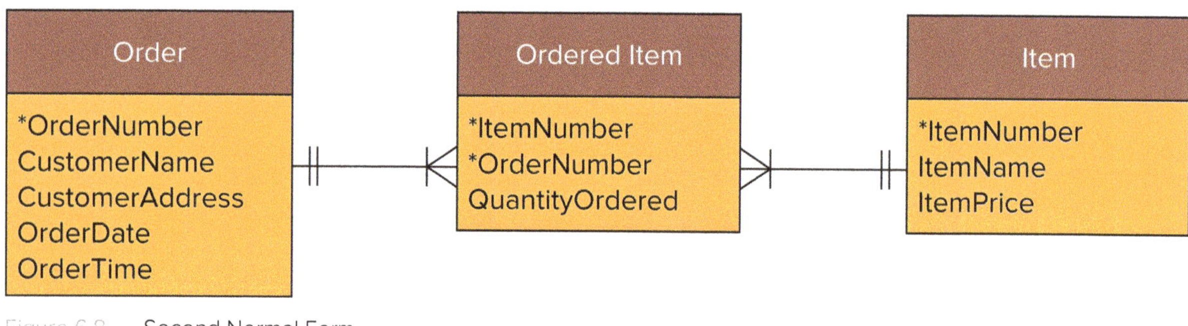

Figure 6.8 Second Normal Form

The second normal form focuses on the entities that contain concatenated primary keys. These entities must be evaluated to determine if any attributes are dependent on just part of the key instead of the entire key. If the answer is yes, create a new entity and move the partially dependent attributes to the new entity (See Figure 6.8).

Once the formation of the new entity is completed, the relationship between the original entity and the newly formed entity is drawn, and the resulting ERD is reviewed. The potential anomaly most likely to exist after the creation of the new entity is that it may contain transitive dependencies. That is to say, several of the nonprimary key attributes may depend on an attribute other than the primary key attribute or attributes. If this occurs, the third normal form rule must be applied.

THIRD NORMAL FORM

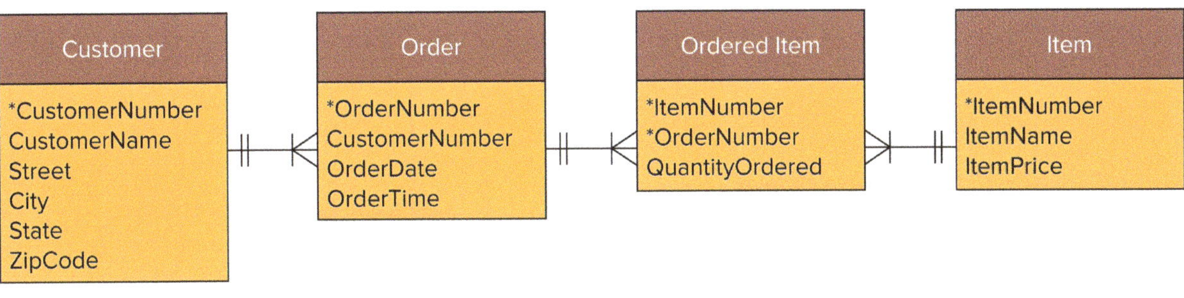

Figure 6.9 Third Normal Form

The third normal form focuses on attributes dependent on nonprimary keys. These attributes must be moved to a newly created entity created specifically for them, making the attribute or attributes they are dependent on the primary key of said new entity.

Once the formation of the new entity is completed, the relationship between the original entity and the newly formed entity is drawn (See Figure 6.9), and the resulting ERD is reviewed. At this point, the ERD should now be normalized.

Transitioning From the Logical to Physical Entity-Relationship Diagram

While the logical ERD is created in the analysis phase in order to denote the business view of the data, the model does not adequately provide the information necessary to build the data storage architecture in the design phase. More information regarding data type and size is required in order to accomplish the actual data design tasks required of the project team. Therefore, the logical ERD will be brought back into utilization in the design phase in order to transform it into the physical ERD that will then be used to assist in designing the actual data structure of the new system.

The physical ERD will take the structure of the logical ERD. However, instead of simply naming entities and attributes, the physical ERD will be rewritten to include enough information to represent the actual design of the new system's database. For this task to be successful, the following steps are taken to alter the logical ERD:

1. Entity names are turned into table or file names.
2. Attribute names are converted to field names. In many instances, the field names will also incorporate the associated entity name.

3. Each field's metadata is defined. The metadata consists of the field's data type and size limit.
4. Primary keys are defined if not already completed in the logical ERD.
5. Foreign keys are defined if not already completed in the logical ERD.
6. System-related tables and fields are added to the physical ERD.

Once all these steps are completed, the logical ERD becomes the physical ERD and assists in designing the actual database that will be used by the system. This process also incorporates all the business rules and process logic that went into defining the logical ERD in the first place. The end result is a data model that incorporates the requirements of both analysis and design into the design of the data structures that will facilitate the successful operation of the new system.

The CRUD Matrix

Table 6.2 CRUD Matrix

	Process A	Process B	Process C
Data Entity X			
Attribute X-1	CRUD		R
Attribute X-2		R	D
Attribute X-3	C	CRUD	R
Data Entity Y			
Attribute Y-1	C	U	D
Attribute Y-2	C	R	D
Attribute Y-3	C	U	D

A CRUD matrix is a graphical and very useful way to display data entity activities within a system. Therefore, the utilization of a CRUD matrix is a key component of data analysis and should be used by the project team once it is believed that the ERD is both complete and accurate.

CRUD is an acronym that refers to the actions taken on a data entity by the system:

1. Create—To create or store new data
2. Read—To retrieve and read data
3. Update—To modify then store data
4. Delete—To remove data

Specifically, these actions are in reference to how the use cases interact with the data defined in the ERD. The CRUD matrix (See Table 6.2) will be developed using each use case and every data entity.

Developing the CRUD Matrix

The CRUD matrix is developed by creating a table. The table is defined as a row labeled for each data entity and a column labeled for each use case. Regarding data entities, it is also sometimes helpful for the attributes to be included in the analysis as well. In these instances, a row will be used for the entity, and subsequent rows below will be used for each attribute.

The use cases are then walked through, and each entity or attribute of each entity is assessed regarding whether it is interacted with during the use case. If there is an interaction, the interaction will be notated in the intersecting cell as a c for create, r for read, u for update, and d for delete. If more than one interaction is identified, then each will be notated.

The end result of the developed CRUD matrix will be to assert that every entity or even every attribute is, in fact, required for system utilization, as well as to provide a basis for how data queries can be developed to access data when the database is actually developed.

It is important to also note that a CRUD matrix will be developed during the analytical phase of the SDLC in order to assess the validity of the logical ERD. When the physical ERD is created in the design phase, the CRUD matrix should be reviewed and updated to match the physical ERD in order to assert the validity of this new model development as well.

Chapter Summary

The data of a system is the cornerstone component of that system. As such, the analytical activities surrounding data development, both in the form of current system analysis and new system data specification, should be both comprehensive and fully developed. Therefore, it is no surprise that the development and analysis of ERDs is a lengthy and involved process. The process not only takes into account the development of data modeling but also the comparison of those developed models against all other analytical developments of the analytical phase.

The analytical phase is intentionally designed to develop system analysis activities that lead up to data analysis as the final step in the phase. This is to both allow for ample identification and enhanced understanding of how the data is incorporated across the entire system, as well as to provide plenty of comparisons for the data development as it relates to all other aspects of the system. By ensuring that the project team is both focused and driven to comprehensively complete all required tasks of the analysis phase of the SDLC, the systems analyst will help to ensure that the foundation of the new system, the data, is both fully understood and will be adequately designed to allow for overall new system development success.

Project Planning Activities

1. Develop the ERD.
2. Develop the CRUD matrix.
3. In the design phase, the ERD will be converted to the physical ERD.

Image Credits

IMG 6.1: Copyright © 2018 Depositphotos/vectorfusionart.
IMG 6.2: Copyright © 2011 Depositphotos/dacasdo.
IMG 6.3: Copyright © 2013 Depositphotos/jntvisual.
IMG 6.4: Copyright © 2019 Depositphotos/GaudiLab.
IMG 6.5: Copyright © 2018 Depositphotos/ursus@zdeneksasek.com.

CHAPTER 7

Design Requirements

Introduction

With the completion of our data analysis for the new system, we have reached a very important turning point in the SDLC. We are transitioning from the analysis phase to the design phase. This is exceedingly important for a number of reasons. Up until this point, we have been focused on justifying the need for the new system, creating a proposed development that will meet that need, and analyzing both the current system and our proposed development to ensure that all requirements, both functional and nonfunctional, are incorporated.

It is only when all of the tasks and assignments of both planning and analysis are completed that the systems analyst can begin to focus on the actual creation of the new system. Hence, the move into the design phase of the SDLC. This migration to design uses all the information and data that has been developed to date in order to make educated decisions on how best to obtain the results that the project team is working toward.

The decisions that are required to be made in the design phase of the SDLC consist of formulating a strategy on how best to obtain the new system. The system itself is broken down into its individual components in order to determine how each aspect will be developed and incorporated into the current operational scope. Eventually, all of these decisions and developments will result in the construction of the hardware and software specification document that will guide the developers to actually produce the new system.

Learning Objectives

1. Explain transitioning from analysis to design.
2. Describe the four categories of system requirement definition.
3. Describe the three main ways to acquire a new system.
4. Explain the risks associated with each way to acquire a new system.
5. Create an alternative matrix document.
6. Create a request for proposal.

Image 7.1

The Design Phase

The design phase of system development is best characterized as the stage where all the technical details of the new solution are developed. Up until this juncture, the systems analyst has focused their team on the development and rationalization of the new system idea. Yes, this idea contains a wealth of information, including functional and nonfunctional requirements that will be helpful in system design; however, the new system is not physically able to be constructed.

Once the new system development leaves the design phase, it will be fully developed into a workable project with direction provided on how to actually construct the final solution. Think of the design phase as developing the blueprints the developers will use to actually construct the new system. These blueprints need to be all-encompassing and focus on all areas surrounding a new system and how it is used.

Too often, people consider system development as simply software development. When we discuss process automation, manual task reduction, and even process re-creation, many people associate software as the mechanism to complete these tasks within business solutions. Many technological systems that are developed are not simply founded on software alone. There are hardware components that must be considered. What does software interact with at a foundational level? The hardware that runs it. Some new systems are a combination of the addition of new software and new hardware to complete a process. Automotive manufacturing is a key example. The vehicle assembly line was transformed from human task completion to robotic task completion with the development of the robots and the software to operate them. Therefore, the design phase must look at both software and hardware requirements and determine the best course of action for obtaining all the requirements for both.

Even with consideration given to hardware and software, there are still many aspects of the new system that are developed in the design phase. The architecture of the solution is a key component. Data is of limited use when at rest. To be valuable in most systems, data must be able to be moved from point to point, and shared with other processes and even associated systems. The speed and accuracy at which data must flow through the environment can have a critical impact on the success of the new system. Therefore, the way the data is stored, transported, and made available are all critical aspects of the new system that must be formally defined. A system's architecture consists of all these components and focuses the development team on understanding and defining network requirements, storage requirements, and even user presentation requirements.

Finally, it is very rare that a new system development works autonomously in a business environment. Even if the system functions are not directly tied to other systems, the technology infrastructure of the organization must be taken into account to ensure that the new system can operate on existing architectures. Therefore, the concept of integration is a primary component of the design phase. While it is very important to ensure that the new system is developed to meet the system requirements that have been defined, it is also just as important that the new system meets the architecture requirements of the organization so that it can operate within the business environment.

All these decision points and considerations must be actively assessed and developed in the design phase in order to provide the best chance of accurate and effective new system construction. The efforts placed in the analysis phase will provide many answers on what development methodologies and design considerations are most appropriate, but ultimately, there will be questions left to answer that further assessment will bring to light as the project team works through the process. The first step in the design process is to determine two key components of the new system construction, those being the development of the **system requirements** and the determination of the **system acquisition strategy**.

System Requirement Development

Much like functional and nonfunctional requirements, system requirements must be established to ensure that the new development will both operate as a functioning system and operate in the organization's technological environment. In order to accomplish this, the system analyst and his or her team must flush out all the system requirements that will affect system design decisions and highlight aspects that must be upheld or maintained within the design.

For example, a company that only runs Microsoft Windows workstations will need to ensure that developed solutions operate on Microsoft Windows. A company developing a connected in-truck technology will need to ensure that a mobile data device and usage plan are included in the development to ensure Internet connectivity while on the road.

System requirements transcend all aspects of the new system development. This includes defining requirements pertaining to the software, hardware, data architecture, and even how the new system is integrated into the current business environment. Accomplishing this task requires evaluation identification and documentation of required conditions. Some of these required conditions will be focused on the organization's existing technological environment, while others will be focused on the needs of the system being constructed.

The best chance for a successful new system construction is to ensure that all system requirements are fleshed out and accounted for as well as incorporated into the actual new system design. Having these requirements fully identified and met will position the new system to be successfully integrated into the organization's operation.

System Acquisition Strategy

While it is clear that there are many considerations that must be made throughout the system design process, one of the foundational decisions that will drive a significant amount of future effort and planning is that of determining the acquisition strategy. When it comes to system design, one decision will impact future decisions, and therefore, it is important to understand which decisions are cornerstones or have the most impact on other decision-making. The acquisition strategy is the most paramount decision and, therefore, must be determined first.

Once again, there is a common misconception that all system development consists of creating that which does not exist today. This is simply not the case. What is determined to be needed and "new" to one organization may already exist for another. Therefore, there are multiple ways to create a "new" system. Technology can be purchased, development can be outsourced to external parties, and yes, technology can also be internally developed. Determining which course of action is best for a given project will create the basis for which all additional design decisions are made.

Finally, it must be noted that many system developments may contain a complement of acquisition strategies. For example, a new payment system may require software to be developed, but a payment terminal to be sourced from a payment terminal vendor. Acquisition strategy must be applied to all aspects of the new system and defined at each level.

System Requirements

System requirements development is done at multiple levels as related to the new system development being undertaken. A formal breakdown of new system component categories is as follows:

1. Software
2. Hardware
3. Architecture
4. Integration

The detailed information developed to formulate each of these categories is first compiled based on the functional requirements, entities, relationships, and data attributes that were developed in the analytical phase of the SDLC. Secondly, requirements related to the current environment are documented in order to identify new development constraints or conditions that must be aligned. All this data allows for design specifications to be built on all aspects of the new system's requirements.

System requirements are essential to fully understand in order to develop a design plan that will be functional. Not only must the system meet the functional requirements determined to be critical to success, but it must operate in the organization's technological environment. Without a clear understanding of all the details that must be incorporated to allow for all these conditions to be met, a functioning system will be impossible to obtain.

Ensuring that the system requirements are fully formed and developed is the key to the systems analyst's ability to write a usable system specification on which the new system construction can be designed.

A lack of development of any of the four primary components of the new system will greatly weaken the chance for overall success.

Software

Image 7.2

As new system development uses data as the cornerstone reason for completing the initiative, it is not surprising that software is a category of system requirements to be developed. Thought must be put into determining how the system being developed will interact with data and, therefore, what software is necessary to provide those data interactions. Based on predefined requirements, some developments will leverage software that is currently in place within the organization, while other developments will require the incorporation of new software packages. In some instances, the software required does not currently exist and must be developed. Determining how this software development will take place compounds even more decision-making requirements.

User interface design is a specific component of software development that requires some special attention. It is important to determine how the user will interact with the new system and from what perspective these interactions should be controlled or limited. Additionally, how the user interacts will often require the incorporation of hardware that the software must be developed for in order to be successful. Therefore, interface design should be allotted specific time and consideration when determining the overall new system software specifications.

Software decisions are essential to ensuring the new system will function, but they cannot happen in a vacuum. The other categories of system requirements will play a part in determining what software options are available to be considered, and ultimately development of each category will result in the review and alteration of other categories as more constraints and considerations are identified. That said, as the software is responsible for data interactions, it is appropriate to develop the software requirements for the system initially.

Hardware

While software is essential to data utilization, hardware is essential to a user's ability to interact with the newly constructed system. Additionally, hardware often provides additional data systems, whether it be environmental monitoring, testing, decision-making, or physical reaction; hardware allows software to interact with the physical environment. Therefore, assessment of the new system's hardware requirements is essential to ensuring that the hardware-based components required are developed or obtained.

Hardware that exists is not always built to be used in every operating environment under any and all conditions. Therefore, understanding the environment in which the new system will operate will allow for the determination of what sourced hardware is available. In certain circumstances, existing hardware that fits the needs of the new system is not available. It is in these circumstances that part of the system development will require new hardware development as well. Therefore, a new system may be composed of developing both new hardware and software to interact with it. Much as it is with other aspects of new system development, system requirement development can and often will lead to increased new component development.

Data is the foundation of the system, and the hardware is the residence of the data. Therefore, data architecture requirements will also be factored into hardware system requirements. It is important to understand how data needs to be stored and used to ensure the hardware incorporation and configuration are appropriate for data requirements. Hardware decisions are tightly aligned to data requirements.

Architecture

A system is made up of many components. While hardware is essential to tie the new system to the physical environment, the technological architecture of the organization is essential to ensure that hardware can work from a community-based perspective. That is to say, the technological architecture provides the ability for individual pieces of hardware to talk to each other, the software developments to interact with the hardware, and even the data to be stored and interact with the software.

A system's architecture will define what hardware stores data, what hardware runs the software, and, thereby, how the software has to be written. Different processing hardware has different programming language requirements that must be understood for successful software development. Additionally, the requirement to move data from one piece of hardware to the next will reflect on networking requirements (data transmission requirements). As not all systems require the same level of performance, the architecture already in place for an organization may be sufficient or may have to be altered.

Architecture-based system requirements are essential, as they must identify limitations and considerations within the organization's technological operating environment. For example, perhaps based on other currently used systems within the organization, architecture enhancement may be limited or impossible. That may change the way the software for the new system is developed or even the placement of specific hardware in order to compensate for identified limitations. In another instance, wireless data transmission may be required, and the current architecture is unable to accommodate this type of data transfer. While adding hardware that allows for wireless data transmission may be possible, further consideration will have to be placed on other factors as well, such as the security concerns related to wireless data transmission. It is not until all aspects of concern are both identified and accounted for that system design can actually begin.

Integration

As already highlighted in the discussion of the new system component categories, there is a high degree of interdependence between what is already used technologically within the organization and the new system being developed. Understanding that the new development needs to operate successfully in the current environment is the basis for integration.

Integration considerations center around compensating for constraints in the current technological environment so that they can either be altered to meet new development requirements or the new development can be tempered to work within the preexisting constraints. There is no sense in building a system that cannot function in the necessary environment. Integration system requirements can sometimes be frustrating, as new system design may have to be throttled back in order to work within architectural constraints. Conversely, architectural changes may be necessary, but then increased analysis of currently deployed systems must be conducted to ensure that they will be able to function after incorporating change into the environment.

Integration-based system specifications can be complex and challenging. However, the effort placed into identifying requirements is essential. This allows for decisions to be made on how to proceed with new system development and to what degree the project team can or will change the organization's current architecture in order to achieve project success. New architectural requirements are defined while at the same time ensuring that any architectural changes do not result in the inoperability of another system that is also required for overall corporate technological success.

System Acquisition

As we are able to see from the steps taken to build all the necessary system requirements, there are multiple ways to compile new system components. However, overall, there are three main acquisition strategies that are employed when designing a new system:

1. Purchase
2. Outsource
3. Custom Develop

This is not to say that for all categories of the new system design, a single method must be chosen. Especially in regards to software and hardware development of the new system, multiple strategies are often employed. An organization may custom develop the software solution yet purchase the newly required hardware from a newly acquired vendor partner. There is no right or wrong way to combine or limit system acquisition. It is through analysis of the developed system requirements that acquisition strategy can begin to be developed.

Even when components need to be developed for the new system, internal development is not the only solution. Organizations exist that will work with your team to develop the required components for you. These development partnerships can be tricky and come with a number of constraints that must be understood in order to determine if this is the best course of action for your development team. Therefore, we must also look at new developments from the perspective of internal or outsourced.

Finally, there is yet another combination of acquisition that should be highlighted as a design potential, and that is purchase with slight customization. With this strategy, a solution, whether it be hardware or software, is purchased, but then slight alterations are made to ensure that the end result will be a system component that meets all functional requirements. Obviously, there are a number of considerations that must be made here, specifically if the solution provider will allow the organization to alter the purchased solution as required. That said, many new system developments will incorporate customization of purchased system components as part of their overall new system development, and therefore, it cannot be ignored.

By looking more in-depth at each acquisition strategy, we are able to determine the strengths and weaknesses of each method. Therefore, it is possible to consider the influences on the system development and ultimately end with an acquisition strategy solution for each category of new system development. As a final reminder, it is not necessary to make an acquisition decision for every system development category. Oftentimes, the architecture component of the organization will remain the same. However, the design specification document should highlight that the current architecture is sufficient to support the new system development.

Purchase

Purchasing either a component of your new system development or an entire system that meets the needs of your project development is an acquisition strategy that can save a significant amount of time and effort. If your team doesn't actually have to develop a solution, time to implementation can be drastically reduced. Additionally, as the solution is purchased from a provider, future support is not dependent on the project team. Finally, as the solution already exists, it can be used and experimented with to ensure it meets all requirements before being implemented, ensuring that all identified requirements are satisfied all at once.

Purchasing comes with many positive aspects regarding system acquisition. Not only can a purchased solution save time and oftentimes costs, but the expertise of the vendor can often be invaluable. Additionally, ongoing system support is not self-reliant because of the ability to call experts when problems arise. However, there are negative aspects of purchasing that must also be understood.

If a solution is available to your organization, it is also available to your competition. Therefore, for solution development that is based on differentiation, this may not be the best strategy to enact. Additionally, while it can be a comfort to have a vendor to call for issues, you are also reliant on that vendor for maintenance and future enhancements. That means if your business needs require system alteration in the future, there is no guarantee these alterations will be possible. Also, as the software is already developed, organizational processes must adapt to how the software operates. Your process flow may have been developed to have users do specific tasks in a certain order, but if the solution completes these tasks differently, the user process must be altered, as the system process is not able to be changed. Finally, the integration component of the system design may have a negative impact on the purchased solution selection. The solution must operate in your environment; if the solution does not meet architectural specifications, either the organization's architecture must be altered, or the solution cannot be integrated.

From a cost-based perspective, there are a few aspects of purchase that must be included in the decision-making process. Many software and hardware providers are moving away from the historical strategy of one-time solution purchases. Whether it be software development, hardware development, or a system incorporating both, many solution providers have migrated to a recurring payment model of varying degrees. Historically, when a solution was purchased, the purchaser would pay a significant amount up front for the solution and then a much lower annual maintenance cost, ranging from ten to twenty percent of the purchase price. However, more and more solution providers have moved away from this strategy in favor of software and even hardware as service models. In these models, the purchaser pays a set monthly fee with little to know additional funding up front. This monthly fee continues in perpetuity, often with periodic rate increases built into the agreement. When the purchaser decides to end the relationship, their access to the system is terminated. These reoccurring cost models must be factored into the purchase strategy over the anticipated system's entire life cycle.

Even with all the stated positives and negatives of solution purchase as an acquisition strategy, there is still another component of purchase that must be considered as well. It is very rare that a predeveloped solution is a perfect fit for an organization. Oftentimes, during system planning, there are unique needs the organization is attempting to meet. This is why a lot of software and hardware vendors will allow for a degree of **customization** to be factored into the developed solution. However, customization has its own set of challenges that must be understood and incorporated into system design in order to be effective.

CUSTOMIZATION

When considering customization of a purchased solution, the systems analyst is looking to make modifications to the existing solution that is unavailable through out-of-the-box functionality. Customization will require custom coding to the application itself or the development of custom code that interacts with the application to provide unique results. Customization may even require a unique implementation of the solution within the organization's technological environment.

The benefit of enacting a purchase and customize strategy is that you can take a solution that exists and adapt it to your specific use case. The outcome of this is to hopefully gain enhanced overall functionality of the solution within the organization's unique environment. This can provide for a purchase strategy that does allow for the potential of some differentiation when using the purchased solution.

The same drivers for the positive aspects of customization also tend to allow for some negative aspects. The more you customize the solution from its original form, the more difficult it may be for the solution provider to support your version of the solution. This can lead to instances where your organization's version is trapped at a specific time, normally that of customization. What this means is that as the provider enhances the base solution, your organization may not be able to take advantage of those enhancements. Furthermore, customization can lead to a situation where the solution will only be supported for a set time frame. This will require future change decisions to be made at the start of the engagement or at least an agreement that the solution life cycle will be predetermined at the time of implementation.

Often, customization allows for an organization to take the benefit of implementing a predeveloped solution but layers in the ability to differentiate to a degree to meet unique business requirements. As long as the potential detractions are understood and accepted, solution purchase and customization is a viable new system acquisition strategy either in part or as a whole of the new system development.

Outsource

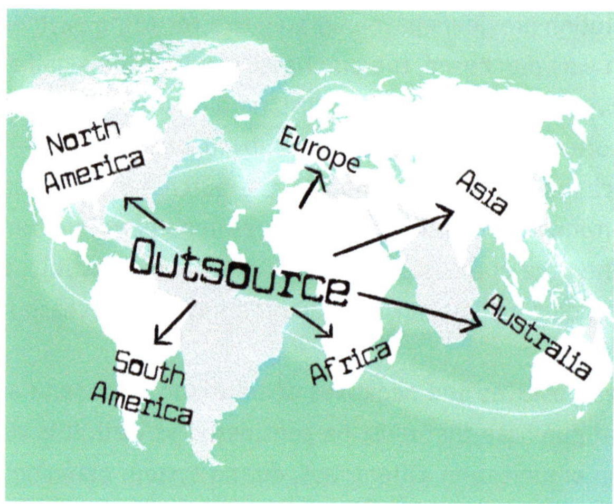

Image 7.3

There are many times when the new system requirements simply cannot be met by a solution that is currently on the market. Additionally, the organization may not have enough experience or development strength to construct a new system from scratch. For times when there is a need for a new system build without the ability to do so internally, or even if the ability exists but current demand dictates an inability to complete the required development in a timely manner, outsourcing is a very real consideration.

Outsourcing has the potential to allow for the development of a new system that meets all the organization's functional and nonfunctional requirements. By leveraging a single vendor or even multiple vendors that have competency in the areas requiring development, the systems analyst is bringing extensive knowledge and technological aptitude to the project team. Securing the "best" vendor partner or partners for the new system development provides the opportunity to complete the new system development potentially faster and at less expense than originally planned. Additionally, as the competencies of the partner vendors are aligned with the requirements of the project itself, ideally, there would be a reduction in overall risk with regard to system creation and alignment to developed requirements.

At first glance, there appears to be a large amount of positive returns when considering an outsourced-based new system acquisition strategy. One might ask why all new systems wouldn't be constructed in this fashion. While there is certainly potential for many benefits in an outsourcing relationship, there is also potential for outsourcing to become less productive, less secure, and even less than fully aligned with all of the documented new system requirements. Some would say there is an art to managing outsourcing relationships, and without a keen understanding of the potential pitfalls of this acquisition strategy, a systems analyst may be hard-pressed to successfully complete the new system development.

In order to better understand why outsourcing relationships are not always as productive as they possibly could be, it is important to understand the potential pitfalls that system development teams encounter when entering into these relationships. Some areas of consideration are as follows:

1. Poor contract development
2. Project scope issues
3. Communication barriers
4. Development quality issues
5. Vendor issues
6. Limited future development options
7. Security concerns

POOR CONTRACT DEVELOPMENT

When a project team is working on a new system development, most often, each member becomes highly invested in the success of the project. A good project team will begin to assimilate the project successes with their personal success and the project setbacks or even failures as their personal setbacks or failures. There are many reasons that drive this personal identification, but the main reason is the investment of time and energy throughout the entire SDLC process. Therefore, when it comes time to bring in an external party to essentially join the team and develop the solution, there is often an expectation that the new partner will share the same passion for the project.

It is important to remember that outsourcing organizations exist to profit from development activities that are unable to be internally completed. Each project is simply a job for most employees of these organizations. There is little to no personal pride or professional development from going above and beyond to ensure that the development doesn't meet but exceeds expectations. Realistically, an outsource organization will look to develop a contract that upholds the expectation that what is presented is developed, no more and no less. If the project team misses requirements, hasn't fully spaced out system requirements, or misunderstood the capabilities of the required new technology development, the outsourcer is not contractually obligated to adjust the development.

It is apparent from the first two phases of the SDLC that system development is a learning process, and mistakes will be made. Even with as much due diligence as possible, items will come to light at each step of the process that requires adjustment to both plan and implementation. If the systems analyst does not develop a contract that requires flexibility and even possibly assistance with issue identification and correction during the system design and construction, there will be very little chance for success.

Ensuring that the outsourcer is more than a hired entity but an actual team participant begins by developing a contract that places some level of outcome success responsibility on the vendor. This can be a tricky process, as most vendors will have boilerplate contracts that are constructed to ensure this type of responsibility from the vendor. It takes negotiation and communication by the systems analyst to overcome objections and develop a contract that assigns greater responsibility to the vendors themselves. If done correctly, this can change the vendor-customer relationship into that of a true development partnership.

PROJECT SCOPE ISSUES

In much the same way as a poor contract development can hinder an outsourcing relationship, so too can an underdeveloped or poorly communicated project scope. Any vendor-customer relationship begins with an assessment of the amount of work to be accomplished, estimation of vendor resources required, resource cost estimation, and the inclusion of a profit percentage that makes the effort worthwhile for the vendor. If the first part of this process, the assessment of work is hindered by incorrect information or a lack of communication of all the requirements; the resulting estimates are misaligned with the actual effort that will be required.

Who is to blame when these instances of poor project scope development or communication occur? The outsourcer will state that the customer, the project team, is to blame, and they will be accurate. However, the assignment of blame is only the first step in what often becomes an adversarial relationship. Misalignment of effort usually translates to increased time and increased recourse requirements. Both of which equate to increased costs for the vendor. Increased cost equates to decreased profit, and most successful organizations will not be satisfied with that result.

When an outsource vendor encounters greater effort being required than expected, they will investigate the reason why. If it is determined to be due to faulty project scope development by the client, the relationship will often degrade from active solution development to development slowdown or even stoppage as the two organizations battle over increased funding requirements, new contract development, or even project abandonment. Just as the organization has many projects working at a given time, so too does an outsourcer, and increased project requirements on a given project may simply not be able to be met, leading to project abandonment.

It is important to understand how a poorly presented project scope can lead to a system development being halted, as it is a common occurrence. Ensuring that the outsource vendor is presented with a realistic project scope that is clearly and fully communicated will go a long way to guaranteeing that the partnership begins and ends positively.

COMMUNICATION BARRIERS

Not only do outsource organizations transcend industries, but they also transcend geographic areas. It is a common occurrence to work with an outsource team that is at least partially composed of international resources. While this can be beneficial from many perspectives, including the incorporation of varying experiences and perspectives, communication challenges can be a very real concern.

Certainly, when one considers communication challenges involving international collaboration, language barriers are a primary concern, and for good reason. Different languages and dialects can sometimes be difficult to understand by both parties involved. Additionally, regional influences such as slang terminology can increase the inability to clearly understand your teammates. The end result is communication efforts that are challenged to effectively and efficiently communicate necessary information to the entire team.

Besides language in and of itself, time zone differences and cultural conventions often provide challenges as well. While asynchronous communication can provide a basis for communication that overcomes these potential issues, we have seen that synchronous communication is often invaluable during system development. Coordinating these events with these constraints requires flexibility, cooperation, and consideration by all members of the project team.

Finally, even though we are more of a globally connected society than ever before, communication systems are not always reliable 24 hours a day, 365 days a year. Especially when tight deadlines are a factor, communication blackout periods owing to international distance and communication infrastructure issues can often result in delays or misunderstandings that can hamper the progress of a development project.

DEVELOPMENT QUALITY ISSUES

Outsourced firms tend to have higher turnover rates for employees than full-time development positions within internal organizations. The availability of global resources is certainly one factor, but so is the baseline financial component of these positions. If a different firm is willing to pay an outsourced employee more, there is little barrier for that employee to migrate to a new company. This is an important aspect of outsourcing that is often overlooked by organizations before entering into a relationship.

Why is this important? As we have seen from our development to date, a large part of success is dependent on team knowledge and growth throughout the development process. Removing even a single team member will make the project team take a step back, as knowledge is lost and must be transferred to that member's replacement. This is the same when it comes to a development resource within the outsource organization. Assuming the systems analyst has taken into account all the predefined areas of concern, losing an outsourced resource is essentially losing a team member, and time must be spent getting the newly assigned resource up to speed.

VENDOR ISSUES

Losing an outsourced resource represents a real setback to solution development but pales in comparison to the setback incurred if the outsource organization itself becomes an issue. Just as with any other business, outsourcers will sometimes have operational issues that result in decreased function or even a cessation of operation altogether. While it may seem farfetched to consider an outsourcer going out of business in the middle of a development project, this does happen. For the partnered organization, it's not simply a setback but can be catastrophic to the system development project.

As the organization depends on the outsourcer for all development expertise, any issue within the outsource organization that results in delays or stoppage of development becomes a very real issue for the organization itself. While the SDLC task success has been internally managed to date, once the outsourcer takes over, control sways to their capabilities or lack thereof. Even in situations where the project is not progressing as defined, it is not easy for a new outsourcer to be brought in as a replacement. The amount of effort required to get the developers up to speed and functional may honestly be impossible.

It is important to remember why the vendor was brought in in the first place. The organization lacks the ability to develop the solution. If the vendor exits the relationship, the organization not only lacks the ability to continue development but may be unable to explain the development to date to a new vendor. This can result in more time wasted while the new vendor deconstructs the development to date, or even worse, the previous vendor's work being abandoned altogether and the new vendor starting from the beginning.

There is no guarantee that the organization will be able to make up for the lost funding or time that an outsourcing vendor change will force them to incur. Ultimately, this type of situation can very easily lead to project failure and the inability for the new system to actually be developed.

LIMITED FUTURE DEVELOPMENT OPTIONS

In instances where the system is successfully developed by the outsourcer, there are still areas of concern surrounding ongoing support and future enhancement. Most outsource contracts cease with the successful rollout of the new solution, leaving the organization to figure out ongoing support. Unlike with a purchased solution, there is not always the ability to rely on the development group to be available for future issues. Conversely, it has already been stated that the outsourcing industry has a high rate of employee turnover. Because of this high turnover rate, it is realistic to assume that in a few years, none of the development teams will still be employed at the contracted organization.

Because of these circumstances, it is important that the systems analyst plan for support and future enhancement aspects of the system at the start of the outsourcing project. Whether this is by developing internal resources to work with the outsourcer to gain knowledge or contracting a support company to do similar activities, if consideration is not given, the end result could be the organization owning a new system they will not be able to support into the future.

SECURITY CONCERNS

Security is always a primary concern when it comes to new system development, and this factor is not to be understated when considering entering into an outsourcing relationship. There are two primary areas of concern when it comes to outsourcing development: privacy of information and actual security of the developed system.

A company's data is often the most profitable component of the organization. As any system development is built with data as a cornerstone for development, it is impossible to construct the system without the organization sharing its data. Additionally, the system development itself can be considered sensitive data if the new system will provide a competitive advantage or a high degree of differentiation from the competition. Therefore, it is imperative that the outsource vendor be vetted regarding their ability to responsibly handle and protect the organization's data, as well as be trustworthy enough not to be tempted to sell proprietary information to an external entity. Even with an organization that has a good reputation, all it takes is for a single employee with access to the project to compromise your organization.

The security of the new solution itself is also paramount. Not only must the systems analyst ensure that the outsourcer is building a system that is both functional and secure, but they must also take into account that there is always a possibility of security weaknesses being intentionally introduced to the system development for future exploitation. While we would like to believe that security issues in systems are due to mistakes or ignorance, this is not always the case. Therefore, when a system is developed by an outsource partner, consideration should be given to using additional resources for security testing that are outside the outsource organization.

Custom Develop

Image 7.4

If the organization has the capability to develop the new system internally, this method is often preferred. The project team will get many of the benefits of outsourcing without the reliance on an external entity that may not be as driven or focused as internal resources.

Just as the rest of the project team tends to associate professional success with project success, so too are an organization's internal development staff most likely to as well. They each have a vested interest in project success and, as such, have a better likelihood of investing all their resources into ensuring the project is successful. Not only will they work harder, but they will push for changes when deficiencies or misconceptions are encountered throughout system development and construction. Additionally, as they are internal resources, it is possible to bring them into the development cycle sooner than you would a vendor partner. This not only increases individual buy-in but also provides a developer perspective in the planning, analysis, and design phases of the SDLC, which can lead to increased benefits such as fewer unknowns during solution development.

It can also be expected that internal development resources will have a better understanding of the organization's current infrastructure and implemented systems. This can be invaluable when it comes to ensuring that the new system's requirements are comprehensive, especially from an architectural and integration perspective. Some of the guesswork will be taken out of the equation when the developers are knowledgeable about the existing infrastructure.

Another area of strength when it comes to internal development is the ability to capitalize on unique situations and requirements. As the development team is familiar with the organization and the unique challenges and potential of its market, this knowledge can be incorporated into the new system itself, sometimes resulting in further strategic advantage. The familiarity of all aspects of the organization will often translate into a more comprehensive solution development than one conducted by an outside organization or through the purchase of someone else's solution.

However, even with all these strengths, there are still some considerations that must be made before deciding to enact a custom development strategy. Internal development requires competency in all areas the new system is meant to deal with. Whether it be a programming language, hardware incorporation, or even architectural change, the internal team must possess the knowledge to successfully complete all tasks. This is can challenging or even impossible in some instances.

Just as with every other aspect of system development, resource allocation can be challenging when it comes to development resources. Even if the competency exists, the system analyst must ensure the capacity is there to allocate the development resources to the project. Overcommitting resources can result in the same project slowdown or even project cancellation that is seen with an outsourcing strategy. Just because the development resources are internally controlled does not fully eliminate this risk.

One factor that is not often considered is that internal development will usually take more time and, therefore, will likely cost more. The reason for this lies in the commitment of the development team. As this commitment was identified as a strength, as it highlights the team's commitment to success, it must also be looked at from a negative perspective. If the development team is committed to being as successful as possible, it is reasonable to assume that they will spend more time in each step of the development process, ensuring that due diligence is thoroughly completed and all development avenues fully thought out before being executed. While the end result will be one of comprehensive thought and focused development, the steps completed to get there will be timely and reasonably more so than with other acquisition strategies.

Finally, as all the dependence for success is placed on internal personnel and not aligned with external resources, which are deemed most appropriate for each aspect of the new system development, there is an elevated risk for overall project failure. It is rare that internal development resources will have all the knowledge required to complete the demands that are placed on them. Often, they must self-educate while developing, and this can lead to misunderstandings or incorrect application. Sometimes, the negative impact on the project can be minor and rectified, while other times, the result can be severe and unable to be overcome. It is important to recognize areas where knowledge gain is required and support educational initiatives as components of the overall development scope.

Influences

By understanding the strengths and weaknesses of each system acquisition strategy, it is possible to categorize influences on the project and make determinations of which strategy to use based on how the specific influence is categorized. It is important to note that no single influence will likely persuade the systems analyst to one particular development strategy. Rather, analyzing each category and looking at the strengths and weaknesses in combination will determine the best strategy or combination of strategies for the system development. These influence categories include the following:

1. Business need
2. In-house experience
3. Project skill development
4. Project management
5. Time frame

BUSINESS NEED

When analyzing business needs as a criterion for acquisition strategy selection, it is important to analyze the uniqueness of the business need the new system satisfies. If the business need is unique to the organization, it is likely that the only way to meet the requirements of the solution is through custom development. This is because a purchased solution would most likely not be aligned to specific requirements, and a lack of privacy concerns for sensitive information would make outsourcing a poor choice. However, if the business need is not unique at all, there is a good chance a solution may exist, and therefore, purchase would be a more accurate choice. Finally, if the business need is not core to the business but also not a standard business need, outsourcing may be the most appropriate course of action.

IN-HOUSE EXPERIENCE

Understanding the capabilities of your internal resources is paramount for making sound acquisition decisions. If you have strong in-house functional and technical capabilities, custom development is possible. If you have strong in-house functional capability only, you are positioned to be able to evaluate purchased solutions and negotiate required customizations, making the purchase a viable option. If you lack both functional and technical capabilities in-house, you will be dependent on outsourced resources to assist in making either a development or purchase decision.

PROJECT SKILL DEVELOPMENT

If a component of the project is to build strong internal skills in order to best support the new solution internally, custom development is positioned to ensure that the greatest amount of knowledge transfer remains in-house. Conversely, if there is little desire for internal competence going forward past solution implementation, solution purchase is the most appropriate strategy. For this consideration, outsourcing can really apply to either instance. As long as the outsourcing contract incorporates in-house knowledge transfer, knowledge development can be facilitated. If knowledge transfer is unimportant, the solution can be taken as developed. However, in this case, ongoing maintenance and support will be a potential issue as internal staff may not have the technical knowledge to support these activities.

PROJECT MANAGEMENT

Project management competence is an important factor when considering acquisition strategy. Both custom development and outsourcing require highly skilled and organized project managers to ensure that the myriad of requirements and considerations are met throughout the development process. However, if strong project management is lacking, purchased solutions can provide these skill sets to ensure successful system implementation.

Even when considering custom development and outsourcing, the characteristics of the project manager will require consideration. If there is a high level of competency in contract negotiation and vendor management, outsourcing may be more attractive as it can save time and cost. However, if the project manager lacks these skills, custom development may lead to a more positive result.

TIME FRAME

The time frame may sometimes take precedence over qualifications. If an organization has the capability to internally develop, but the time allocated is not sufficient, purchasing or outsourcing may need to be considered. When each acquisition strategy is compared from strictly a timing perspective with the expectation that all other aspects of the specific strategy will go as planned, the purchase is the least time-consuming, outsourcing is the second quickest, and custom development is the slowest.

Time frame requirements can easily sway a systems analyst from one strategy to another, and rightly so. Time is a primary component for project success in many circumstances and, as such, will often be given precedence. However, it is still important to gauge all the influence categories to ensure that time-based pressure does not result in an acquisition strategy selection that is doomed to fail.

Selection

With all the variations of influence factors that are contained within a development project, how is it even possible to decide on a final course of action? As stated previously, especially in large-scope projects, there may not be a single acquisition strategy that fits the entire new system development. Components of the new system may have to be broken down by competency, complexity, differentiation requirements, and even time allocation. Then, each component will need to be analyzed for the best development strategy. This can easily result in projects that will incorporate all three acquisition strategies in combination to achieve a successful result.

Even in situations where the entire solution can be built internally, the systems analyst must ask the question of what is the most efficient and effective course. Simply having the internal resources and even the bandwidth does not mean that in-house development makes the most sense. Development projects are rarely completed singularly, and the systems analyst owes it to the organization to do as much due diligence as necessary to ensure that the system is developed comprehensively, efficiently, and cost-effectively.

To accomplish this, even small-scale projects should be analyzed against all three acquisition strategies to select the most appropriate path forward. This means that while analyzing internal capability, the systems analyst must also look for external resources in the form of available solutions and outsource partners. This will allow the systems analyst to develop each acquisition strategy and, therefore, be able to compare the positive and negative components of each method on the project as a whole. Additionally, this allows for the analysis of whether it is more appropriate to break the project down into specific development areas of focus and use multiple acquisition strategies.

Not only should the acquisition strategies be compared, but there should be an analysis of vendor partners used for each strategy as well. Multiple vendors should always be researched for each acquisition strategy, and therefore, being able to compare vendor responses is important. To accomplish these tasks, it is important for the systems analyst to develop standardized project requirements that can be distributed to multiple vendors. Ensuring that each vendor obtains the same requirements will allow for a more accurate comparison of differing vendor quotes. The tool that many systems analysts used to develop this standardized document is the **request for proposal (RFP)**.

While the RFP will assist in ensuring that consistent project requirements are distributed to potential vendors for analysis, allowing for the selection of the most appropriate vendor per acquisition strategy, there is still the requirement to compare the acquisition strategy developments themselves against one other to determine the most appropriate acquisition strategy to use. Just as the RFP is a tool for vendor comparison, there is also a tool that systems analysts use for acquisition strategy method comparison, the **alternative matrix**. The alternative matrix will take the strengths and weaknesses identified in each strategy development and tabulate them to demonstrate which strategy has the highest level of competency and, therefore, the best chance for success.

So, how is the system acquisition strategy determined? The answer is to develop an analysis of each strategy as it relates to your specific project. Determine the most appropriate course of action and, when necessary, the best vendor to assist. Finally, compare each strategy development against each other and select the one that ranks the highest. Whether done for the entire project or component by component, the end result will be an acquisition strategy that is developed to provide the greatest potential for project success.

REQUEST FOR PROPOSAL

Image 7.5

An RFP is a document that will be used by solicited vendors in order for them to analyze their ability to support the project and, if they are able to do so, ultimately create a quote for their services. While it sounds like a simple enough process, the ability of a vendor to effectively understand your project needs and identify areas of concern can be challenging. Additionally, it can prove difficult to provide a realistic estimate of the effort (cost) to complete the project. The ability of a vendor to complete these tasks effectively is directly proportional to the amount of accurate and effective detail that is developed within the RFP itself.

The RFP needs to tell the full story of the development to be undertaken. It is important to **define your project and needs** to paint a picture of the full scope of work to be accomplished. Introduce the reader to both the history of your organization and the project itself to communicate the reason for the development and the level of importance to the organization. **Document all of the project requirements** to ensure that there can be an assessment of capability by the vendor. **Explain how the vendor should respond** so that each vendor development is uniform and can be compared with other vendor submissions. Oftentimes, this can be accomplished by creating a response template that guides the vendor to incorporate specific information in a specific way. Outline your **selection criteria** and your **time line**, so there is no question of what the vendor must agree to in order to be considered.

By putting effort and thought into your RFP, you are positioning assessed vendors with every opportunity to present you with proposals that are comprehensive and meaningful. This is exceedingly important, as this will be the foundation of the vendor relationship should you determine to partner with them. While they must hold up to what they agreed to, your RFP must hold up to all the challenges they will encounter in the actual development of your new system.

ALTERNATIVES MATRIX

An alternative matrix (Table 7.1, p. 148) is a chart that allows for the comparison of system development criteria as compared to the perceived importance of each criterion and the level to which each acquisition strategy can effectively meet each criterion. Put in more general terms, an alternative matrix will look at the feasibility analysis of each acquisition strategy. These feasibility groupings will be broken down into technical, economic, and organizational components.

For the project, the systems analyst will weigh each feasibility component by overall importance to the project. For example, a project that is extremely cost-constrained will put more importance on cost efficiency and, therefore, a higher weight on economic feasibility. Consequently, for this project, the weights may look like technical feasibility 20, economic feasibility 50, and organizational feasibility 30.

Next, the systems analyst will assign a score to each feasibility component for each acquisition strategy based on the degree to which that strategy is able to effectively meet the requirements of that strategy. So, for example, on a scale of 1 to 5, with 5 being the most appropriate, when analyzing the outsourcing strategy for the project, a systems analyst may say that its ability to meet the technical requirements is 5, economic requirements 1, and organizational requirements 2.

The scores are then factored in combination with the weights and finally totaled to get a total. The totals of each acquisition strategy are then compared, and the strategy with the highest number is determined to be the best option. Of course, it is important to state that the final outcome is only as accurate as the analysis that is put into the component development for each acquisition strategy. This is the only way that accurate weights and scores can be assigned to each component of the alternative matrix.

Chapter Summary

While the systems analyst and his or her project team are only just beginning the activities required to successfully design the new system, it is already apparent that a significant investment of time and effort is required. Just as with every previous phase of the SDLC, the level of detail and commitment to ensuring that every effort is made to enact all required due diligence when assessing both design requirements and acquisition strategy is critical to project success.

When it comes to designing the new system, developing the design requirements completely and fully understanding all the implications of each design decision will greatly strengthen the quality of the new system construction. The acquisition strategy is truly the foundation of the design and cannot be accurately selected without both a firm understanding of design requirements and a comprehensive analysis of the potential incorporation of each strategy as the designation for system development. It is only through the development of each model that a comparison can be conducted and the most appropriate selections made.

This is a significant amount of effort being enacted by the development team prior to actually building the design specifications that will be used to physically construct the new system. However, if the systems analyst builds a faulty foundation, the resulting construction will most likely crumble. So every effort and consideration given to these tasks will pay off when actually developing the design specifications.

Project Planning Activities

1. Develop an RFP for vendor analysis.
2. Develop an alternatives matrix to better determine system acquisition strategy.

Table 7.1 Alternatives Matrix

Evaluation Criteria	Importance (Weight)	Alternative 1	Score 1–5	Weighted Score	Alternative 2	Score 1–5	Weighted Score	Alternative 3	Score 1–5	Weighted Score
Criteria 1	20	Info	3	60	Info	1	20	Info	5	100
Criteria 2	10	Info	2	20	Info	2	20	Info	3	30
Criteria 3	30	Info	4	120	Info	1	30	Info	2	60
Total	100			200			70			190

Image Credits

IMG 7.1: Copyright © 2016 Pixabay/geralt.
IMG 7.2: Copyright © 2014 Pixabay/geralt.
IMG 7.3: Copyright © 2016 Pixabay/Jirehg.
IMG 7.4: Copyright © 2019 Pexels/ThisIsEngineering.
IMG 7.5: Copyright © 2016 Depositphotos/Bakhtiarzein.

CHAPTER 8

Design Development

Introduction

Now that the project team is able to determine the appropriate acquisition strategy for acquiring the new system, the next step is to create the instructions for the development team to actually be able to facilitate the new system acquisition objective. To do so, the systems analyst will guide their team through the process of defining all necessary components of the new system, designing the required specification documents for both hardware and software requirements, developing interface designs to facilitate user-system interactions, and compiling all of these developments into the final system specification document.

The system specification will become the guide to which the project team will actually build the new system. Based on the acquisition strategy chosen, these tasks may include product selection, vendor instruction, or specifications for custom development. Regardless of the acquisition strategy or strategies employed, the system specification will be the road map that will finally bring the new system from concept to creation. The successful completion of the system specification will also mark the completion of the design phase of the SDLC and the transition to the implementation phase.

Learning Objectives

1. Describe the required components of a technology system.
2. Explain architectural design considerations.
3. Explain how nonfunctional requirements affect architectural design.
4. Explain the importance of user interface design.
5. Explain the incorporation of user perspective in user interface design.
6. Create a user interface design.
7. Create a hardware and software specification.
8. Create a system specification.

Image 8.1

Architecture Design

Architecture design is the process of correlating the software components of the system to the hardware components that will run them. This process must take into account many factors for the system construction to be successful. Initially, every component that makes up the new system's complete software development must be fully understood to most appropriately define how it will be implemented in the physical environment. The physical environment is represented by the hardware selected to "bring the software to life" or act as the medium between the software and the end user. The hardware is also broken down into primary components that each function in such a way as to support the software's intended utilization. Additionally, operational factors surrounding the interaction between the hardware and software components based on both functional and nonfunctional requirements are factored in as well.

The software aspect of a technology system architecture is broken down into four basic functions. **Data storage** defines how the data is to be stored at rest in the system. **Data access logic** defines what is required to access the stored data. That is to say, what processing requirements must the system have to effectively use the data contained within the system's data storage? The **application logic** is the process that the software is designed to complete. This is a culmination of the logic defined in the functional requirements and highlighted in both the use cases and design flow diagrams. Finally, the **presentation logic** defines how the information is displayed to the user and how the user's commands are interpreted. Essentially, the presentation logic is the definition of the system's user interface.

The hardware aspect of the technology system architecture is broken down into three basic functions. The **servers** are the devices that store the software and data. These devices can be used for a single purpose or configured to be used for multiple purposes. That is to say, a single hardware server can be matched to one function of the software development or multiple based on nonfunctional requirements. The **client devices** are the devices that interact with the users. They present data from the software to the user and receive input from the user that is processed by the software. Both functional and nonfunctional requirements will be used to select the appropriate client device to be used for the system. The **network** is comprised of the devices that connect the servers and client devices together. The network consists of components, such as switches, wireless access points, and cellular routes, whose purpose is to appropriately transmit data from one hardware component to the next. Once again, both functional and nonfunctional components will factor into the most appropriate selection of network components.

Architectural Components

To better understand the importance of correctly aligning both the functional and nonfunctional requirements to both software and hardware component design, each architectural component must be looked at in more detail.

SOFTWARE

The software is the heart of the system. It is the facilitator of how the data is used and, therefore, defines how the necessary processes are completed. As such, the software is key to ensuring that the system is not only producing the necessary output that is anticipated by the user but is doing so as efficiently as possible. To best ensure that this is the case, each software component must be designed to all the functional and nonfunctional requirements developed in the analysis phase. This will position the new system to produce the expected results.

Software can be written in many ways. A single application may contain all the functions required for the new system. This means that all the coding for processing data, storing data, and interfacing with both users and hardware are programmed as a single development with all the application components contained within a single framework. This type of development is common in small- to midsized application development projects.

For more complex systems or even for multiple smaller systems that are to be developed using similar components, a different approach may be used. For example, two systems that will complete different processes but will share the same user interface design, breaking out the software components into separate applications to be developed independently and then combined to create the new system, are preferred. The way in which software development is broken down in order to be developed can be varied based on a number of factors. Some factors include code reuse, developer aptitude, nonfunctional system requirements, and even the type and size of data that is to be used by the system.

The many ways that software can be developed to meet not only current system development goals but also future system development strategy is both diverse and also lends software design to having its own set of architectural design considerations. Only by understanding all the demands and constraints on not only the current system being developed but also future developments that may benefit from a specific development strategy can the systems analyst determine the best method for software creation.

Data Storage

Data storage, at first glance, seems somewhat simplistic. Many assume that data at rest is the least technical aspect of a technology system. However, this would be very inaccurate. There are a multitude of factors to consider in order to design accurate data storage components in a new system. If software is the heart of the system, data is the blood. It is the ultimate reason why every other system component is developed and is the cornerstone for the justification of the system development itself, ensuring that data is available when needed and able to be referenced, altered, created, and deleted not only successfully but also to meet the needs of all established constraints dictated by both functional and nonfunctional requirements.

In even simple systems, there is often a need for multiple different data storage methods to be employed. Take, for example, an ATM machine. Cardholder data is stored at the associated banking institution and must be accessed by the software via communication channels. However, a record of each transaction is maintained by the machine as well. This data is stored in a transaction file on the machine itself. The requirements for each data type are different. The cardholder data must be accessed quickly, and as the transaction is multistep, it must also act as a communication with data going back and forth multiple times. The transaction record, on the other hand, is only used as a future reference of the transaction. Therefore, it only needs to be written to the file once the transaction is complete. It also doesn't need to be accessed, so constant communication between the transaction file and the system is not necessary. This example demonstrates the consideration that each data storage component must take into account to ensure that data is designed to meet process requirements is essential.

Another factor that will influence data design is data security. Not all data needs to be secured in the same manner. There are varying levels of confidentiality when it comes to a system's data, and determining security requirements for each data type will allow the systems administrator to design data storage structures that not only facilitate operational efficiency but also data security requirements. It is important to understand that data security and data agility can often be at odds. The more secure the data is, the slower that data is to access and use. Even if the lag in data access speed is in milliseconds, this can have overall reduced system performance consequences as related to a nonsecure system. So, ensuring that data security needs are well defined and designed is imperative to ensure that the system is not only usable but also protects the organization.

One activity that is completed by the project team during data storage design is the construction of the **physical data model** or physical ERD. The physical data model takes the logical ERD developed in the analysis phase of the SDLC and adds references as to how the data will be stored in the system. Essentially, the following changes are made to the logical ERD:

1. Entity names are changed to file or table names
2. Attribute names become field names
3. The primary key field is identified
4. The foreign key field is identified
5. Field type and size are added

Data Access Logic

Data access logic has already been touched upon in the example given when discussing data storage. That is to say, data access logic is the design of how the data will be transmitted to and from data storage and the application. As previously defined, speed and reliability are nonfunctional requirements that will certainly impact how the data access logic is designed. However, there are also many other factors as well.

It has been shown that not all data is used the same way within a system. Therefore, not all data needs to be accessed in the same way. Understanding the way each piece of data is used will greatly assist in determining the most appropriate way to access it. To make this objective manageable, the systems analyst will group like data into data objects and define access logic based on the object as a whole. For example, customer information may need to be constantly accessed by the application for a retail sales application. Even though not every single piece of customer data is used in these application interactions, the data will be grouped together, and the access logic will be developed for the group. This not only keeps the design organized but also ensures that functional and nonfunctional requirements developed for data access are applied.

Data access logic design ensures that data objects are made available to the application in such a way as to allow for successful data utilization. Even in small systems, multiple data access logic developments are reasonable, as data objects will have varying requirements that need to be met.

Application Logic

The application logic design component has also been touched upon in the software discussion. The demonstration of consideration that must be undertaken when defining how the software will be constructed is directly correlated to the design of the application logic. Application logic design takes into account the modules to be developed, the granularity to which each development must be defined, the responsibilities of each module, and even the potential reuse of the developed module in both the current system and additional corporate systems.

When considering application logic design, the systems administrator must consider the **purpose** of the module, the **audience** to which the design will be provided, the **content** of the module itself, and the **naming** of the module in order to provide clarity of purpose. All of these consideration factors, coupled with the alignment of the application logic to defined functional and nonfunctional requirements, will ensure that the application is developed in the most appropriate method(s) for successful system operation.

Presentation Logic

Presentation logic is the basis for defining the interactive experience between the user and the new system. In essence, presentation logic design is the focus of defining how the information is presented to the user as effectively and efficiently as possible. Everyone who has ever used a technology system has had exposure to presentation logic design.

All of us have had varying degrees of success interacting with technology systems. Some systems seem very intuitive, and the placement of the system data is well thought out and useful to the user. Other systems are seen as lacking in one or more of these areas. Effective presentation design development is critical for new system success. The application can be the best development ever created, but if it is not presented to the user in an understandable and effective manner, the capabilities of the system will appear less than adequate. Conversely, if the user feels that the data presentation is well thought out and intuitive, both their desire to use the new system and trust in its capabilities are likely to increase.

Understanding what the user expects the system to do for them is not sufficient enough to design effective presentation logic. The systems administrator must also understand how the user expects to view the data itself. This is important from both the perspective of data display and data entry. Effective user interaction assists in defining system success, and the presentation of user data is a primary component of how effective the user interaction will be.

HARDWARE

Hardware is a critical component of an effective technology system. Each system will differ in requirements for what specific hardware is required; however, there are three main categories of hardware that are often deployed. These categories consist of **client devices**, **servers**, and the **network hardware** that connects the two. While there are applications that are built solely for client computing devices, such as mobile phones, laptops, or even appliances with digital components, the vast majority of technology systems incorporate more than a single piece of hardware in order to function, and as such the interdependence of these components must be fully understood.

Client Devices

Image 8.2

Client devices are technological devices that are used to access and interact with the technology system. Essentially, the client device is the hardware component that implements the presentation logic in order for the user to interact with the system and its data. While client devices used to encompass a rather narrow defined set of devices—namely, computers, workstations, or terminals, today, they have expanded into a vast amount of "connected devices." With the advent of the Internet of Things, client devices range from cell phones to washing machines and every piece of technology in between. If a device allows for the receipt and/or input of data, it can be considered a client device.

The systems analyst must first ensure that the client device selected for the new system is appropriate to meet both the functional and nonfunctional requirements of the system. Secondarily, if no current client device exists, then the systems analyst must consider developing new hardware in order to meet the demands of the new system.

Ensuring that the client device chosen most accurately implements the presentation logic is essential. As this is the hardware the user will interact with, being able to operate it effectively and intuitively is very important.

Servers

While client devices have become seemingly infinite in today's technological environment, this hardware diversification has been made possible, in part, due to a decrease in the amount of computing power that these devices require. This is facilitated by the use of servers. Servers are hardware components that contain the application logic. Essentially, these devices run the application processes, accessing and manipulating the system data, coupled with transmitting data to and from the client devices, in order to complete the functional requirements of the system.

As these devices complete the "heavy lifting" of the system or, in other words, leverage large amounts of computing power in order to complete digital tasks, this allows for the client devices to be far less sophisticated. Servers play a vital role in a technology system. They must be designed to meet all the system's functional and nonfunctional requirements and structured to ensure that they are supporting the new system as effectively and efficiently as possible.

Just as in other aspects of system design, servers can be leveraged in different ways. A single server can be designed to run the entire new system. In this instance, the data storage, data access logic, and application logic will all be designed on this single piece of hardware. While this may be possible for small or even some mid-level systems, server hardware has nonfunctional limitations in which not every system can be developed in this way.

Just as software design can be partitioned, so can server utilization. In larger or more complex systems, multiple servers will be employed. Take, for example, data storage. Multiple servers may be used to store various data types for the new system. Additional servers may be used for access logic and application logic. Even these aspects of the new system may be spread across multiple servers.

The degree to which multiple-server devices will need to be used will be correlated to the software design decisions and the nonfunctional requirement definitions as they pertain to the limitations of the server hardware. Aligning these requirements and device limitations will allow the systems analyst to define a server structure that is most appropriate for the new system.

Network Hardware

Image 8.3

The roles of client devices and servers are essential for new technology systems to function. By focusing design efforts on each component, the effectiveness of the overall system is able to be enhanced. However, both of these components have a cornerstone reliance on the ability of the data to be transported between them. It is this function that network hardware is essential to ensuring overall new system success.

Network hardware is the set of physical devices that are essential for interaction between client devices and servers. These devices are diverse in their utilization and purpose, and often, a combination of network hardware is used in new system development. For example, a new system may require servers to communicate between themselves and are located in the same data room. As they are in the same physical space, network switches with physical network cables are employed to facilitate this communication. However, the client devices are all remote and installed in vehicles. Cellular modems are, therefore, used to connect the client devices to the servers. While this is one small example, the importance of network hardware design is paramount to ensuring each hardware component of the new system can communicate as required.

Network hardware is becoming more diverse every day. Advancements in wireless technology, faster-wired technology, and even more rapid buildout of communication infrastructure all play a part in defining new methods of possible hardware communication strategies for new systems. Employing the right network hardware to meet both functional and nonfunctional system requirements is critical to ensuring the effectiveness of the new system.

Client-Server Architecture

Through understanding the basic hardware components of a technology system, you begin to see the development of the client-server architecture. This architecture depends on the design and implementation of client devices, servers, and network hardware in order to successfully build the new system. Each component works in strictly defined roles to complete the functional requirements of the system.

The client devices interact with the user. Displaying system information and receiving user input. These devices will have varying degrees of intelligence developed. This means that in some instances, these devices will simply display what the server presents to the user and transmit what the user inputs to the server. In other instances, application logic will be developed on the client device so that processes can be completed independently of the server and then periodically sent to the server once completed.

The degree to which processes are developed on the client device will affect the amount of computing power the device itself must have. However, in this architecture, the vast majority of the application logic is designed and implemented to be completed on the server or servers themselves. This is because these devices are developed to contain the majority of the computing resources to effectively store and process data.

The networking devices are used to facilitate data communication between the client devices and the servers as well as between the servers themselves. The networking devices will take into account the geographic, physical, and functional data communication constraints to define the most adequate component technologies to be employed—for example, fiber versus cellular versus coax cable versus network cable communication infrastructures. In many systems, a single communication infrastructure is not sufficient, and therefore multiples will be employed. Each communication infrastructure requirement will affect the network hardware components selected.

Client-server architectures are widely used in many technology system developments as they allow for flexibility of hardware configuration. Additionally, this architecture supports the ability to right size each component to its intended purpose and establish functional and nonfunctional requirements. However, there are some issues with client-server architectures. As the development is structured to and dependent upon understanding the anticipated system workload, unpredictable workloads can create challenges for certain system components.

Mobile Application Architecture

Image 8.4

While it is true that a mobile device can be classified as a client device, the operating systems these devices use put unique constraints on developing new solutions for them and, therefore, have resulted in the development of a unique mobile application architecture. Mobile application architecture refers to the rules, techniques, and processes required when developing mobile applications.

The two primary operating systems for mobile devices are Android and Apple's iOS. Each operating system has developed over time to create rules and standards for developing on each platform. As you are likely to assume, there are differences in regard to these rules and standards between the operating systems, and this must be taken into account when considering mobile application development. In fact, there are many considerations to be made regarding the incorporation of mobile application development with your system.

Perhaps the first consideration is if your application can be consolidated to either Android or iOS. If this is possible, then the design requirements will be simplified to that of a single mobile architecture. If both operating systems must be incorporated, the system architecture must incorporate the constraints of each operating system. As one can imagine, this can make for a much more complex solution development.

In order to understand the complexities, one must understand the high-level definition of each operating system's architecture. Android applications are developed in Android-supported languages like Kotlin and Java and must support devices from a variety of device manufacturers. iOS, on the other hand, is strictly for use by Apple products and is developed using Object-C and Swift programming languages. As you can see already, a single application development is not possible, as different programming languages must be used.

To develop mobile applications that can be developed singularly and deployed to both operating systems, a hybrid mobile application architecture has been developed. This architecture consists of developing native apps as "shells" for the back end. However, the front end is developed using JavaScript, HTML, and CSS, which are platform-neutral. This front-end development then leverages vendor-supported plugins to access native platform features for each operating system.

With the complexity of cross-platform development required to successfully use the vast majority of mobile devices as client devices in the new system, it is not surprising that this design requires its own architecture. However, with the vast availability of these devices to the public, working through the development complexities has the potential to result in the new system having a client device component that is far-reaching and ultimately cost-effective. The new system interacting with the user on a device that they are comfortable with and already own has many potential advantages.

Virtualization

Just as mobile application architecture plays a part in user device design strategy, so too does virtualization play a part in server design strategy. Server virtualization is the process of dividing a physical server device into multiple unique virtual servers. Each virtual server can be used by the new system in the same way that a physical server device can be. Virtualization is powerful as it allows for increased server utilization at a decreased cost. This is because there is no longer a correlation between the number of servers and the number of purchased physical devices. While this used to be a one-to-one correlation, it now becomes possible for a many-to-one relationship.

Virtualization certainly provides for a more cost-effective multiple-server system architecture. However, there are additional benefits related to virtualization as well. Historically, physical servers were overprovisioned, meaning that the computing power in the physical device was more than the application being run on it. This was to ensure that the device could handle the workload of the developed system. Most often, the end result was computing power not being used over the life of the system. Virtualization allows for more efficient partitioning of physical resources, ensuring that each physical device is actually using the computing resources to its fullest potential.

Virtualization also allows for an increase in system redundancy. Historically, if a server had a hardware failure, the system component contained on that server would be unavailable until either the hardware was fixed or replaced. However, due to virtualization and with the assistance of software that manages virtualization, when hardware becomes inoperable, the virtual servers can automatically be moved to other hardware within the system. This allows for the entire system to remain active even when hardware failure is encountered. It is important to note that a reduction in physical server resources can result in less than optimal system performance. However, most organizations would prefer a system running slower than to be unavailable altogether.

Virtualization has become a powerful tool in new system architecture design. It allows for more powerful system architectures to be deployed at less cost. Couple this with increased system redundancy, and it is no surprise that many technology development teams have incorporated virtualization as a primary component of their new system design.

Cloud Computing

Image 8.5

Cloud computing is a phrase that has become very popular in the technology industry. Many look at cloud computing as magic in that there appears to be an unlimited amount of computing power available to a development team, with the main constraint simply being cost. However, cloud computing is not mysterious or magical at all. Cloud computing is essentially server virtualization on a much larger scale.

Cloud computing providers maintain massive data centers with large numbers of physical servers. Each server is virtualized into a number of virtual servers. The entire development is then connected to an extremely fast networking infrastructure that allows for resource access globally. The provider then sells virtual server space to organizations looking to develop or house technology solutions. Instead of the organization's server infrastructure being physically contained and, therefore, maintained by the organization, it is simply accessed through the provider.

Cloud computing allows organizations to remove themselves from having to purchase and maintain physical data centers either in totality or for new system development. There are many potential benefits related to this architecture. Less effort needs to be spent on the right sizing server requirements for system development. If a system requires additional server resources, the organization can simply purchase more from the provider. Additionally, locally hosted servers come with considerations regarding remote access and availability. If the server infrastructure already exists online, then theoretically, it is much more simplistic to access it from anywhere in the world.

For all the potential benefits, cloud computing is not without risks or limitations. For one, the availability of the servers is limited to the organization's access to the Internet. Especially in times of natural disasters, external Internet connectivity disruptions can result in complete system unavailability. Additionally, sensitive corporate data is being stored on another organization's hardware. While cloud computing providers will make attestations regarding data security, security compromise is always possible. Add to this that while a threat actor may not be specifically looking for your data but going after another organization's data contained in the cloud service provider's environment, once that environment is compromised, your data is compromised as well.

Cloud computing is an important architecture design component to consider when designing a new system. By understanding the strengths and weaknesses of this architecture, the systems analyst can determine if the new system will ultimately benefit from cloud computing utilization or not.

Hardware and Software Specification

Now that there is a better understanding of all the components of the system architecture, it is more clearly seen that hardware and or software acquisition may very well be required for system development. It is for these instances of component acquisition that the systems analyst will require the development of hardware and software specification documents. The purpose of these documents is to communicate project needs. Not only will this facilitate a better understanding of the needs of vendors, but it also allows the project team to turn over acquisition tasks to the organization's purchasing department in some instances.

For both hardware and software specifications, it is important to include key pieces of information so that the most aligned solution may be acquired. The more robust the specification document, the more information that can be taken into account when completing acquisition assessments both from the organization and vendor perspectives. For each component to be acquired, the project team will construct a list of requirements that must be met. For example, if software needs to run on the Windows operating system, this will be noted. If a laptop needs to have a cellular modem, this also will be noted. These details are the bare minimum information required to ensure that the appropriate solution is sourced.

However, as we have seen throughout the development process, the more information provided, the more assessments that can be completed, and ultimately, the best selection can be made. Therefore, the hardware and software specification document will benefit from including additional information as well:

1. Introduction Section

    a. Purpose of the required component
    b. Intended audience meant for the specification document
    c. Definitions and acronyms for industry or organizational language contained within the document
2. Description Section
    a. User needs for the component
    b. Assumptions and dependencies for component integration
3. System Features and Requirements Section
    a. Functional requirements of the component
    b. Nonfunctional requirements of the component
    c. System features required of the component
    d. External interface requirements of the component

By developing hardware and software specifications to a greater extent, the project team is positioning the vendors to be able to put forth their best products to meet the demand. This will assist in selecting system components that will meet all the functional and nonfunctional requirements of the system, as well as ensure that competing technology benefits can be reviewed and the best selection made.

User Interface Design Development

Now that the physical infrastructure of the new system has been assessed and is able to be fully designed, the next priority is developing the user interface. The user interface is the connection between the user and the system, and it is imperative that all the functionality of the system not only be brought out to the user but done so in such a way as to ease the use of the system and provide the maximum benefit possible to the user.

User interface design is not only a function of bringing the presentation logic to life but doing so in a creative, cohesive, and intuitive way so as to enhance the user's experience with the functionality of the new system itself. Doing so is a challenge of not only assessing data placement on the client device but also considering details and aspects of the user environment that may assist or hinder the user's utilization of the system. For example, if a user must enter numbers into the system, displaying a number pad on the client device is a good user interface design choice. However, if the user is wearing thick work gloves and needs to input a number, displaying a large format number pad on the client device that takes into account the thickness of the gloves and minimizes incorrect number selection is an optimal choice.

Looking at every aspect of not only how the system and user need to interact but also all of the external conditions in which the user operates is going to provide the strongest basis for user interface design that is not only functional but appreciated. These are the aspects of user interface design that must be assessed:

1. Layout
2. Aesthetics
3. Usage
4. Consistency

5. Minimization of user effort

Layout

Image 8.6

When considering the layout of the user interface, the systems analyst must consider how the user will successfully interact with the system. When you consider how technology systems are structured from the user's perspective, there are four design elements that must be considered.

The first element of user interface functionality is **navigation**. These are the components of the user interface that allow the user to traverse the system. Whether it be menu by menu, page by page, or the use of slide bars, search fields, or back arrows, even simple systems will have more data than can be displayed in a single screen view. How the user gets from one object to the next must be thoughtfully considered and positioned. Simply having these elements is not sufficient. Placement of them in locations that are easy to find and use is paramount for a user to feel comfortable going from one portion of the user interface to the next.

The next element related to interface functionality is **input controls**. User interfaces are about displaying information to the user and receiving information from the user. Input controls consist of items such as text fields, checkboxes, buttons, or even image or voice prompts. Fully understanding how the user needs to interact with the system and developing input elements that allow for ease of communication is important.

Informational components must also be considered in terms of layout development. Everyone has used a system that simply appears to be stuck. There is no indication that anything is happening. These situations can lead to users taking action that can be detrimental to system process completion. The incorporation of items such as progress bars and pop-up windows allows for the system to communicate with the user and minimize unintended user interaction. These items also provide relief to the user by him or her knowing that the system is operating as intended during periods of little to no user and system interactions being undertaken.

Finally, **containers** assist in content organization by arranging content in easily digestible sections. This layout item is often preferable to endlessly scrolling down a single page, especially when the user has time constraints or requires a quick lookup of specific data. Incorporating containers into the user interface allows for a much more organized presentation of large amounts of data to the user.

Aesthetics

While the layout of the user interface is important, the aesthetics will often impact the user's perception of the effectiveness of the interface to an even higher degree. It is important to understand that how a user interface is presented will go a long way to either inviting the user to interact with the system or repelling them altogether. Not only must the user interface be functional, but it also has to be inviting. Think about applications you yourself gravitate toward. What are your thoughts on their appearance? How much does that factor into your perception of the overall quality of the application? It is interesting to consider just how much we, as individuals, associate welcoming imagery and data presentation with quality development.

Color and pattern choice are also aesthetic components that have a realized effect on user acceptance of the new system. Certain color combinations can make it difficult to look at the application, especially for long periods of time. Background patterns can either highlight information or detract from it. Additionally, while some of these combinations may simply not be pleasing to users, others can be in violation of the American Disabilities Act requirements.

The project team must ensure that the screen space available is best used. Information overload can give the perception of disorganization and ineffectiveness. Also, font choice and size can factor into user perception of the overall aesthetic. Clean and crisp information presentation will have a better user response than hard-to-read, small type. Additionally, users associate capitalization with yelling. While capitalization of every letter can be perceived as easier to read, it can be off-putting to many users.

Choices in how the system information is presented to the user are as important as ensuring the correct information is presented. If the user cannot effectively process what is displayed in front of them, they will not be able to gain the overall benefits of the new system.

Usage

A user's usage level of the new system is also a consideration that must be made for strong user interface design. If the system is to be used heavily by the user, they will become knowledgeable of layout components quickly. This user type will be focused on having components that enhance ease of use. Shortcuts, searches, and hot key incorporation are all items that this user type will appreciate and gravitate toward from a usability perspective.

Conversely, infrequent users of the system will focus more on quick and easy ways to figure out how to use the interface. Even if an infrequent user is trained on the new system, there is a good chance there are aspects of the user interface that they will forget or not be shown. Having integrated user assistance components will allow these users to be more self-reliant regarding successfully using the system. Intuitive menu design, well-thought-out help menus, and even informational pop-ups are all components that will assist this user type.

Whenever possible, the project team should ensure that the needs of both user types are met in the user interface development. That said, it is important to ensure that for both types, the appreciated components are user initiated. This will assist in ensuring that a heavy system user is not slowed down by receiving unnecessary assistance and that an infrequent user is not further confused by unintuitive shortcut functionality.

Consistency

Another key component of good user interface design is consistency throughout the application. Users are comforted by knowing where to look for interface components. Ensuring that each component exists in the same location as the user traverses the system is helpful in increasing comfortability with the system itself. Additionally, having the same look and feel on every menu or page will highlight the similarity of content arrangement. If the user can begin to establish an understanding of the form and function of the new system, ease of use will begin to increase for the user.

For consistency to be established in the user interface, the project group must take care to structure layout components across all aspects of the interface. This incorporates not only navigation controls but also presented terminology and even the standardization of form and report design. Interface aesthetics should also be incorporated on every menu or screen to ensure continuity of design presentation.

Minimization of User Effort

The key for a user interface to appear intuitive is to minimize the effort required by the user to interact with the system. The less interaction between the interface and the user, the greater the perception of the user will be influenced to view the application as easy to use. This will go a long way for overall user acceptance of the new system. Here are some recommendations for minimizing a user's cognitive effort when interacting with a user interface:

1. Keep the interface simple.
2. Provide quality feedback to the user.
3. Use visual hierarchy.
4. Use familiar patterns.
5. Reduce choices.

Reducing complexity related to the user's interactions with the system will greatly assist in the user viewing the new system as user-friendly. The ultimate measure of success between user and system user interface is the user believing that the system is intuitive and knows what they are looking for prior to them heavily interacting with the system itself. Minimization of user effort will greatly assist with users associating the interface as being intuitive.

User Interface Design Process

It is impossible to discuss user interface design without also discussing user experience. Historically, user interface design has focused on the visual and interactive elements of the new system that facilitate user interaction. However, looking at the cognitive components of a user's assessment as to the quality of a user interface design, these design elements must be paired with elements of a good user experience. Essentially, it evaluates how the interface provides an overall experience for the user. This assessment takes into account the user's emotions, perceptions, and responses when interacting with the interface.

By considering not just the functional interaction but also the emotional components of the user interaction, the project team can develop a user interface that not only meets the functional and nonfunctional requirements of the new system but does so in a way that the user appreciates the interactions with the system overall.

Understand the Users

In order to develop a user interface that appeals to the system users, it is imperative that the project team understand the users. This can be difficult, as different users will have different goals and intentions for system utilization. However, by interacting with multiple users and talking through expectations and perceived challenges, the project team will find commonalities in user expectations from which to develop. Additionally, these user interactions can be valuable for highlighting aspects of user interaction that may be segmented by job function and can point to interface developments that will be tailored to specific user group requirements.

If the project team is going to humanize the interface development, then it makes sense to develop user personas that develop characterizations of various user groups. These personas will integrate user interests, behaviors, goals, objectives, and expectations that can be expanded to a specific group of users. By aligning the user interface to the developed persona of each user group, the intended result is to provide a user experience that meets both the functional and emotional needs of the user.

In addition to incorporating user traits into the interface design, it is equally important to ensure the intended process completion is incorporated into the interface. The user interface can look visually appealing, but if the steps the user is expecting to complete are not aligned with how the interface operates, the user will lose faith in the system overall. Therefore, referring to the DFDs and building use scenarios that highlight the steps the user performs and then ensuring that the interface encapsulates both in the developed user interaction is key to overall interface acceptance by the user.

Organize the Interface

To this point, the components of the user interface have been discussed in detail. Now, they must all be assembled into a cohesive structure that the user can walk through in order to interact with the system. For this, it is important to organize all the components. This is accomplished by developing an interface structure diagram (ISD).

The ISD will demonstrate how all screens, forms, and reports contained within the system are related. By following the diagram, the project team can evaluate how the user moves from one interface component to the next. The ISD is similar to the DFD in that boxes are used to represent specific screens. Lines demonstrate the navigation from one screen to the next. The diagram, in totality, becomes a visual representation of the user's possible paths through the user interface.

The ISD equivalent for web development is the site map. The site map demonstrates the hierarchy of information on the site and can be used to complete user walkthroughs of the website navigation.

Both ISDs and site maps provide a visual representation of user navigation. This allows the project team to ensure that all user interface components are accessible by the user and that they are assessable via a logical path that will make sense to the user.

Define Standards

In order to achieve consistency across all components of the user interface, it is important to establish standards that are to be followed when developing each segment of the user interface. Some components of the interface need to remain the same across all menus or site pages. Other components can change. By looking at each developed interface component, assessing the level of change allowed, and recording the decision, the project group is essentially defining design standards for the user interface.

In order to best understand this process, let's look at an example. A project team is assessing the placement of a navigation bar that will allow the user to traverse from one screen to the next. The project group determines that for user acceptance, this item needs to always be located in the top right corner of the screen. They have just created a standard for the placement of the navigation bar throughout the entire interface. Conversely, the team is evaluating pop-up windows that provide tool tips. It is determined that as the user is initiating the pop-up to appear, there is no need to create a uniform size or location for the window. Therefore, the pop-up can be sized dynamically based on the amount of content contained within the window.

Defining standards for user interface design development will assist in ensuring that the user has a consistent and recognizable experience as they traverse from one component of the user interface to the next. However, this effort will also allow for dynamic development, where appropriate, to assist with enhancing data presentation as well.

Interface Design Prototyping

With the level of importance of creating a user experience that resonates with the user and assists in resulting in overall user acceptance, simply incorporating user analysis into the user interface design is not sufficient to guarantee success. Therefore, aligning the interface design with prototyping development is appropriate to determine what overall interface development will provide the greatest chance of user success.

User interface design prototyping can be accomplished in many ways, but three main categories of prototype development are common. These types consist of:

1. Diagrams
2. Storyboarding
3. Software

Diagrams

Diagram development as a form of user interface prototyping consists of developing diagrams that visually represent the screens, webpages, forms, or reports the user interface will use. These diagrams can be developed manually by sketching on paper or leveraging software to create wireframes or wireflow diagrams.

Regardless of the level of technology used to develop the diagram, the intended use is the same: to provide a visual representation of the interface to be developed and allow users to walk through the proposed development in order to ensure the process flow is accurately captured.

Storyboarding

Storyboarding is a prototyping method that requires the project team to develop the interface progression in the form of pictures. Each picture shows a step in the process that will be encompassed by the developed user interface. The purpose of each individual picture is to answer the why, what, and how of what is being done in the moment. While it may seem like a huge task to answer those questions with a simple picture, it has been stated that a picture can contain a thousand words. Therefore, the prevalent thought behind using storyboarding is that it can communicate much more information than diagraming alone. This is assuming that the pictures can be developed to a level that conveys all these components.

Software

Image 8.7

One of the most comprehensive and ever increasingly easy-to-use methods for prototyping user interfaces is through the aid of software. Software packages exist that allow a user not only to develop a user interface design mostly by point-and-click technology but also assemble the process flow of the system into the design. The end result is a prototype that looks and functions just as the project team intends to develop the actual user interface. This allows for not only a demonstration of the perceived interface but also the ability for the users to see and interact with the prototype as well. All this is completed well before the user interface is actually developed.

This method of prototyping is becoming increasingly popular, as it really brings to life the user interface and allows for user interaction ahead of development. Changes to the proposed design are easy to complete in the software, and the results of the changes are quickly available for assessment. While it still may make sense for diagraming and storyboarding in the early stages of user interface design, the utilization of software-assisted interface prototyping is the one clear way to actually bring your interface to life prior to development.

Interface Evaluation

Even with the power of software-aided prototyping, it is still essential to evaluate the user interface design development prior to actually creating the interface. There is always the possibility of mistakes in the development of the actual interface design. Additionally, aspects of the interface may have been missed in the prototype simulation that will come to light through enhanced evaluation of the developed interface.

There are multiple evaluation methods for reviewing user interface design. While not every method needs to be used for each interface development, it is common for multiple evaluation methods to be used in combination. The evaluation methods that will be looked at in more detail are as follows:

1. Heuristic evaluation
2. Walkthrough evaluation
3. Interactive evaluation
4. Formal usability testing

Heuristic Evaluation

Heuristic evaluation involves the comparison of the design development with that of the final user interface design. When the design development tasks are being completed, at points where the project team agrees on specific inclusions into the user interface design, these inclusions are recorded. Once all aspects of the user interface design have been developed, the inclusion items are used to create an interface design checklist.

At the completion of the final user interface design, the checklist is brought out, and each item is assessed to ensure that it was incorporated into the final interface design. Missing items are analyzed, and the design is altered to incorporate the missed component. When all of the checklist items are verified to be included in the user interface design, the design is approved to proceed to development.

Walkthrough Evaluation

Another evaluation technique used by project teams is walkthrough evaluation. Essentially, the team will refer to the user interface design and simulate a user's actions as they relate to the interface. Each user action is played out by the team as they walk through the entire interface.

Walkthrough evaluation techniques will often employ not only the developed user interface but also the DFD to provide process mapping for guidance on how the expected user interactions are to be ordered. The walkthrough will either verify that the user interface design meets the process flow requirements or that it does not. If there is a misalignment, the process is compared to the interface design, and required alterations to the interface design are made.

Interactive Evaluation

Interactive evaluation takes the walkthrough evaluation method one step further by employing actual system users to interact with the new interface design. Much like the walkthrough method, users are guided through each interface design component, and they are allowed to make assessments as to the level at which they feel the development meets their needs.

One of the challenges of interactive evaluation is that the user is getting a premature look at the user interface prior to it actually being developed. This can allow the user to develop preconceived notions as to the quality or lack of the new system being constructed. This has the potential to negate user support for the new system even before the new system is constructed. However, with that said, this method also allows for valuable user feedback to be taken into account. This can provide for design assessment and alteration that will better align the user interface to the needs of the user.

Formal Usability Testing

Formal usability testing requires the inclusion of trained inspectors who develop structured activities and define steps in order to ascertain if the developed user interface design is appropriately aligned with organizational and user requirements. This testing method is highly focused and specialized. However, because of the amount of effort required to develop and implement, it is also very expensive.

This method of testing is normally reserved for complex system development that places a high degree of importance on comprehensive user interface design as a primary component of new system success. This method of testing is costly and time-consuming and is not normally used in situations where other testing methods are deemed adequate.

System Specification

The system specification document is the culmination of the design phase activities. This document will act as the blueprint that the development team will use to construct the new system. All aspects of the new system design will be assembled in an inclusive document consisting of both an **introduction section** and a **system requirements section**.

The introduction section is meant to provide pertinent information regarding the system to be developed. The **purpose** of the project, **scope** of the new solution development, and **roles and responsibilities** of the project team are all included in this section. None of the information should have to be created but rather reiterated from previous developments.

The system requirements section of the system specification defines all the specifications developed in the design phase of the SDLC. The **functional specifications** section defines the following:

1. Functional system specifications
2. Software specifications
3. Hardware specifications

The **operating specifications** section defines the following:

1. Hardware environmental specifications
2. User characteristic specifications

The **security specifications** section defines the following:

1. Hardware security specifications
2. System security specifications
3. Network security specifications

The remaining specifications defined in the document are:

1. User interface specifications
2. Regulatory specifications
3. Manufacturer specifications
4. Data specifications
5. Infrastructure impact specifications

The development of the system specification document marks the culmination of the design of the new system. The project team will now present the development team with the completed specification documentation so that new system creation can begin.

Chapter Summary

The tasks required in the design phase of the SDLC are numerous and detail oriented. However, the development of the documents necessary to develop a new system acquisition strategy and then define the overall new system design is essential for ensuring the new system is constructed in such a way that the system requirements are fully met.

The hardware and software specification documents are critical to ensuring that sourced vendors are evaluated, and the most appropriate solutions are secured for system construction. The development of the user interface is critical to new system adoption by system users. The system specification document is the blueprint from which the development team will construct the new system. All of these developed components are essential for ensuring that the new system not only functions but functions to meet or exceed expectations.

Whether the construction of the new system is the assembly of purchased components, the development of new technology, or a combination of both, the efforts placed in completing the design tasks in the design phase of the SDLC will go a long way to ensuring that the project team is about to construct a new system that is both functional and intuitive. The efforts enacted on the new system development today will make the system construction that is about to happen in the first part of the implementation phase not only possible but successful.

Project Planning Activities

1. Create the physical data model.
2. Create the hardware and software specifications.

3. Create the user interface.
4. Create the system specification.

Image Credits

IMG 8.1: Copyright © 2018 Pexels/Christina Morillo.
IMG 8.2: Copyright © 2020 Pexels/Polina Zimmerman.
IMG 8.3: Copyright © 2016 Pexels/Pixabay.
IMG 8.4: Copyright © 2020 Pexels/Liza Summer.
IMG 8.5: Copyright © 2015 Depositphotos/scanrail.
IMG 8.6: Copyright © 2019 Depositphotos/VitalikRadko.
IMG 8.7: Copyright © 2014 Depositphotos/radoma.

CHAPTER 9

Development and Testing of the New System

Introduction

The time has finally come to construct the new system! By using the system specification document that was completed in the design phase, the systems analyst will now compile a development team that will actually construct the new system. Whether new system construction is the assembly of purchased products, custom development of hardware and software components, or a combination of both, the systems analyst still has a number of important tasks to complete in order to ensure that the new system is compiled effectively and efficiently.

Many people think of implementation as the initiation of the new system into the organization's technology environment. However, within the SDLC, implementation begins with the construction of the new system. While it is true that development resources will play a critical role in actually developing the new system, the systems analyst is not able to take a break from their responsibilities. Throughout the implementation phase, the systems analyst will play a critical role in ensuring that all the development resources remain on task and on schedule throughout the construction and testing of the implementation phase.

Learning Objectives

1. Understand the system construction process.
2. Explain various testing methods and when to use them.

Translating System Specification Into System Components

One of the very first tasks that must be completed in the implementation phase is translating the system specification document into actual development tasks. As we have seen in the design phase of the SDLC, there are a vast amount of components that make up a new system. The systems analyst will lead the development team in first breaking each system specification down into associated component requirements. For example, if a hardware specification dictates the need for a number of PCs to be required with a defined set of specifications, an acquisition resource must be assigned to source this equipment.

The systems analyst will lead the development team in systematically traversing the system specification document, identifying each required system component, and assigning the system component to a development resource. As you might expect, resource allocation management is imperative to ensure that development resources are not overloaded with development items. The project schedule clearly denotes the allotted time for new system construction, and all component development activities must fit within this pre-defined time frame.

One key to maintaining a balance between managing the project time line and managing a finite number of development resources is fully understanding the capabilities of each resource. Take, for example, a purchasing agent. He or she should be able to manage the sourcing of multiple pieces of equipment in a given time period. Having a clear understanding of just how many different pieces of equipment the purchasing agent can manage at one time will allow for efficient distribution of sourced system components. This logic remains true for all types of development resources, from contract negotiators to software developers. Knowing your team and their capacity limits will allow the systems analyst to distribute component development tasks in groupings that can be facilitated by each resource without overloading them.

The process of identifying and matching system components to system development resources takes a lot of knowledge of both what is required to develop each individual component as well as the strengths and weaknesses of each development resource. This is yet another area where the systems analyst will have to be enough of an expert on both in order to make these assessments.

The new system development is ready to begin once every specification has been analyzed, a resulting system component identified, and a resource assigned. At that time, the development schedule is analyzed to ensure that development resources are positioned to meet time-line requirements for component development. While this is just the beginning of system construction, the systems analyst will be tasked with a variety of management objectives throughout system construction to ensure that the project remains on schedule and the development is aligned to meet all the project requirements.

Managing New System Construction

While the systems analyst does not construct the new system themselves, they are still responsible for ensuring that the project is moving forward as expected. This means that not only is development occurring, but that it is on budget, on time, and meeting all the defined requirements. However, with the vast amount of resources completing multiple development activities in unison, how is it possible to assess progress and align to plan? The answer lies in organization, communication, and structure. The systems analyst must develop plans and initiatives that allow for assessment of current progress, analysis of the quality of work being completed, and allow for ample communication across all resources to ensure that everyone is on the same page regarding all aspects of the project.

In addition to management of the development resources, the systems analyst must also be aware of potential scope creep and development changes that often occur during system creation. As development resources are given guidelines in the form of system specifications, as opposed to step-by-step directions on what is to be created, there is a potential for component development that is altered by the developer from the original intended development. In some instances, this can enhance the overall solution, but in other instances, it can be a hindrance. Therefore, the systems analyst must make an effort to search out when development activities are diverging from the intended plan.

In order to better understand the areas of focus of the systems analyst during the construction of the new system, we will break down management responsibility into these classifications:

1. Risk management
2. Quality management
3. Activity coordination
4. Development schedule management
5. Meeting coordination

Risk Management

Image 9.1

System development, whether implementing purchased solutions or developing new ones, is comprised of many activities that can affect the organization in different ways. First and foremost are the activities focused on constructing the new system. Many resources will work on component development of the new system, and coordination of these activities is critical. If there is no assessment of each resource's efforts, it may become difficult to assemble each component into the final system successfully. Also, development estimations that are inaccurate will lead to time-line challenges that may not be able to be overcome. Changes to the original component development plans can lead to scope creep, challenging both the time line and budget of the project. While all these potential risks need to be understood and managed by the systems analyst, the new system construction is only one potential risk factor.

As we have seen from the new system design, there are many infrastructure components that are affected by the integration of a new system into the environment. Datacenters will often need to be altered or enhanced to meet the new system processing requirements. Changing the configuration of a data center can be risky. Even in a virtual environment, hardware additions and server reconfigurations can potentially interrupt core business functions.

Networking infrastructure is another area that is often impacted when a new system is introduced into an environment. As networking components are constantly being enhanced, it makes sense that developers will want to take advantage of newer technologies and push for networking alterations as a requirement of new system implementation. Just as with the data center, anytime a core networking hardware component is altered or replaced, there is the risk of downtime. Managed and communicated downtime is very manageable, but unexpected downtime from incorrect configuration, hardware failure, or even simply a longer transition time than anticipated can have adverse effects on the organization.

In some cases, completely new back-end infrastructures will need to be developed and integrated into the environment. This creates a potential risk of adverse consequences of legacy components not interacting as intended with the new infrastructure. This can sometimes lead to annoyances such as system slowdowns or critical issues like complete system failure.

Human resources are another risk factor that must be acknowledged. Project members may become unable to work for periods of time or may even leave the project mid-completion. Some resources can easily be replaced, while others, especially those with critical knowledge, may be difficult or impossible to replace. Ensuring that the human resource pool has enough depth to overcome these issues is a necessary function of the systems analyst.

Most new systems require some form of procurement. This places reliance on suppliers and, therefore, is another form of risk to be managed. Ensuring that component acquisition is facilitated along the project time line and cost requirements can be critical. Even when the best vendor partner has been selected, there can be unexpected issues that arise and must be handled. The systems analyst has to be ready for these unplanned occurrences and ready to support issue resolution in this area as well.

Communication challenges between development resources but also any parties associated with the new system construction can lead to both quality and productivity-related risks. Effective communication is often difficult but is essential during system construction. Each member of the development initiative, both primary and secondary, needs to be kept informed of project positioning, challenges, and change. Without effective communication, the risk of successful project completion exponentially increases.

Risk management is no small task the systems analyst must undertake throughout the implementation phase of the project. The key to success is to first understand the many facets of risk that may be encountered throughout the system development and implementation activities. Second, there needs to be the development of methods that will assess potential risk and allow for the development of a strategy that will mitigate said risk. In essence, the systems analyst must remain vigilant throughout the development process to proactively identify issues and work with his or her team to develop solutions when issues are encountered.

Quality Management

Along with overall risk management, there is a need to ensure special emphasis is placed on quality management. With all the potential for change throughout the new system development, there are significant opportunities for the quality of the final product to suffer. Therefore, the systems analyst must work on strategies to assess developmental efforts throughout the development and compare against key system components and functions in order to ensure that system quality is not being negatively affected. However, aligning the development to project requirements is only one facet of quality management.

Along with ensuring the development will operate as expected, there is a futureproofing component to quality management. In system development, there are best practice methods for both software creation and hardware incorporation. When development is conducted using best practices, it makes it easier to support. One reason for this is that support vendors who may be necessary to contract down the road if internal competencies are ever reduced will be better prepared to work with a solution that is developed as they would expect it to be. But what does "as they would expect it to be" mean?

When programming in specific coding languages, there are expected ways to write code, incorporate software libraries, document developed code, and assemble the developments into an application. The more the developers adhere to the expected development methods, the more understandable the development will be to a third party who might be brought in to support it one day. This same methodology holds true for all other aspects of new system creation. Hardware components will often have a generally acceptable utilization that, when followed, will be easier to support. Networking and communication components will be more understandable when they are implemented as expected.

System development is fascinating from the perspective that there are often a hundred different ways to get to an end result. However, some of those ways will be more effective than others. Whether it be from a time, cost, or, in this case, quality perspective, the systems analyst must be able to ascertain throughout the development areas where the current actions may have a negative impact on the overall quality of the development and be able to institute change to correct these actions.

Activity Coordination

When looking at what is required to manage risk and quality within a system development project, coordination of activities is shown to be a primary component. The diverse responsibility scope of resources throughout the development activities makes coordination of effort essential for forward progress. Coordination can be viewed as directing individual efforts toward achieving a common goal. In this instance, it's the development of the new system to meet all functional and nonfunctional requirements.

So, how does the systems analyst effectively coordinate project resource activities throughout development and implementation? It once again starts with effective communication. Setting formal meetings where information is exchanged and discussed is paramount. Based on the project size, one regularly scheduled meeting where all aspects of project development are discussed may be sufficient for small projects, whereas large projects may require multiple regularly scheduled meetings where each meeting is more focused. For example, a large project may require a weekly status meeting where each resource shares where they are in the project development, a weekly requirements meeting where the systems analyst will align efforts to both the development schedule and project budget, a weekly change management meeting where any required changes by development resources are highlighted and discussed to provide awareness to all project resources. While the content of each meeting is limited and focused, the overall project communication is diverse and cohesive.

In-person meetings are not always feasible or productive, so reporting is also a key factor in activity coordination. Status reports, challenge and roadblock reports, change requests and change reporting, budgetary reporting, resource allocation, both present and future reporting, and prioritization reporting are all communication developments that facilitate coordination.

Live dashboarding and key performance indicator incorporation are other toolsets that facilitate coordination. Sometimes, report distribution is too slow based on development speed requirements. Leveraging technology to communicate immediate requirements and focus initiatives can also be productive when it comes to the coordination of activities to immediate requirements. This method can also be interactive and allow collaboration between the project resources. However, when there is dynamic information sharing, there is also the risk of change incorporation, so this method needs to be monitored to ensure it is enabling coordination more so than enabling change and possible scope creep.

The key to coordination is awareness and communication. By incorporating both, the systems analyst can conduct development activities in much the same way a conductor conducts a symphony. In both instances, the result is music to the ears when completed successfully.

Budgetary Management

Budgetary control during system development is a required function of the systems analyst. With all the potential vectors for change during the development cycle, the potential for cost overruns is always a viable risk. Understanding where the project is positioned at the start of development and including cost forecasting in change management discussions are primary activities the systems analyst will undertake to ensure that the project budget remains a focus of the development team.

It is very easy for the development team to focus on the functional aspects of the system and look to enhance development through the alteration of the development plan. At times, change has the potential to strengthen the final product, but how change impacts the project constraints must always be factored in. If a requested change to the project scope may lead to a budgetary overrun, there needs to be discussion and approval of the additional spending. In some instances, even if the change has the potential to enhance the final product, it may be rejected due to budgetary constraints. The systems analyst is not responsible for making change decisions alone, but he or she is responsible for ensuring that actions that may have an impact on the defined budget are brought up for review so informed decisions can be made.

Project Schedule Management

As is demonstrated in every other management function, management of the project schedule is crucial to project success. All of the SDLC activities to date have led up to developing a schedule that is provisioned to provide the best chance of development success. It is now the responsibility of the systems analyst to ensure that this schedule is carried out as intended by the project resources.

Effective project management requires careful scheduling to ensure that tasks are completed on time, on budget, and of the highest quality. Additionally, this schedule will organize each task into not only the most efficient hierarchy for completion but also take into account dependencies so as to ensure that no task is completed before a related required task is completed. Additionally, this schedule will define what resources are to be working on what task, not only to ensure each task gets completed but to align resource strength with task completion demand.

All these reasons for schedule utilization have already been communicated previously in the SDLC; however, they are being restated to emphasize the importance of aligning the development to the schedule. The schedule was tailored to the new system development through painstaking analysis and design activities. It has been determined by the project team to be the best chance to successfully complete the project, and it is up to the systems analyst to ensure it is adhered to.

Meeting Coordination

As already established, one of the best ways to ensure compliance with the project schedule by the project team is through the coordination of regular meetings. Aligning meeting requirements to project schedule focus will ensure that the project schedule remains a primary focus of every project resource. As the project schedule is the primary guide to gauge development alignment to success, incorporating schedule components at every meeting reinforces its importance.

Effective Communication

TEAM COMMUNICATION

Image 9.2

Incorporating the project schedule into the meeting discussion is not sufficient to ensure that project resources are aligned with task requirements. The systems analyst must structure the meeting discussions to incorporate all the project schedule information into the conversation where appropriate. He or she must highlight where individual resources are supposed to be in their development cycle and encourage conversation to determine if this is the case or not. By using the project schedule as a tool for discussion of resource task positioning, it will become very clear to the development team if they are on schedule or need to exert additional effort to get back on schedule. Even in situations where there is diversion from the overall project plan, these discussions can facilitate changes to the overall plan with a focus on maintaining project success.

Even wIth all of the effort taken on schedule development to date, it is not to say that items will not come up during development that will require assessment of the current schedule and possible alteration. This is a realistic possibility for a number of reasons. However, it is important that the project schedule act as a guide and that any alterations to it be communicated to all project resources. Risk management, quality management, coordination, and, ultimately, project success depend on the adherence of the project team to the developed project schedule.

Managing Software Development

Internally developing new software has many advantages. However, in terms of managing the development process, there are many challenges that the systems analyst must be aware of in order to successfully manage the development of software that will be on time, on budget, secure, functional, and supportable in the future. While organizations that have internal software development capabilities are at an advantage from the perspective of knowing their development resources and capabilities, there are still a number of factors to consider when setting up the development strategy. Additionally, all the responsibility classifications that the systems analyst must adhere to in all other aspects of the new system development also apply to the software developers, and therefore, the structure must be enacted to facilitate managerial requirements.

When it comes to managing internal software developers, there are a few areas of consideration that the systems analyst can develop processes for in order to have the best chance of a successful development outcome. These areas of focus include the following:

1. Assigning developers
2. Defining milestones
3. Managing code review

Assigning Developers

When it comes to assigning developer resources to a software development project, one might consider that the more developers involved in the project, the better. It does stand to reason that the more the software development can be sectioned off, it should allow for more development to happen simultaneously and ultimately reduce development time. If time were the only factor, this theory would hold true. However, when it comes to software development, development time is only one factor.

Just as with every other aspect of system development, communication is a primary component of success. The more developers you have working on a project, the more communication paths need to be managed to ensure everyone is on the same page. However, when it comes to development, communication requirements are heightened. This is because work done separately needs to be combined in the end to form a cohesive system. However, software development requires that code be developed in such a way that the data can be worked with inconsistent methods. Therefore, software development requires consistent development methods that are only possible through developer collaboration. In essence, collaboration needs to be facilitated among every member of the development team.

Let's take a look at what these collaboration requirements mean when related to communication paths. If I have two developers, we will call them Developer A and Developer B. I only have two communication paths: Developer A can talk to Developer B, and Developer B can talk to Developer A. However, if I add two more developers to the project, Developer C and Developer D, the number of communication paths does not simply increase to four. With 4 developers, the number of communication paths actually increases to 12 paths. The paths are as follows:

1. A to B
2. B to A
3. A to C
4. C to A
5. A to D
6. D to A
7. B to C

8. C to B
9. B to D
10. D to B
11. C to D
12. D to C

This is important because the more communication paths, the greater the chance that communication gets missed, altered, or otherwise degraded. Communication is imperative for comprehensive software development, and the more communication paths, the more challenging it is to communicate effectively.

Along with communication considerations, the systems analyst must also take into account developer competencies. Many developers will focus on specific programming languages or technology developments. It is important to align developer strengths with software development requirements. By understanding what technologies are being incorporated and what developer characteristics will be important for each development role, these decisions can be made.

Once the appropriate number of developers has been determined and individual resources assigned based on competency, there are a few activities the systems analyst can conduct in order to provide the best chance for project success. These activities include the following:

1. Weekly meetings
2. Create standards
3. Develop change control mechanisms
4. Develop program log
5. Organize work areas

WEEKLY MEETINGS

From project initiation, it is important to schedule weekly meetings. These meetings do not need to be long in duration but should act as the conduit for maintaining both coordination of development activities as well as effectively communicating the current standing of each development resource and the development status as it relates to the development schedule.

CREATE STANDARDS

Ensuring that all the developers are clear on the aspects of their developments that must align in order for the final software solution to function is essential. By creating development standards that solidify these conditions and act as a guide for the developers it will set them up for the best chance of compiling each individual development into a final cohesive software solution. These standards should encompass all aspects of software development, ranging from variable assignment to programming language used. If an item is required in order for the code to be combined, then it must be included in the standards definition.

DEVELOP CHANGE CONTROL MECHANISMS

Change is a constant in software development and, therefore, must be managed. Ensuring that there are change control mechanisms in place is the best way to ensure that change awareness is propagated across all developer resources. Change control mechanisms include a structured process for developers to notify the systems analyst and development team of their belief change is required, a process for reviewing the proposed change, a process for accepting or denying the change request, and, finally, a process for updating all developer resources of the specifics of an accepted change. Change within a software development project must always be visible, considered, and communicated if the decision to allow the change is made.

DEVELOP PROGRAM LOG

Maintaining a program log will ensure that all accepted program changes are formally tracked. While ensuring that when change is accepted, it is communicated to all developers is important, it is also just as important to have a single source for all changes that can be referenced as necessary. The program log will not only act as a reference for accepted change but can be used to highlight software development changes that may be encountered as unapproved so corrective action can be taken against the responsible party.

ORGANIZE WORK AREAS

Software development requires collaboration to be effective. Organizing developer work areas to facilitate development, testing, and production activities is a good way to assist in keeping developers organized and on task. With the large amount of software components being developed and assembled, structured organizational activities, such as defined work areas, can be very beneficial.

Defining Milestones

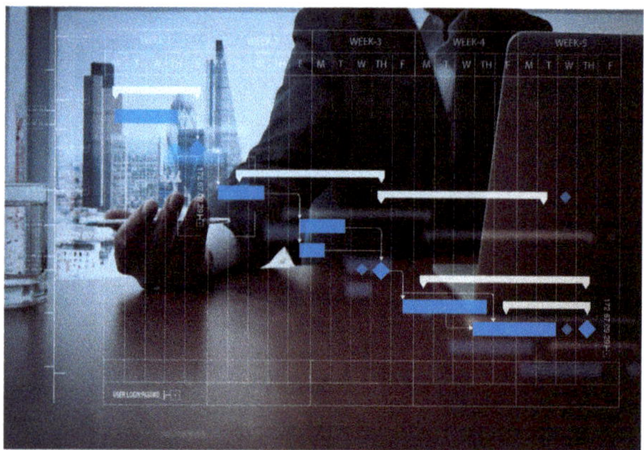

Image 9.3

Incorporating project schedule adherence into development groups can be challenging. There is a great deal of unknown at the start of any software development project as the end product is being created as you go. Therefore, it is important that the systems analyst have a basis for evaluating how the development team is aligning their development to the project schedule. This is accomplished through the definition of development milestones. By looking at the development schedule and defining key component completion dates, the systems analyst can begin to gauge how well the development team is progressing as related to the amount of time allocated to development.

Milestone definition is as much an art as a science and takes project experience to truly perfect. It is challenging to determine what aspects of the overall development will be a good barometer for overall development and schedule alignment. Some tasks may appear complex and, therefore, a good identifier, but in reality may end up being much more simplistic than others and, therefore, not a key component. The only way to accurately select completion activities that are meaningful is through experience and understanding of required developmental efforts.

Managing Code Review

One final aspect of software development that is critical to manage is code review. It is often too late to find out at software development compilation that the code developed by each developer will not work once combined. Therefore, it is imperative that the system analyst have a way to verify throughout development that standards are being adhered to and developments appear to meet all the requirements in order to be assembled at the end.

While no software development project is 100% guaranteed to function once compiled, instituting regular code review sessions will help. This allows for the developers to meet with both the systems analyst and periodically as a complete group to look at developments and ensure alignment. Areas of concern can be brought to light much earlier in the development process, analyzed, and altered, if necessary. The end result is a due diligence process that allows for the best chance of a successful implementation of each developer's work into a fully functioning software system.

Vendor Management

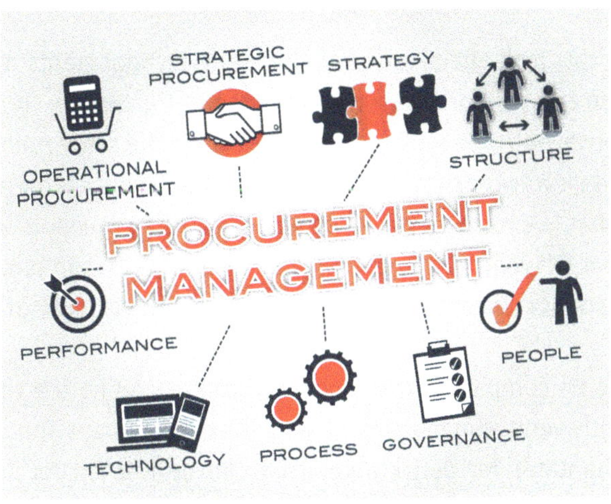

Image 9.4

When vendors are required to fulfill components of the new system development, there is always a requirement to ensure that the vendor is both coordinated with and overseen. Vendors essentially become part of the development team as they are contributing to the new system build. As such, their staff will need to be updated on requirements, expectations, constraints, change, and communicating roles and responsibilities throughout the engagement. Additionally, it is important to monitor vendor performance and ensure that the vendor is meeting or exceeding expectations and doing so in a cost-effective manner. Often, there will be a contract defined at the start of the vendor engagement that will provide the guidelines to which the vendor must be held.

The systems analyst is very well qualified to act as the vendor manager for the project. They may participate or even head the vendor selection process and then further the relationship by being the primary point of contact for the remainder of the development process. Other times, the systems analyst will be brought in after vendor selection but tasked with ensuring that vendor obligations are met and that necessary communication between the partners is consistently facilitated. When the systems analyst assumes the role of vendor manager, there are a few areas of consideration that will assist in the overall success of the management process. These areas of consideration include the following:

1. Project scope
2. Roles and responsibilities
3. Vendor performance reviews

Project Scope

In order to be able to hold the vendor responsible for expected performance, the systems analyst must first define the required scope of the vendor's participation in the development project. Additionally, the vendor must be in agreement with the scope requirements and attest to their ability to complete all activities assigned to them.

In order to accomplish this task effectively and efficiently, arrangements must be made to have meaningful conversations between the vendor and the project team. If possible, in-person meetings are always preferred, as much can be conveyed when individuals are sitting in the same room. However, if this is not possible, virtual meetings with telepresence capabilities will suffice. The systems analyst must come prepared to discuss every aspect of what is expected of the vendor. Then, the request must be made to the vendor to provide an honest assessment of what they are able to and not able to complete. It will sometimes help to develop a formal scope of work document to ensure that there is full visibility of all items being agreed to by both parties.

Along with the tasks to be completed, it is also important to define the time line for work to be completed. In order to assist with vendor management activities throughout the development, this time line should include key milestone dates for deliverables that can be tracked for schedule adherence reasons. These milestone deliverables should be highly detailed so there is no question as to whether they are accomplished or not on the agreed-upon deliverable date.

Finally, the cost for agreed-upon scope completion should be formally documented as well. This will ensure that if there are challenges to scope completion, there is evidence of agreed-upon pricing. When a vendor is required to put more effort into a project than originally estimated, they may attempt to increase costs to compensate for the increased effort. This will allow the systems analyst to push back and maintain budgetary requirements for the project.

Roles and Responsibilities

Another area of vendor interaction that can cause friction between the two partners is understanding who is responsible for what components of the development. By formally establishing roles and responsibilities between the two parties, there will be an increase in understanding of the expectations of both parties throughout the engagement.

The best way to accomplish this task is by working with the vendor to formally create a document that outlines the individual tasks defined in the scope of work and assign which party is responsible for each task. Work as a team to develop this document so that there is conversation and agreement between both parties on each item.

Assign individuals who act as task owners and who can answer for progress or challenges to time-line requirements. This will increase personal responsibility within both organizations and clarify who should be communicating with the development team and at what times.

Ensure that all of the developed roles and responsibilities are communicated to all parties involved, as well as any oversight entities within both organizations. This will allow for both understanding that there is agreement on the specifics of the partnership as well as provide clarification on who should be approached with questions or concerns regarding any one specific task.

Finally, ensure that there is a formal process in place for altering the established roles and responsibilities. As we have seen, there are many potential instances of change that will occur throughout the development. There must be flexibility in altering task items, but also a structured way to do so in order to ensure that all parties are in agreement to all changes that must be enacted.

Vendor Performance Reviews

While system development is a partnership between the organization and the vendor, it must still be understood that this is a provider/customer relationship. The organization is the customer and, as being in this role, is the one paying the vendor for their services. As such, the systems analyst has a responsibility to ensure that the vendor is meeting the objectives that they agreed to from the perspective of quality, time frame, and cost.

An effective way to promote communication and transparency throughout the development process is to establish performance review sessions throughout the development time line. Aligning these performance reviews to milestone deliverable dates will assist in providing evidence of vendor performance. In addition to time-line adherence, any issues or concerns regarding the interactions of both organizational and vendor team members, billing inaccuracies, quality concerns, or communication challenges can be discussed, and agreements reached on how to proceed.

It is also important to remember that these reviews are not solely meant to highlight challenges. This is also an opportunity to address aspects of the partnership that are going well or that are exceeding expectations. Positive reinforcement of efforts within both organizations has the potential to strengthen the effec tiveness of the entire development team and foster more effective development for the remainder of the project.

New Development Testing

Once the new system has been successfully developed, the systems analyst must direct the project team to transition from the role of development to testing. It is imperative that all parties involved in project development reengage for the testing of the new system. Not only will this bring multiple perspectives into the testing environment, but using the resources that developed the new system processes and requirements along with the resources that developed the new system will allow for the assessment that all requirements for the new system have been successfully met.

It would be ideal if new system testing went as expected and the accuracy of the new system was validated. However, most often, there will be issues brought out by testing procedures. By having all project resources available during testing, collaboration between system design and development resources allows for more effective and efficient issue remediation. Knowledge is always power, and ensuring that the knowledge base for both system design and construction are able to collaborate as necessary is supportive of being able to finalize the new system development fully.

In regards to how testing is to be conducted on the new system, there must be thought and consideration given to the process and methods to be conducted. The goal of system testing is to ensure that the system performs to the developed system specifications. However, there are numerous variables that can affect system performance. There are numerous processes contained in a new system, with many of them having multiple decision points. The only way to truly know if the system is functioning correctly is to fully test every process path possible in the system. Additionally, it is not sufficient to simply test through each process with expected system interaction, meaning providing the data to the system that is expected, but processes should also be tested by entering inaccurate or completely incorrect data. The system must be robust and able to handle unexpected user interactions. Bugs and development errors will often surface during incorrect data entry, even if the expected data entry is handled correctly.

With the vast amount of testing variables required, it is important for the project team to develop a **testing plan**. The testing plan should provide a roadmap for all the tests that must be completed on the system. The testing plan should take into account each user interaction, system process, and decision point within the process logic, and from that, testing scenarios should be developed that incorporate every possible combination. The testing plan then becomes a checklist of activities to be performed on the system in order to assess the degree to which the system will perform as expected.

In combination with the execution of the testing plan, it is important to ensure accurate documentation of the sequence of events being enacted on the system and the results of those actions. If an unexpected result is produced by the system, it can often be difficult to reproduce the sequence of events that caused it. Documenting each and every interaction it makes it possible to reproduce the sequence that caused the issue to see if it happens again.

Testing Techniques

Image 9.5

When it comes to facilitating testing procedures, it should be noted that there are both manual and automatic testing procedures that can be implemented. Manual testing requires project members to manually interact with the system in order to complete process interactions. This can be a very time-consuming and trying process, as each step must not only be completed by the user but documented fully as well. Automatic testing is performed by developing test scripts that are run by machines on the system. The test scripts mimic user action and elicit the necessary system responses. Automatic testing still requires a significant amount of effort to set up the scripts; however, the scripts themselves become the documentation of the process enacted on the system. The system results can be more easily aligned to the actions performed on the system by correlating the results with the test scripts run.

Testing the new system needs to be undertaken in phases in order to ensure that every aspect of development is vetted and assessed for both completeness and correctness. In order to successfully test all aspects of the new development, there are a number of testing techniques that will be used by the project team. Different techniques will focus on different aspects of the new system and, when combined, will allow the project team to complete a comprehensive testing cycle in order to determine if the new system is ready to be used by the organization or if alterations need to be made. The testing techniques used by system development teams consist of the following:

1. Unit testing
2. Integration testing
3. System testing
4. Acceptance testing

UNIT TESTING

Unit testing is low-level testing that consists of testing individual methods and functions within the modules of the software. Unit testing incorporates system components to verify that each software module actually performs the function it was designed for. Unit testing consists of **black box testing** and **white box testing**.

Black Box Testing

Black box testing focuses on whether the method or function being tested meets the requirement of its associated specification. Black box testing is focused on system results and their alignment with the requirements denoted in the specification.

White Box Testing

White box testing takes the assessment made in black box testing one step further by looking at the code that was developed to complete the method or function. This testing procedure is not only focused on the method or function result but also on how that result is completed by analyzing each process step.

INTEGRATION TESTING

Integration testing is focused on the interaction of different services or modules within the new system and how they operate in combination. These tests are more involved in development as they require thought to be put into how the modules interact and the definition of procedures to be enacted that will trigger these interactions in the system. Integration testing consists of **user interface testing**, **user-scenario testing**, **data flow testing**, and **system interface testing**.

User Interface Testing

User interface testing tests every component of the user interface. Not only are data entry methods looked at, but also data presentation methods. This testing will validate that system interactions not only exist for every expected user function but that the interactions are logically arranged.

Use-Scenario Testing

Use-scenario testing essentially uses the use cases to ensure that both the user and system interactions are as expected, but so too is the system result. This testing focuses on the existence of the system components that align to the use cases and not necessarily that each step of the process aligns to the normal course defined in the use case.

Data Flow Testing

Data flow testing builds on use-scenario testing in that it focuses on the step-by-step completion of each process. Again, using the use cases and, in this instance, both the normal course and exception developments of the use cases, each process is tested for compliance with the defined correct course of system interactions and resulting actions by the system.

System Interface Testing

System interface testing focuses on the data interactions between systems. This testing will focus on how the systems have been integrated to work in conjunction with each other and that the expected data is flowing between each system.

SYSTEM TESTING

System testing is focused on the correlation between the system software and all other components of the system. This testing will not only focus on the correct completion of functional tasks but also incorporate all nonfunctional requirements in order to ensure that each one is met in the new system. System testing consists of **requirements testing**, **usability testing**, **security testing**, **performance testing**, and **documentation testing**.

Requirements Testing

Requirements testing is focused on asserting that the integration of the new system into the organization's technology environment does not cause any new errors. Anytime a change is made to a technology environment, there is the risk of unintended consequences. Requirements testing verifies that the implementation of the new system does not result in any adverse effects on the technology environment.

Usability Testing

Usability testing focuses on the ease at which the system can be used. How the processes and user interactions flow, and the degree to which the user experience is intuitive and understandable. This testing also focuses on ensuring that users are able to traverse the system completely and without issue. The easier it is for the user to be able to understand how to use the system, the more successful the new system will likely be.

Security Testing

When it comes to technology systems, strong security positioning is essential. Security testing focuses on the security functions of the new system and how accurate and well developed they are. Security testing will leverage best practice information, threat assessment tools, and often even outside vendors to assist in attempting to break security developments. Comprehensive security testing is the only way to be reasonably sure that your new system will be able to protect the data it uses.

Performance Testing

Performance testing is focused on the ability of the system to work under demand. That is to say that performance testing simulates a high volume of system demand in regard to aspects such as simultaneous users, anticipated peak transaction volume, increased network traffic, and even multiple report generation in order to gauge the level of performance the new system is capable of.

Documentation Testing

System developers are tasked with documenting the code within the new system in order to support future support of the system. Documentation testing reviews the documentation created as part of the system development process. The documentation is analyzed in order to determine if it is comprehensive enough to be helpful in the future. In order to ascertain if the reporting is adequate, the project team will look at it from the perspective of being used to assist support staff that are not familiar with the system construction.

ACCEPTANCE TESTING

Acceptance testing is structured to ensure that the new system meets the needs of the organization and that the organization is prepared to utilize the new system. Once this level of testing is reached, there is a high degree of certainty that the new system has been developed correctly and is ready to be turned over to the actual users of the new system. Acceptance testing consists of **alpha testing**, **beta testing**, and **sign off**.

Alpha Testing

Alpha testing incorporates a small amount of users, normally those with the most knowledge of the functional requirements the system is supposed to meet. Often, test data is entered into the system for these tests. The users will work with the new system to repeat earlier tests and gain confidence that the system is performing as anticipated. Alpha testing will conclude when this sample set of users confirms that they accept the new system as usable.

Beta Testing

Beta testing will expand on the alpha test by increasing the number of actual system users and using real corporate data. The test group will work through all their required tasks with the new system to ensure that they are receiving the expected results. Errors or lack of process completion will result in further analysis and system correction if necessary. Beta testing will conclude when the user group confirms that they accept the new system as usable.

Sign Off

Often, a sign off process is implemented during beta testing. This requires each beta user to formally sign off that they have tested all the necessary processes and system functions under their purview and have verified all results as being accurate. The systems analyst will also sign off on the successful testing of the new system once he or she has verified that all beta users have successfully signed off. At this time, the new system is ready to be implemented into the live environment.

Testing Strategies

Not every testing technique is used for every new system testing strategy. While ideally, testing would be completed at every level and comprehensively at that, this is not always possible. It is common to see development teams combine techniques or omit ones that they feel are not necessary. For example, a project team may forgo unit testing by arguing that these test requirements will be captured in integration testing.

It is important to remember that the reason for completing testing activities is to ensure that the system that was just created will be successful in its function within the organization. Success is not only dictated by meeting the functional requirements of the project but also ensuring nonfunctional requirements are met, user experience is positive, the system is secure, and system integration does not have a negative impact on the technology environment of the organization.

It will be the responsibility of the systems analyst to ensure that the developed testing strategy is comprehensive enough to provide reasonable assurance that all these conditions are met. However, project constraints such as time, budget, or external factors may limit the testing scope, and therefore, compromises may need to be made.

Chapter Summary

The activities required to successfully develop and test a new system are numerous and diverse. However, so are the responsibilities of the systems analyst during the implementation phase of new system development. At first glance, one might think that system construction is an opportunity for the systems analyst to take a step back and regroup while others take the lead; however, it should now be apparent that this is not the case.

The systems analyst takes a leadership role at every phase of the project, and implementation is no different. To be a project champion, one needs to assert themselves and assist at every level. The management tasks and requirements during system construction provide ample opportunity for the systems analyst to do just that. Successful projects are created through dedication, and this will certainly be seen during the new system implementation.

Project Planning Activities

1. Refine the implementation phase of the project plan if necessary.

Image Credits

CHAPTER 10

Transitioning to the New System

Introduction

Once the system has been vetted and the project team believes it is ready for full implementation, there are still a number of critical tasks that must be facilitated by the systems administrator. The true success of the new system rests in the ability of every user to be able to transition with as much ease as possible. By facilitating an educated and thereby empowered user base, the organization has the best possible chance for the new system to be used to the best of its abilities. This means that the full benefits built into the new system will be realized by complete utilization of the new system.

In order for the systems administrator to ensure that every possible chance is given for user migration to the new system, efforts are placed on creating documentation and comprehensive training. These developments focus on not simply imparting the function of the new system but aligning the functions to the user roles and effectively imparting the knowledge required to become comfortable completing the required functions.

Additionally, once training is completed and the new system is fully functioning, the systems analyst has a responsibility to lead the project team in after-action analysis efforts in order to ascertain what aspects of the project went well and what could have been done more effectively or efficiently. The knowledge gained from these activities will assist in better decision-making for future project development.

Learning Objectives

1. Describe how to develop documentation.
2. Describe the different user training methodologies.
3. Describe how to develop and implement a training plan.
4. Describe how to effectively identify important takeaways from the project.

Image 10.1

Documentation Development

Documentation development begins during system creation and continues through system testing. Documentation for new systems happens in many forms, and it is the systems analyst's responsibility to ensure that what is created is not only comprehensive but usable by the intended audiences. Not all documentation is created for the same audience.

System documentation assists system administrators and third-party support vendors with support and future development initiatives. This is accomplished by providing detailed information on the purpose and development methods for each system component. Whether it be code, hardware, or networking, system documentation should provide the necessary data for an individual with no previous knowledge of the system to be able to understand how the system was created and, therefore, work with it.

User documentation provides the information necessary for the user to be able to successfully interact with the system. Effective user documentation does not simply state the steps a user must take when interacting with the system but also provides context as to what functions are being performed by the system. This will assist with user understanding and should lead to an ability to analyze system output and make determinations if the results provided by the system are anticipated and, therefore, likely correct.

Benefits of Digital Documentation

Documentation will take many forms in the new system. Physical hard copy documents are still developed, even today, as some feel there are associated risks of retaining critical documentation in a digital format only. For example, if an organization's entire data center were to incur downtime, access to critical documentation that could assist with bringing individual systems back online would not be available. This does lend some credence for at least printing off components of digital documentation and storing it in a secure location.

However, the vast majority of documentation is developed and used digitally today due to the following benefits:

1. Accessibility
2. Searchability
3. Multiple format presentation
4. Multiple interaction methods

ACCESSIBILITY

One of the main reasons digital documentation is preferred is that it then becomes easily accessible. By creating an online document repository, intended audiences can be given access to required information from anywhere around the world. This is especially appreciated when external resources such as outsourcers are used by the organization. Having global access to new system documentation can facilitate more time-conscious external support of the new system.

SEARCH ABILITY

Another large benefit of digital documentation is the enhanced ways the documentation can be searched. Key words, interactive table of contents, and even artificial intelligence (AI) integration can allow for more ease of interaction with the documentation by the intended audiences. This not only pertains to each individual document but also the ability to search all documents at the same time in order to compare results as well.

MULTIPLE FORMAT PRESENTATION

Digital documentation also allows for multiple presentations of the data contained within the documentation. Components can be described in written form but also shown through pictures, charts, graphs, etc. The ease at which data can be presented allows for diverse inclusions that may assist viewers in different ways. As the main intent of documentation is to provide information, using multiple methods to present data only enhances this ability to do so.

MULTIPLE INTERACTION METHODS

In regards to audience interaction with the documentation itself, there are, again, benefits to using digital documentation. This allows for multiple presentation strategies for the document material. Animation, interactive tool tips, narration, professionally produced video tutorials, or even AI-developed content are all possible. This level of audience interaction allows for information to be digested in more meaningful ways, adding additional value to the overall documentation itself.

Creating Documentation

Documentation is a time-consuming and resource-intensive process. Developers, vendors, allocation specialists, and the project team will be used in combination to develop all the information to be documented. High-quality documentation can take hours to develop each page of information. When you consider the hundreds of pages developed for new system documentation, the time requirement is certainly significant. However, that time estimation is based on searching out the required information, verbalizing the information, developing the most appropriate communication method, and compiling everything into the final product.

To ensure that documentation requirements are fully met and the project schedule is maintained, it is important that the systems analyst not wait to accomplish every task at the end of the project. Information gathering and organization should be completed in combination with system development and testing. System documentation would be primarily developed during creation. User documentation would begin to be defined in development but fully organized in testing.

This methodology will result in the bulk of the effort coming out of system testing to be on the assembly of the documentation information into user-friendly organization and interaction method development. As user documentation specifically will be necessary for adequate user training, it is important to put time into the project plan for user documentation development and testing. Simply ensuring that there is enough time to develop documentation is not sufficient to gauge success; the developments must be tested with both the development team and pertinent system users, most likely the same users who participated in alpha and beta stage system testing.

DOCUMENTATION SOFTWARE

Technology has the ability to assist in documentation tasks. Software has been developed that can be overlaid on the new system devices and essentially record the actions being taken by the user. Many of these software packages incorporate AI in order to make educated guesses as to what is actually being performed by the user interactions to develop detailed descriptions of task steps. The software also records screenshots of the system interactions that are automatically captured and displayed in the document, with imagery inserted to highlight areas of user focus and system interaction.

The end result is a system-generated, step-by-step guide as to how each user task is completed in the system, complete with visualization components. While it is important to note that the description development is done with a degree of educated guessing, this does leave some inaccuracies potentially being incorporated into the development. That said, it is much less effort for the project team to review these developments and adjust inaccurate information than it is to create all the content from scratch.

Software also exists that does much of the same documentation development from the system perspective. Processes are analyzed, and information is recorded for each system process. Documentation is then created by the software from the information collected, incorporating detailed system information that is accurate at the time the process is being completed. This information includes items such as processing power required, memory allocation, system component interactions, configuration specifics, and even security protocols encountered.

In much the same way as software-assisted user documentation creation, software-assisted system documentation creation does encounter a degree of error when recording system conditions. For example, multiple processes running at the same time may affect system status, whereas the software may attribute the status to be wholly composed of one of the processes. However, just as in user documentation creation, the project team verifying documentation creation accuracy takes less overall effort than creating all the documentation from scratch.

Overall, documentation software can assist in a more efficient documentation creation process. However, the inclusion of this technology does not make sense for every system development project. These solutions come with a cost, as well as specialized resource competencies, in order to use them effectively. If the project team is not prepared to understand the limitations and potential pitfalls of these solutions, the end result of using them will be developments that are less than fully reliable. Also, when developing less complex projects, the funds required to acquire development software may not offset the time savings of the resources required to develop the documentation.

System Documentation

System documentation is meant to assist future resources who will be tasked with maintaining and potentially enhancing the new system development after initial implementation and throughout the new solution's full life cycle. This documentation will normally consist of the **requirements document**, the **architecture design**, **source code**, **testing information, and test results**, as well as developed **maintenance and help guides**.

REQUIREMENTS DOCUMENT

By now, you should be very familiar with the requirements document developed by the project team. While it is true that the development team is also intimately familiar with this document, that is not going to be the case for future resources that are brought in to support the system. Just as it was important to understand the functional and nonfunctional requirements that were critical to the development team, so too is this true for future support resources. Understanding the why of the system will greatly assist in issue identification and accurate resolution in the future. By the time system documentation is finalized, there should be little to no additional effort needed to be placed on this document. Simply including it as a component of the overall system documentation will suffice.

ARCHITECTURE DESIGN

The architecture design component of the system documentation will also be pulled from already created materials. The combination of the hardware and software design developments coupled with the interface design materials will provide the basis for the architecture design. The project team will also review the fully developed systems specification document and include any aspects specifically related to the architecture components of the system that are pertinent to system support. This can be tricky, as it takes a practiced eye to ascertain what aspects of the specification document will support architecture clarification. That said, when making decisions, it is best to include more items than restrictions. If information is deemed as potentially helpful, include it.

Likewise, when referencing the interface design documentation, while the information is valuable, the design creative such as mappings, charts, graphs, and even prototype development can be invaluable. Including interface creativity can assist in communicating design intent and architecture capability.

SOURCE CODE

The source code document is a technical document that explains how the code works. Not every aspect of the source code needs to be included in this document. However, aspects of the code implementation that are complex, critical, or unique to the solution should all be developed. The source code document will not only contain a description of these aspects of the new system software but may also include code snippets with reference highlights as well. The more clarity the document can provide to future programmers, the more easily the solution will be to support.

TESTING INFORMATION AND TEST RESULTS

The testing information that was used to validate the system development can be very informative when it comes to supporting the system in the future. By reviewing what tests were developed, it provides a basis for what the developers were attempting to accomplish. The inclusion of the test results demonstrates system performance at the time of system acceptance, and from this, support resources can create a baseline of how the system was expected to function. This baseline can then be compared to the current system function, and alterations can assist in highlighting areas of issue or concern for future exploration.

Testing data also provides additional system information, such as performance and security requirements at the time of testing. These configuration contexts can also be useful to better understand how the system was configured to get the expected results. Over time, configurations get altered and can potentially become misaligned to how the original developers expected the system configuration to be set. When encountering unexpected system performance, sometimes going back to historical configuration settings can assist in uncovering where change has had unintended consequences and promote strategies for successfully dealing with it.

MAINTENANCE AND HELP GUIDES

Maintenance and help guides can be viewed as user documentation for the support resources of the new system. These documents should explain known issues, as well as provide step-by-step instructions for administrators to troubleshoot and resolve them. These documents should also contain all the best practice information related to maintaining and updating the new system. Security requirements and assessments should also be developed and included in this documentation, as well as any known limitation to security implementation at the time of system implementation. Finally, these documents should provide a comprehensive outline of the system's architecture and functionality in an easy-to-understand format. This should be a highly detailed outline that is able to communicate essential information for ensuring that the system can be adjusted back to functional configurations.

User Documentation

Image 10.2

User documentation is developed to support system users. User documentation is meant to support user training, provide reference for users throughout the system life cycle, and overall document how the system users and administrators interact with the new system. While system documentation is technical, with little emphasis placed on creativity, user documentation needs to be more creative. As the intent is to educate, user documentation should enhance the user experience. It needs to be easy to understand and logically structured. The verbiage needs to be lower level, meaning that it can be understood by an audience of varying degrees of experience and education. The incorporation of visualization aids will assist in presenting material in creative and more easily remembered formats.

User documentation serves multiple purposes and, therefore, has multiple classifications. Additionally, all user documentation is developed separately for two classifications of users: end users and administrators. The information developed for user documentation development can be assembled into knowledge bases in the form of FAQs, video tutorials, system-embedded assistance processes, or even entire online support portals, but the material can be classified under three general categories:

1. Troubleshooting guides
2. Manuals
3. How-to help guides

TROUBLESHOOTING GUIDES

Troubleshooting guides focus on identified issues that have been encountered while using the system and provide suggestions on how to resolve the encountered issue. There are limitations to troubleshooting guides, mainly that they will rely on only known issues. That said, these documents are not simply developed at the implementation stage. They are created at implementation but updated regularly throughout the system life cycle. As new issues are identified and solutions developed, they are added to the system's troubleshooting guides.

MANUALS

Manuals are created that document how to perform the business tasks that the system was designed to complete. These documents are developed by analyzing the user's business tasks, the commands and menus contained within the user interface, and by reviewing the functional requirements list. These documents provide a step-by-step guide for not only how the user interacts with the system but also what order system interactions must occur.

Manuals are not simply text instructions but have evolved into interactive media developments that will often contain integrated components within the system software. As the user is interacting with the system, the user manual will respond with pertinent information. With the incorporation of AI technology, user manuals can be developed to anticipate user action and not only provide information on the current step in the user process but also provide advice for contemplating the next steps as well.

HOW-TO HELP GUIDES

How-to help guides attempt to satisfy the user's preference for self-help. These documents are created to provide additional guidance regarding user task completion, provide clarification of aspects of the system that may be confusing to the user, and enforce transparency of what the system is expected to provide to the user at any given point in user/system interaction.

How-to help guides have also become much more interactive, with integrated system components allowing for quick and easy access to related information. Information presentation is also often multifaceted, with users having the option to view information in print, video, or sometimes even spoken format.

Defining New Operating Procedures

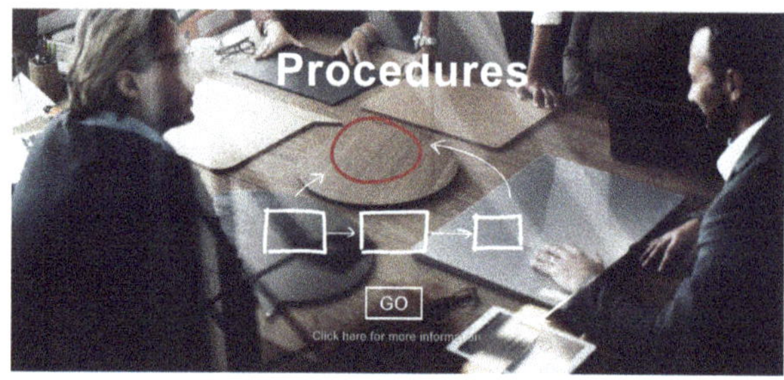

Image 10.3

Systems are developed to enact change in the organization. While this change is anticipated to provide benefit to the system users, it is change nonetheless. With change comes worry, anticipation, anxiety, or all-out fear of the unknown. All of these natural negative human responses to change have the capability of potentially hindering or even derailing the successful integration of the new system into the organization's operational environment.

Therefore, it is imperative that the systems analyst take a dedicated and structured approach to ensure that user education is prioritized, creatively developed, comprehensive, and easily understandable. While it is easy to emphasize that user education be developed and implemented with all these traits incorporated, actually doing so is much more difficult. There is no single educational development that will work for every single employee. In fact, there is no single educational structure that will adequately convey the required information to all necessary parties of a new system. In reality, user education must be broken down by many different points of consideration and then developed to meet criteria that are developed from multiple combinations of each consideration. These considerations include the following:

1. Differentiation of group tasks
2. Level of experience
3. Responsibility scope
4. End-user or administrator responsibility
5. Appropriate interaction method

Differentiation of Group Tasks

Just because there are a specific number of user groupings that are defined to interact with the new system does not necessarily mean that there needs to be an equal number of unique user educational developments. By comparing how each user group completes their unique tasks by interacting with the system, it is possible to determine where process differentiation may be required. For example, if the project team is developing an educational development for a new system dealing with employee information, both the human resources staff and accounting staff may need to use the system for employee information access. While their positions differ in responsibility, their need to access and review the employee information in the system will be the same. Therefore, a single educational development for accessing and reviewing employee information will be all that is required to educate all employees.

Analysis of positional requirements is important because while some system processes can be all-inclusive and, therefore, education can be developed and communicated at the process level, other times, there will be differences that require education to be developed at the group level in order to accurately define the process around group constraints. The end result is the ability to classify what user groups share educational consistency, and therefore, the project team can begin to align user groups for consolidated training development purposes.

Level of Experience

The level of experience a user has can affect the way in which educational materials are developed. If there is a high level of experience, educational developments can focus on the specific change the new system is enacting and omit aspects of the user and system interactions that remain the same. However, if there is a low level of user experience with the previous system process, then a more comprehensive educational development incorporating all steps in the user process will be more beneficial.

It is important to keep in mind that new system educational development is an opportunity to not only focus on educating users about the new system but also reinforce best practices for user task completion.

If it is beneficial to incorporate best practice aspects to task completion as opposed to simply educating on what changes to task completion the new system will require, include the best practice components in the educational development.

Responsibility Scope

The responsibility scope of the user group is another consideration when developing educational processes. Users who oversee other user groups or migrate between user groups will not only need to be educated on their user-specific tasks but also the tasks of those groups they oversee or periodically step into. Sometimes, it becomes a simple decision to include these users in participating in multiple educational paths, while other times, it may make sense to create a unique educational path that is developed specifically for these users. While each organizational environment will dictate different developments, it is important to identify these users and plan an educational method that positions them for success.

End-User or Administrator Responsibility

It is important to understand that the difference in the roles of end users as compared to administrators will result in very different approaches to educational development. End users are interacting with the system from a task completion perspective. Administrators are interacting with the system from a maintenance and enhancement perspective. As these perspectives vary greatly in activity, perspective, and responsibility scope, educational development so too must vary.

When it comes to new system educational development, this is the biggest differentiator of development strategy. The systems analyst will ensure that two unique educational developments take place in order to facilitate rollout to these two unique groups of users.

Appropriate Interaction Method

Defining how the educational development will be developed to interact with the individuals being educated is a consideration that must also be given much thought. Not every individual learns in the same way. Some are more visually stimulated, while others prefer documentation and highly structured presentations. Understanding the preferences of the users and being able to group those preferences based on user group classifications will allow the project team to define educational presentation methods that have the best chance of enhancing user retention. Ultimately, the more information the user is able to retain, the more prepared they will be to take on the required interactions with the new system.

User Training

Image 10.4

Once the project team has developed the necessary new system documentation, the next focus needs to be on developing quality user training. User training development will pull from the developed user documentation in terms of information assessment, identification of documentation content, the ability to collaborate with documentation resources, and best practice guidance on how the user will use these documents. However, user training development must go far beyond user documentation to comprehensively prepare new system users for how to use the new system to the best of its potential.

Implementing new technology is more than simply installing new software and hardware components, providing directions on how to complete tasks, and expecting users to embrace the new system and flourish. There are cultural considerations within any organization that need to be understood and confronted by way of user training development. Without understanding that many people are resistant to change, that they find comfort in understanding and completing the same tasks day after day, and incorporating this into user training, the project team will find themselves at a disadvantage when it comes to converting to the new system.

Additionally, while change is significant at the time of conversion to the new system, it does not end there. Software upgrades, system enhancements, bug fixes, and additional system integrations will ensure that users encounter change throughout the entire system life cycle. Developing training that is change focused will not only assist with initial user training at the time of conversion to the new system but can reinforce future system utilization with periodic reinforcement training throughout the system life cycle.

Another challenge to effective training is a lack of depth. The project team has been focused on the new system development for such a significant period of time that it becomes difficult for team members to objectively identify what items need to be included in user training and what can be omitted. The systems analyst needs to ensure that there are controls in place in the user training development initiative that recognize and balance this challenge. Incorporation of key system users, third-party assistance, or even reservation of project team members to only be included in the user training components of the projects are all ways that the systems analyst will enact controls over potential inadequate training development.

So, how does the project team develop effective user training? Incorporation of the developed documentation will act as a road map in assisting with how user groups should be segmented and provide an understanding of just how many different training programs should be developed. Additionally, the user group assessments will also highlight the most appropriate communication methods of the training materials for each identified training segment. This will allow for each user segment to have a training program developed that is tailored to their unique functional requirements, as well as their identified most appropriate aptitude for learning. However, while this addresses the organization and differentiation of user training development structure, there are still additional strategies that should be factored in order to provide the most comprehensive development possible.

To enhance training proficiency, each user training development needs to incorporate these five user training program development strategies:

1. Educate the change
2. Timed training
3. Time allocation
4. Availability
5. Reoccurring training structure

Educate the Change

In order to facilitate increased user acceptance of the new system, it is important to not ignore the potential resistance to change. In order to change culture and assist in user acceptance, create training that communicates the need for change. Provide users with the reasoning for the new system and educate them on the new process and what is to be expected. Highlight areas where the user experience has been enhanced and where previously manual tasks have been automated. Take the time to fully demonstrate the reasons why it is in the user's best interests to embrace the new system.

It is impossible for every new system transition to go smoothly and effortlessly from the user's perspective. By educating on the reason and benefit of the change prior to actually training the user on the new system, the project team is creating an environment that asserts the user's personal stake in being an active and positive part of the process. Users are more likely to embrace a solution that they believe will personally benefit them. When issues are encountered, they are more likely to work toward a solution with the project team as opposed to using the issues encountered as reasons for pushing back against the new system entirely.

Whenever possible, incorporate interactive components into this aspect of the user training development. By allowing the users to provide their feedback, opinions, or contributions to the training program development, you are asserting their personal ownership of the initiative itself. If they assimilate themselves with the training development, the user is more likely to push for the success of the initiative.

Timed Training

Timing of user training is important. Not every user of the new system will begin to use the new system at the same time. Additionally, the longer the duration of time between user training and system utilization, the more chance that necessary information is not retained by the user when they need it most. This can lead to a negative experience with the new system from the very beginning and should be avoided whenever possible. Therefore, developing a training schedule that takes into account the phasing in of each user group and aligns training program completion as close to new system adoption as possible is always preferable.

The greater the degree to which the user can be educated on how to use the new system and then empowered to take that information and apply it directly, the more at ease he or she will feel. Retention of training information makes for a much smoother transition for not only the individual user but for all users of the new system, as each user will play a role in the overall success of the system itself.

Time Allocation

It is important to note that often, when a user is being trained on a new system, they are still operating and, therefore, responsible for task completion on a current system. It is important to take into account the overall demands on the user and develop a strategy that frees up enough time for them to adequately train on the new system. By ensuring that the user is able to focus on the training being presented without the distraction of other duties, the project team will be positioning the user for the highest degree of information retention possible.

This may sound like a simple task, but the limitation of organizational resources, operational demands, and additional factors not able to be controlled by the project team can make this a very difficult strategy to adhere to. That said, it is in the best interest of the organization to ensure that each and every user is given ample time to focus on the task at hand, a successful migration to the new system.

Availability

There needs to be an intuitive aspect to how the training material is integrated into the new system. The user needs to be empowered by having access to the training materials necessary at the appropriate time. This means that the less effort required to find pertinent information both when first moving to the new system, as well as at any time when an unfamiliar aspect of the new system is encountered by the user, the more at ease the user will be with operating in the new system environment. People dislike the feeling of helplessness, and therefore, providing methods for users to execute self-service assistance as part of the training program development will put the power of knowledge in the hands of the user in training.

Reoccurring Training Structure

The most appropriate time to consider an organization's need for periodic reinforcement of employee training is at the time of the creation of the training program itself. The most effective system training programs take into account that training is not a single initiative, meaning that it is not simply to be undertaken when a user is new to the system. Just like every other aspect of technology, effective system utilization contains a lifelong learner component. In order to accommodate lifelong learning for the system user, the project team must factor in periodic reinforcement training that emphasizes aspects of the system that are critical to ensuring system utilization, which results in optimal system performance.

There must also be a component that incorporates future system changes into the reoccurring training model. While fear of change is most detrimental at system initiation, unexpected change throughout the system life cycle can undermine user trust in the system. Incorporating change explanations into every aspect of user training will assist in minimizing this risk.

The project team is best positioned to identify key components of the initial user training that are most appropriate for continuous reinforcement to the user at the time of initial training development. Therefore, incorporating these tasks into the overall training development initiative will help to ensure the best result possible.

Training Methods

At this juncture, the project team has most of the necessary components to assemble the most comprehensive training programs possible. However, there is one more decision that must be considered prior to the training programs actually being constructed. The training method to be employed in order to most effectively impart the training materials is an important decision point. While each training program can be implemented using a different method, the systems analyst must have a clear understanding of the nuances of each method. The training methods to consider are as follows:

1. Individual training
2. Group training
3. Train the trainer

INDIVIDUAL TRAINING

The development of an individual training program can be broken down into two strategies. The first strategy would be to define a training program that is facilitated by an instructor with a single user being trained at a time. This is a highly intensive training structure, as it limits training resources to a one-to-one ratio. Systems containing a large number of users would either require a large number of associated trainers or a large duration of time to complete user training requirements.

However, instructor-led one-on-one training is usually reserved for training programs that are limited in user scope and focus on extremely complex or highly specialized user requirements. It is important to consider the level of training complexity and employ this method in situations where the user role is both complex and essential to system success.

The second strategy that involves an individual training approach is self-directed training. In this configuration, the training program is designed to be taken by the user in the user's own direction. No live instructor is involved. Technology systems are usually leveraged in order to provide an interactive user experience designed to enhance the retention of information by the user.

Self-directed training programs can be efficient to administrate when developed accurately, as they do not require live training resources to interact with the users. This allows for large numbers of users to be trained simultaneously. However, success requires the user to have some capacity for being a self-directed learner. Additionally, as the user is most often interacting with a digital training technology, the success of this method is directly dependent on the user's ability to successfully operate the training technology itself. However, with all that being considered, self-directed individual training is the primary method of implementation of reinforcement cyclical training programs.

There are training resource and user competency tradeoffs to leveraging an individual training approach to a system training program. However, in certain circumstances, this method is not only viable but the most accurately aligned for user training success.

GROUP TRAINING

Group training is a training development method that leverages assembling users of defined user groups and training as a collective group. This method is most often instructor-led and interactive in nature. There are many benefits from this type of training development. Some key strengths include the ability to train a larger number of system users simultaneously, the enhanced ability for user understanding due to collaboration and directed discussion between the trainer and training group, and the ability to develop a support structure of users throughout the training experience and relationships made throughout the training.

However, with a group training methodology, there are a few potential issues to be aware of. Not every member of the training group will learn at the same rate. Therefore, users who are having trouble retaining information have the potential to slow down the rate of information transfer to the group and result in other group members becoming disconnected from the training. Also the ability for collaboration can also lead to situations where the training can become sidelined or even derailed by questions and discussions that are not pertinent to the actual training at hand.

Group training is one of the most popular methods of new user training and is highly effective when training user groups who do not have a high degree of differentiation in system task requirements. This training method can be effectively structured and scheduled within the confines of most development timelines and is a go-to for most new system training program developments.

TRAIN THE TRAINER

Train the trainer is a variation of the group training method, which incorporates the individual training method as well. In this method, organizational resources are selected to be the facilitators of the training program developments. These resources are paired with instructors who will train them individually on the new system. However, these resources are not only expected to retain the training information but to then go out and train the remainder of the system users. This essentially makes the pre-selected group of users the trainers for the remainder of the user groups.

This method has a number of strengths. As actual system users are empowered to become the trainers to the bulk of the associated user group, the strengths of the group training method are retained, but with the added benefit of the instructor remaining within the organization post-go live. This means that users requiring future clarification or retraining have an in-house resource that they can go to in the future. Additionally, there is usually increased familiarity among organizational staff, so the user selected as trainer will have enhanced knowledge of individual user's strengths and weaknesses. This can allow them to tailor training initiatives to users in ways that will allow for the highest level of user retention possible.

Conversely, there are some potential issues with this method that must be considered. For this method to be effective, the selected user must not only be able to retain the vast amount of information that they are required to then teach the remaining user group but also have the personal characteristics that make a trainer successful. Communication skills, patience, ability to handle diverse personalities, group dynamic management skills, and even the ability to manage a lack of user support for the system are all aspects of the chosen user that must be considered in order to select a successful trainer candidate.

Train the trainer is heavily reliant on the internal resources within the organization and, more importantly, the inclusion of resources that have the aforementioned personality traits that make for a strong trainer. However, assuming that this resource exists within the organization, training the trainer can have lasting benefits that simple instructor-led group training is unable to facilitate.

Training Development and Implementation

Now that all components of effective training program development are understood, the systems analyst and their team are ready to actually develop the necessary training programs. It is important to prioritize the training requirements, as not all training programs need to be fully developed to begin training. In fact, oftentimes, as there is a finite number of training development resources, project teams will develop a single training program, deploy, and develop the next training program while the currently developed program is being implemented.

Successful training development and implementation require thought, structure, and comprehensive scheduling. Training is given a set time allocation in the overall project schedule, and it is essential that the systems analyst ensure that all development and implementation activities conform to the overall time allocation for this component of the overall system development.

However, ensuring that training is developed comprehensively and implemented efficiently is the goal of the systems analyst. By doing so, he or she will ensure that the new system users will be well prepared for the final step of the implementation phase, the actual migration to the new system.

System Migration

Image 10.5

Once training has been developed and implemented, it is now time for the organization to finally migrate to the new system. Even with all the preparation and planning, this can often be a risky endeavor and requires strong management of all activities in order to come to a successful completion. It is important to realize that oftentimes, there is a current system in place that is being wound down at the same time as the new system is being brought online. This can present both challenges and opportunities that must be well understood.

System migration relies heavily on a well-thought-out and developed migration plan. The migration plan must include the formal listing of all technical tasks that must be completed to bring the new system online and sunset the current system and in what order these tasks must be completed. Potential risks that may be encountered throughout this technical process must also be identified and tasks defined for both identifying a risk occurrence and remediation of the risk should it be incurred. Additionally, user roles, tasks, and timing for entering the new system need to be developed and highly detailed. Finally, an actual system cutover strategy needs to be determined. When all these components are formally developed, the migration can begin.

System Cutover

The system cutover defines how the organization will actually transition from the legacy system to the newly developed system. In some instances, the project team will have a high degree of confidence in the new system development to the extent that they recommend an immediate system cutover.

What this means is that a cutover date and time will be defined by the project team and communicated to the organization. This time frame will also be communicated as being when both the legacy and new systems are unavailable. At the aforementioned time, the legacy system will be shut off. The system data will be copied to the new system, and the new system will be turned on. Validation processes will be run on the new system to ensure that the migration of data is completed as expected and the new system is ready to be used. At that time, the new system users will be enabled in the new system, and communication will go out that the system is now ready to be used.

Not every situation allows for an immediate system cutover to take place. In situations where the project team has less confidence that the newly developed system will operate as intended or that the function of the system is highly critical to the overall success of the organization, a **parallel operation** cutover strategy will be enacted.

Parallel Operation

In a parallel operation system cutover, a new system implementation date and time are still announced. This time frame still results in a period of downtime for both the legacy and new systems, with the data from the legacy system being copied to and verified in the new system. However, upon verification of accurate data transfer, both systems are brought back online. From this point forward, every action taken in the legacy system is repeated in the new system.

The reason for this duplication of effort is twofold. It allows for analysis of the functioning of the new system and comparison of the results to the old system in order to reinforce or disprove the accuracy of the operation of the new system. It also ensures that the legacy system remains in effect should there be issues with the new system that result in it being unreliable or even unusable. Should either of these results occur, the organization can continue to function as usual on the legacy system.

This method is not without its drawbacks, however. As every action must be duplicated in both systems, the end result is a significant increase in the workload on the system users. When it comes to user acceptance of the new system, doubling the user workload is not the best way to build support for the new system. Also, there is additional effort required by the project team to analyze and compare the processes and results of both systems in order to ascertain the degree of new system success. Finally, there is likely to be additional functionality or changes in the new system as compared to the old system. These expected alterations must be fully understood and well documented to ensure that encountering these differences does not result in a false positive of an issue being brought up by the project team.

Additional System Migration Criteria

Communication has been essential throughout the system development process and is critical through the system migration. All affected organizational resources must be kept apprised of the migration status from initiation through completion. Additionally, as users are brought on to the new system, they must be provided with methods for communicating issues, challenges, or bugs that they encounter. These communication channels must allow for efficient and timely communication, as this information could be critical to overall implementation success.

Project team members need to be structured to be able to monitor and assess new system functionality as the move to the new system occurs. While the users can assist in providing feedback on potential issues with the new system, the project team needs to ensure they are taking a proactive approach to system monitoring and issue identification. As the organization moves to the new system, it becomes increasingly dependent on the new solution functioning as intended. If there are any aspects of the system that are not doing what is expected, the sooner the issue is identified, the better the chance it can be corrected with minimal overall disruption to the organization.

When all these factors are taken into account and a well-defined migration plan is put into effect, the end result is the successful conclusion of a long-awaited outcome. The transition of the organization from a legacy system that has identified limitations to a new system that is much better prepared to increase overall value to the organization.

Project Closeout

Once the new system has been successfully migrated to the organization's environment and the users are fully operational, there are still a couple of tasks remaining for the systems analyst. While the project team is able to celebrate a successful new system development and deployment, there are always lessons to be learned from the project that was just undertaken, and the best time to pull out these lessons is when all aspects are fresh in the mind of every member of the project team.

Therefore, the systems analyst will attempt to create additional value from the project by completing two activities that will result in the creation of two formal documents. These documents can be referred to by future development teams, which can hopefully gain both perspective and benefit from understanding the challenges encountered in the current system development and the solutions that were developed to mitigate those challenges. The two activities consist of the following:

1. The executive summary

2. After-action meeting

Executive Summary

The executive summary is developed to provide an overview of the system development project. The document will analyze the problem requiring the new system development, highlight the proposed development to solve the identified problem and explain the actual new system development in a complete but brief synopsis.

This document is intended to provide readers with a complete yet concise explanation of the development project so that they may determine if the documentation of said project will provide guidance regarding the current project they are working on. As time is always of the essence, it is important to remember that this development must efficiently provide necessary project information without overexplaining the details of the project.

After-Action Meeting

Image 10.6

The systems analyst will also arrange for an after-action meeting to take place shortly after the new system implementation is complete. The intent of this meeting is to assemble all members of the project team and discuss as a cohesive unit both the successes and challenges of the new system development.

The intent is to create a record of what went well during the project and what could have possibly been improved. For items identified as having possible improvement, the project team will be asked to reflect on circumstances surrounding the challenge and identify potential courses of action that could have led to a more positive result. The systems analyst will document the results of this meeting in order to create a **project lessons** learned document.

PROJECT LESSONS LEARNED

The project lessons learned document is the final formal creation of the project team. This document formally records the results of the after-action meeting and provides a written record of what aspects of the development went well for the project team, what could have been improved, and even potential alterations to the project that could have led to a more positive result.

The combination of the executive summary and project lessons learned documents will allow future project development teams to assess if the findings of this current project may have value in overcoming challenges incurred by the future development teams. An organization retaining these developments at the completion of each project provides a basis for ensuring that past project challenges are not repeated in the future, or at least not to the same degree.

Chapter Summary

For every member of a new system development project, transitioning to the new system marks the culmination of a significant amount of effort. Reiterating that the majority of technology development projects fail emphasizes just how important reaching this phase of development truly is. Looking back on all the tasks, compromises, effort, and focus that everyone contributed to developing a successful new system, transitioning to the new system is not simply completing a final set of task requirements but actually getting to see the fruits of your labor in action.

While the systems analyst has every right to take a moment and feel accomplished for actually reaching this stage, they must keep in mind that the job is not yet completed. There is still a level of risk to the success of the new system. While it has been vetted by the development team and some key users, the true success of a new system rests in the successful adoption of said system by the entire intended user base. If the systems analyst is not able to successfully achieve complete utilization of the system by all intended users, there is still the chance that the organization will not see the optimum benefit of the new implementation.

Therefore, it is important that the systems analyst focus their team on comprehensive documentation and training development to ensure that every user has the tools necessary to comfortably interact with the new system. Throughout the rollout process, when bringing on new users, it is important to monitor the effectiveness of the transition process, identify any areas that appear to be causing issues or confusion, and make adjustments as necessary for interacting with additional new users.

Additionally, as there are always lessons to be learned from every development project, both good and bad, it is always beneficial for the project team to do a formal after-action analysis of the completed project and document the lessons learned from undertaking the project. Many times, future projects will encounter similar challenges, and having reference to previous decision-making, both good and bad, can assist in making more concise decisions during these future projects.

Treating every system development project as a knowledge-gathering opportunity for future projects allows a systems analyst to build a depth of knowledge that can be crucial for making tough decisions in the future. These positions carry with them the cornerstone requirement of being true lifelong learners, and the on-the-job learning requirement is often an invaluable asset when ensuring this requirement for success is met.

Systems analysis is not for everyone. You must have a strong organizational aptitude, the inherent ability to successfully interact with many different types of personalities, the desire to succeed to such a degree that you are willing to stake your reputation on the success of the project you manage, and the depth of knowledge to be able to interact with all aspects of technology development, as well as the myriad of resources both internal and external to the organization. However, if you are an individual who possesses these aptitudes, the feeling of accomplishment you experience seeing firsthand the usefulness of a system you championed from conception to implementation is very powerful. These experiences can contribute to making becoming a systems analyst a very worthwhile and fulfilling career choice.

Project Planning Activities

1. Develop the executive summary document.
2. Develop the project lessons learned document.

Image Credits

Bibliographies

Chapter 1 Bibliography

Barrier, T. (2003). Systems analysis. In H. Bidgoli (Ed.), Encyclopedia of information systems (pp. 345–349). *Elsevier.* https://doi.org/10.1016/b0-12-227240-4/00177-5

CareerExplorer. (2023). What does a systems analyst do? https://www.careerexplorer.com/careers/systems-analyst/

Dennis, A., Wixom, B. H., & Roth, R. M. (2018). *Systems analysis and design (7th ed.).* John Wiley & Sons.

Eby, K. (n.d.). The ultimate guide to understanding and using a system development life cycle. *Smartsheet.* https://www.smartsheet.com/system-development-life-cycle-guide

Kay, R. (2002, May 14). *System development life cycle.* Computerworld. https://www.computerworld.com/article/2576450/app-development-system-development-life-cycle.html

Kendall, K. E., & Kendall, J. E. (2013). *Systems analysis and design.* Pearson.

Kumari, R. (n.d.). *What is system analysis and design? Analytics Steps.* https://www.analyticssteps.com/blogs/what-system-analysis-and-design

Reference for Business. (n.d.). Systems analysis—organization, definition, business, project proposal. https://www.referenceforbusiness.com/management/Str-Ti/Systems-Analysis.html

IIASA—International Institute for Applied Systems Analysis. (n.d.). *What is systems analysis?* https://iiasa.ac.at/options-magazine/winter-2021/what-is-systems-analysis

Chapter 2 Bibliography

Bogavac, L. (2023, May 29). *How to create a software development plan.* Plaky. https://plaky.com/blog/software-development-plan/

Cleary, S. (2023, May 30). The teamwork guide to software development project management. *Teamwork.com.* https://www.teamwork.com/blog/software-development-project-management/

Dennis, A., Wixom, B. H., & Roth, R. M. (2018). *Systems analysis and design (7th ed.).* John Wiley & Sons.

Font, V. M., Jr. (n.d.). *The project management method and the SDLC.* The Ultimate Guide to the SDLC. https://ultimatesdlc.com/project-management-method-sdlc/

Green, D. (2022, November 21). 7 steps of agile system analysis process. *Apptio.* https://www.apptio.com/blog/7-steps-of-agile-system-analysis/

IIASA–International Institute for Applied Systems Analysis. (n.d.). *What is systems analysis?* https://iiasa.ac.at/options-magazine/winter-2021/what-is-systems-analysis

Kendall, K. E., & Kendall, J. E. (2013). *Systems analysis and design.* Pearson.

Landau, P. (2023, June 29). *Project selection: Use these 8 selection methods for better strategic results.* ProjectManager. https://www.projectmanager.com/blog/project-selection-for-better-strategic-results

Monday.com Blog. (2023). Project management for software development: A complete guide. https://monday.com/blog/project-management/project-management-for-software-development/

Monnappa, A. (2023). 11 Project selection methods for project managers in 2023. *Simplilearn.com.* https://www.simplilearn.com/project-selection-methods-article

Nishanth. (2023). Create a perfect software development plan [with template]. *NeoITO.* https://www.neoito.com/blog/create-software-development-plan/

Chapter 3 Bibliography

Dennis, A., Wixom, B. H., & Roth, R. M. (2018). *Systems analysis and design (7th ed.)* John Wiley & Sons.

Kendall, K. E., & Kendall, J. E. (2013). *Systems analysis and design.* Pearson.

Oatley, M. (2021). Activity 3—requirements analysis. *Software Development Life Cycle (SDLC).* https://sdlc.uconn.edu/activity-3-requirements-analysis/

Shergil, A. (2023, June 23). What is requirement analysis phase of SDLC? Detail guide. *TopDevelopers.co.* https://www.topdevelopers.co/blog/requirement-analysis-in-sdlc/

Simplilearn. (2023). What is requirement analysis: Overview, applications, and more. https://www.simplilearn.com/what-is-requirement-analysis-article

Tutorialspoint. (n.d.). *System analysis & design—system planning.* https://www.tutorialspoint.com/system_analysis_and_design/system_analysis_and_design_planning.htm

Udoagwu, K. (2022). How to carry out a requirements analysis. *Wrike.* https://www.wrike.com/blog/how-carry-out-requirements-analysis/

Upadhayay, D. (2022). SDLC requirement analysis—all you need to know. *OpenXcell.* https://www.openxcell.com/blog/sdlc-requirement-analysis/

Valacich, J., Valacich, J. S., & George, J. (2019). *Modern systems analysis and design.* Pearson.

Visual Paradigm. (n.d.). Requirement analysis techniques. https://www.visual-paradigm.com/guide/requirements-gathering/requirement-analysis-techniques/

Chapter 4 Bibliography

Dennis, A., Wixom, B. H., & Roth, R. M. (2018). *Systems analysis and design (7th ed.).* John Wiley & Sons.

Kendall, K. E., & Kendall, J. E. (2013). Systems analysis and design. Pearson.

Larson, E. & Larson, R. (2004). Use cases: What every project manager should know [Paper presentation] PMI® Global Congress 2004—North America, Anaheim, CA, United States.

Saylor Academy. (n.d.). *Use case concepts in object-oriented analysis: 1. Use case concepts.* https://learn.saylor.org/mod/book/view.php?id=33013

Inflectra. (2023, January 17). *Use cases and scenarios: Their importance, how to write them, & more.* https://www.inflectra.com/Ideas/Topic/Use-Cases.aspx

Penn State College of Earth and Mineral Sciences (n.d.). *Use cases in a nutshell | GEOG 468: GIS analysis and design.* https://www.e-education.psu.edu/geog468/l8_p3.html

Software Testing Help. (2023, June 30). *Use case and use case testing complete tutorial.* https://www.softwaretestinghelp.com/use-case-testing/

Valacich, J., Valacich, J. S., & George, J. (2019). *Modern systems analysis and design.* Pearson.

Visual Paradigm. (n.d.). *Use case analysis: How to identify actors?* https://www.visual-paradigm.com/guide/uml-unified-modeling-language/how-to-identify-actors/

Vpadmin. (2022, February 25). Use case analysis tutorial. Cybermedian. https://www.cybermedian.com/use-case-analysis-tutorial/

Chapter 5 Bibliography

Dennis, A., Wixom, B. H., & Roth, R. M. (2018). *Systems analysis and design (7th ed.).* John Wiley & Sons.

Eby, K. (n.d.a). Beginners guide to business process modeling and notation (BPMN). *Smartsheet.* https://www.smartsheet.com/beginners-guide-business-process-modeling-and-notation-bpmn

EWSolutions. (2021). Business processes and logical process modeling overview. *EWSolutions.* https://www.ewsolutions.com/business-processes-logical-process-modeling-overview/#:~:text=Logical%20Process%20Modeling%20is%20the,to%20reaching%20the%20desired%20outcome

IBM. (2021). What is business process modeling? https://www.ibm.com/cloud/blog/business-process-modeling

Nishadha. (2023). Business process modeling techniques with examples. *Creately.* https://creately.com/blog/bpm/business-process-modeling-techniques/

Javatpoint (n.d.). Software engineering data flow diagrams. https://www.javatpoint.com/software-engineering-data-flow-diagrams

Valacich, J., Valacich, J. S., & George, J. (2019). *Modern systems analysis and design.* Pearson.

Visual Paradigm (n.d.). What is data flow diagram? https://www.visual-paradigm.com/guide/data-flow-diagram/what-is-data-flow-diagram/

Yoo, S. (2003). Data flow diagrams. In H. Bidgoli (Ed.), Encyclopedia of information systems (pp. 455–468). *Elsevier.* https://doi.org/10.1016/b0-12-227240-4/00031-9

Chapter 6 Bibliography

Agile Data. (n.d.). *Data modeling 101—the agile data (AD) method.* https://agiledata.org/essays/datamodeling101.html
Brewer, T. (2023, March 10). What is an entity relationship diagram and how do they work? *Functionly.* https://www.functionly.com/orginometry/org-charts/what-is-an-entity-relationship-diagram-and-how-do-they-work
Coursera. (2023). What is a relational database and how does it work? *Coursera.* https://www.coursera.org/articles/relational-database
Dell Technologies. (n.d.). *Unstructured data—data storage.* https://www.dell.com/en-us/dt/learn/data-storage/file-storage.htm
Dennis, A., Wixom, B. H., & Roth, R. M. (2018). *Systems analysis and design (7th ed.).* John Wiley & Sons.
Duh, K. (2022). What is a relational database? Airtable. https://blog.airtable.com/what-is-a-relational-database/
Smartdraw. (n.d.). *Entity relationship diagram (ERD)—what is an ER diagram?* https://www.smartdraw.com/entity-relationship-diagram/
Gaur, C. (2023, June 23). What is data modeling? Types, steps and tools. *XenonStack.* https://www.xenonstack.com/insights/data-modelling
Knight, M. (2022, October 7). *What is data modeling?* DATAVERSITY. https://www.dataversity.net/what-is-data-modeling/
Loshin, D., & Lewis, S. (2021). Data structures. Tech Target Network. https://www.techtarget.com/searchdatamanagement/definition/data-structure?Offer=abt_pubpro_AI-Insider
Pedamkar, P. (2023). Multidimensional database. *EDUCBA.* https://www.educba.com/multidimensional-database/
Redis. (2023, June 7). *What is NoSQL. Redis.* https://redis.com/nosql/what-is-nosql/
Simplilearn. (2023). What is data modelling? Overview, basic concepts, and types in detail. https://www.simplilearn.com/what-is-data-modeling-article
Team, P. B. (n.d.). What is data modeling? *Powerbi.microsoft.com.* https://powerbi.microsoft.com/en-us/what-is-data-modeling/
Valacich, J., Valacich, J. S., & George, J. (2019). *Modern systems analysis and design.* Pearson.

Chapter 7 Bibliography

Bak, T. (n.d.). *5 step decision-making process for build vs buy software.* Soft Kraft. https://www.softkraft.co/build-vs-buy-software/
Dennis, A., Wixom, B. H., & Roth, R. M. (2018). *Systems analysis and design (7th ed.).* John Wiley & Sons.
Halwai, S. (2021). SDLC design phase—everything you need to know. *OpenXcell.* https://www.openxcell.com/blog/design-phase-in-sdlc/
Hoekstra, R. (2023). Top 10 problems of outsourcing: How to avoid them. TechMagic. https://www.techmagic.co/blog/top-10-outsourcing-problems-and-how-to-avoid-them/
InterviewBit. (2023, June 22). *System architecture—detailed explanation.* https://www.interviewbit.com/blog/system-architecture/
Kendall, K. E., & Kendall, J. E. (2013). *Systems analysis and design.* Pearson.
Martins, J. (2021, October 30). 7 quick steps to create a decision matrix, with examples [2023]. Asana. https://asana.com/resources/decision-matrix-examples
Rasmussen, R. (2022). How to write an effective data acquisition strategy: An in-depth guide. *UrbanLogiq.* https://urbanlogiq.com/how-to-write-an-effective-data-acquisition-strategy/
Ropp, M., & Ropp, M. (2022). The RFP process: The ultimate step-by-step guide. *RFP360.* https://rfp360.com/rfp-process-guide/
Schaffer, E. (n.d.). *The complete guide to system design in 2023.* Educative. https://www.educative.io/blog/complete-guide-to-system-design
SEBOK. (n.d.). Procurement and acquisition. https://sebokwiki.org/wiki/Procurement_and_Acquisition
Shergil, A. (2023a, January 19). The significance of the design phase in SDLC. *TopDevelopers.co.* https://www.topdevelopers.co/blog/design-phase-in-software-development-life-cycle/

Chapter 8 Bibliography

Adobe. (n.d.). *User flow diagram—what it is, why it's important, and how to create one.* https://business.adobe.com/blog/basics/how-to-make-a-user-flow-diagram
Bak, T. (n.d.). *UI design process—7 easy steps to make great UIs faster.* Soft Kraft. https://www.softkraft.co/ui-design-process/
Bose, S. (2023). UI testing: A detailed guide. BrowserStack. https://www.browserstack.com/guide/ui-testing-guide
Citrix. (n.d.). What is virtualization? Virtualization definition. https://www.citrix.com/solutions/vdi-and-daas/what-is-virtualization.html
Dennis, A., Wixom, B. H., & Roth, R. M. (2018). *Systems analysis and design (7th ed.).* John Wiley & Sons.
Freshcode. (n.d.). How to create a perfect system requirements specification? https://freshcodeit.com/freshcode-post/how-to-create-a-perfect-system-requirements-specification
Hamilton, T. (2023). What is interface testing? Types & example. *Guru99.* https://www.guru99.com/interface-testing.html
Interaction Design Foundation. (2023). What is user interface (UI) design? https://www.interaction-design.org/literature/topics/ui-design
InterviewBit. (2023, June 22). *System architecture—detailed explanation.* https://www.interviewbit.com/blog/system-architecture/
Kendall, K. E., & Kendall, J. E. (2013). *Systems analysis and design.* Pearson.
Lane, C., & Kruger, G. (2023). How to write a software requirements specification (SRS document). *Perforce Software.* https://www.perforce.com/blog/alm/how-write-software-requirements-specification-srs-document

Lteif, G. (2023, June 30). *Part 5: High-level solution design documents: What is it and when do you need one.* SoftwareDominos. https://softwaredominos.com/home/software-design-development-articles/high-level-solution-design-documents-what-is-it-and-when-do-you-need-one/
Molloy, J. (2023, June 6). A comprehensive overview of the client-server model. *Liquid Web.* https://www.liquidweb.com/blog/client-server-architecture/
Ranjan, R. (2023). The mobile app architecture guide for 2023. *Net Solutions.* https://www.netsolutions.com/insights/mobile-app-architecture-guide/
Valacich, J., Valacich, J. S., & George, J. (2019). *Modern systems analysis and design.* Pearson.
Terra, J. (2023). What is client-server architecture? Everything you should know. *Simplilearn.com.* https://www.simplilearn.com/what-is-client-server-architecture-article

Chapter 9 Bibliography

Boogaard, K. (2022). How to manage a software development team. *Wrike.* https://www.wrike.com/blog/non-techies-can-successfully-manage-development-team/
Bryce, I. (2023, April 20). *How to manage vendors in 2023.* Gatekeeper. https://www.gatekeeperhq.com/blog/how-to-manage-vendors
Craig, D. (2023, June 6). *Your step-by-step guide to successfully manage every construction project.* Procore. https://www.procore.com/library/construction-project-management-guide
Dennis, A., Wixom, B. H., & Roth, R. M. (2018). *Systems analysis and design (7th ed.).* John Wiley & Sons.
DOOR3. (n.d.). *Risk management in software development: 7 common risks.* https://www.door3.com/blog/understanding-risk-management-in-software-development-7-common-risks
Great Learning. (2022, January 13). *Systems analyst guide—great learning.* Great Learning. https://www.mygreatlearning.com/blog/systems-analyst-guide/
Keates, C. K. (2018, September 10). The five C's of effective communication. *Forbes.* https://www.forbes.com/sites/forbescoachescouncil/2018/09/10/the-five-cs-of-effective-communication/?sh=6c1f6f2c20c8
Kendall, K. E., & Kendall, J. E. (2013). *Systems analysis and design.* Pearson.
Kochalski, D. (2022, July 26). How to deal with project risk management in software development. *Gorrion.* https://www.gorrion.io/blog/how-to-deal-with-project-risk-management-in-software-development/
Osbourn, T. (2022). How to manage a software development team: 17 tips for success. *TextExpander.* https://textexpander.com/blog/how-to-manage-a-software-development-team-17-tips-for-success
Semah, B. (2023, March 16). Ultimate guide to the different types of software testing in 2023. *Hackr.io.* https://hackr.io/blog/types-of-software-testing

Chapter 10 Bibliography

BLEICH, C. (n.d.). *How to train employees on a new system or technology: 5 tips. EdgePoint Learning.* https://www.edgepointlearning.com/blog/how-to-train-employees-on-new-system/
Dennis, A., Wixom, B. H., & Roth, R. M. (2018). *Systems analysis and design (7th ed.).* John Wiley & Sons.
Eby, K. (2023, June 1). How to write standard operating procedures: Experts provide tips and free templates. *Smartsheet.* https://www.smartsheet.com/content/standard-operating-procedures-manual
Editor. (2019, December 9). Technical documentation in software development: Types, best practices, and tools. *AltexSoft.* https://www.altexsoft.com/blog/business/technical-documentation-in-software-development-types-best-practices-and-tools/#:~:text=System%20documentation%20provides%20an%20overview,and%20maintenance%20or%20help%20guides
Hanson, K. (2021). How to write documentation for your next software development project. *FreeCodeCamp.* https://www.freecodecamp.org/news/how-to-write-documentation-for-your-next-software-development-project/
Kendall, K. E., & Kendall, J. E. (2013). *Systems analysis and design.* Pearson.
Meij, S. (2020, March 9). End user training: How to get it right from start to finish. *GoSkills.com.* https://www.goskills.com/Resources/End-user-training
Momentum. (2019, August 6). *The insider's guide to implementing a new system.* https://www.m-inc.com/article/the-insiders-guide-to-implementing-a-new-system/
Oragui, D. (2023). Software documentation best practices [with examples]. *helpjuice.com.* https://helpjuice.com/blog/software-documentation
Wharton Executive Education. (2021, June 21). *After-action reviews: A simple yet powerful tool. Wharton.* https://executiveeducation.wharton.upenn.edu/thought-leadership/wharton-at-work/2021/07/after-action-reviews-simple-tool/
Wheeler, R. (2022, August 5). The ultimate project closeout checklist. *The Motley Fool.* https://www.fool.com/the-ascent/small-business/project-management/articles/project-closeout/
Yıldırım, H. (2023, May 21). End-user training—everything you need to do it right in 2023. *UserGuiding.* https://userguiding.com/blog/end-user-training/

www.ingramcontent.com/pod-product-compliance
Ingram Content Group UK Ltd.
Pitfield, Milton Keynes, MK11 3LW, UK
UKHW050141280726
14058UKWH00006B/769